The work of the German philosopher Manfred Frank has profoundly affected the direction of the contemporary debate in many areas of philosophy and literary theory. This present collection brings together some of his most important essays, on subjects as diverse as Schleiermacher's hermeneutics, the status of the literary text, and the response to the work of Derrida and Lacan. Frank shows how the discussions of subjectivity in recent literary theory fail to take account of important developments in German Idealist and Romantic philosophy. The prominence accorded language in literary theory and analytic philosophy, he claims, ignores key arguments inherited from Romantic hermeneutics, those which demonstrate that interpretation is an individual activity never finally governed by rules. Andrew Bowie's introduction situates Frank's work in the context of contemporary debates in philosophy and literary theory.

MANFRED FRANK is Professor of Philosophy at the University of Tübingen, Germany. His many books and articles include studies of the problem of time in early German Romantic philosophy and literature, and a study of Schelling, Hegel and Marxist dialectic. His major work on contemporary literary theory appeared in English in 1989 as *What is Neostructuralism*. He is an editor of the *Revue internationale de philosophie* and has published widely in German and English language journals on both philosophical and literary topics.

ANDREW BOWIE is Professor of European Philosophy at Anglia Polytechnic University, Cambridge. His books include *Aesthetics and subjectivity: from Kant to Nietzsche* (1990), *Schelling and modern European Philosophy: an introduction* (1993), *F.W.J. von Schelling: on the history of modern philosophy* (1994), and *From Romanticism to Critical Theory: the philosophy of German literary theory* (1996).

THE SUBJECT AND THE TEXT

THE SUBJECT
AND THE TEXT

Essays on literary theory and philosophy

MANFRED FRANK

Edited, with an introduction by
ANDREW BOWIE

Translated from the German by
HELEN ATKINS

CAMBRIDGE
UNIVERSITY PRESS

PUBLISHED BY THE PRESS SYNDICATE OF THE UNIVERSITY OF CAMBRIDGE
The Pitt Building, Trumpington Street, Cambridge CB2 1RP

CAMBRIDGE UNIVERSITY PRESS
The Edinburgh Building, Cambridge CB2 2RU, United Kingdom
40 West 20th Street, New York, NY 10011-4211, USA
10 Stamford Road, Oakleigh, Melbourne 3166, Australia

All German edition © Manfred Frank and Suhrkamp Verlag 1989

These essays were first published in German in 1989 as part of
Das Sagbare und das Unsagbare (Suhrkamp Verlag, Frankfurt am Main 1989)

First published in English by Cambridge University Press in 1997 as
The subject and the text: essays on literary theory and philosophy.

English translation © Cambridge University Press 1997

Printed in the United Kingdom at the University Press, Cambridge

Typeset in Baskerville 11/12.5pt, using Poltype™   [VN]

A catalogue record for this book is available from the British Library

Library of Congress cataloguing in publication data
Frank, Manfred, 1945–
[Sagbare und das Unsagbare. English]
The subject and the text: essays on literary theory and philosophy /
Manfred Frank; edited, with an introduction by Andrew Bowie;
translated from the German by Helen Atkins.
p.   cm.
Includes bibliographical references and index.
ISBN 0 521 56121 3 (hardback)
1. Discourse analysis.   2. Hermeneutics.   3. Semiotics.
I. Title.
P302.F7313   1997
401′.41–dc21
97-6243   CIP

ISBN 0 521 56121 3 hardback

Contents

Introduction

Andrew Bowie

THE ROOTS OF LITERARY THEORY

'Literary theory'[1] has long since ceased to be of importance only
to those concerned with the study of literature. The growth in the
importance of literary theory might, however, seem somewhat
surprising, given that it is predicated on an assumption which had
already informed American 'new criticism', namely that the aim
of recovering the intended meanings of the author could no
longer form the main basis upon which literary texts were to be
interpreted. Attention to the 'verbal icon' in new criticism did
lead to considerable controversy. It did not, though, as literary
theory has, set in motion a whole series of new research projects
which affect nearly all areas of the humanities. What really
helped bring home the key change of methodological perspective
now associated with literary theory was the radicalisation and
dramatisation of anti-intentionalist assumptions, in the work of
Michel Foucault, Roland Barthes and others, which crystallised
in the idea of the 'death of the author'. This radicalisation made
visible formerly hidden links between theoretical reflection on
literary interpretation and central issues in modern European
philosophy. In the light of these consequences literary theory also

[1] By 'literary theory' I mean the work of those theorists who have had the most noticeable
influence on the humanities since the 1960s, such as Roland Barthes, Michel Foucault,
Jacques Lacan, Jacques Derrida, Gérard Genette, Paul de Man and others. This is clearly
a largely arbitrary designation, but its significance will become apparent in the focus of
Frank's essays and from the contexts in which I discuss it here. Frank himself refers to
'French textual theory' in relation to what I term 'literary theory'. This is in many ways a
more apt designation, as many positions in literary theory tend to exclude the very notion
of 'literature', in favour of the idea that there is no reason for privileging particular texts
by honouring them with the label of literature.

began to play a controversial role in mainstream European and analytical philosophy.

The 'death of the author' was the perceived result of the 'subversion' of the intended meaning of the author – and, by extension, of any language user – by the workings of a language which the author did not invent and over which he or she had only limited control. Roland Barthes claims that it was Mallarmé who was 'the first to see . . . the necessity to substitute language itself for the person who until then had been supposed to be its owner' (in David Lodge (ed.), *Modern Criticism and Theory*, London and New York: Macmillan, 1988, p. 168).[2] In conjunction with the assimilation into the study of literary and other texts of ideas from Saussure's linguistics and from a variety of other theoretical sources, such as the work of Freud and Heidegger, this view of language and the subject became a central assumption in many areas of what now goes under the name of 'literary theory'. Along with the supposed demise of the author went a related suspicion of the very notion of interpretation, as well as of the idea that literary texts have a special aesthetic status that other texts lack (see e.g. Terry Eagleton, *Literary Theory. An Introduction*, Oxford: Blackwell, 1983). Debates over the effects of this incursion of such theories into the study of literature continue, as do the philosophical debates over the validity of the work of Derrida and others. The point of the present selection of translated essays is to make available some new perspectives that have often been ignored in these debates, perspectives which, furthermore, widen the scope of the discussion to include the most important areas of contemporary philosophy.

Manfred Frank is at present Professor of Philosophy at the University of Tübingen, having studied philosophy and German studies at a variety of German universities and been Professor of Philosophy at the University of Geneva. Frank's work is initially

---

[2] Whether Mallarmé was really the first is at least open to doubt. Novalis maintains, for example, that 'The artist belongs to the work, and not the work to the artist' (Novalis, *Band 2 Das philosophisch-theoretische Werk*, ed. Hans-Joachim Mähl, Munich and Vienna: Hanser, 1978, p. 651), as well as maintaining that 'a writer is really only one who is enthused by language [*ein Sprachbegeisterter*, which has the sense of one who is "in-spirited" by language]' (*ibid.*, p. 439): the context makes it plain that we are in certain ways subject to language. Novalis does not go so far, though, as to invert the roles of subject and language as Mallarmé can be said to do: this will be significant in Frank's appropriation of the Romantic position represented by Novalis.

significant in the context of debates over literary theory because it is directed both against the idea of the 'death of the subject', and towards a revaluation of hermeneutics which gives a central role to aesthetics. Unlike Jürgen Habermas, whose criticisms of post-structuralism (e.g. *Der philosophische Diskurs der Moderne*, Frankfurt am Main: Suhrkamp, 1985, English translation: *The Philosophical Discourse of Modernity*, trans. Frederick Lawrence, Cambridge: Polity Press, 1987) have sometimes betrayed a lack of hermeneutic sympathy which leads him to misinterpretations of Derrida and others, Frank's critical responses to Derrida, Foucault, Lyotard and others are all the more telling because of his partial sympathy with and concern to do hermeneutic justice to what he criticises. The lack of an adequate response – or, indeed, any direct response at all – on the part of the main proponents of post-structuralism to many of these criticisms can suggest just how telling Frank's criticisms are. However, although it is sometimes critical of contemporary literary theory, Frank's work does not constitute a regression to the unreflective approach that still dominates many areas of literary study even today.[3]

Frank's theoretical work emerged from two essential sources in post-war German philosophy that played a major role in his earlier academic career: the tradition of hermeneutics associated with Heidegger and Hans-Georg Gadamer, and the tradition of research in German Idealism associated with Dieter Henrich. Frank has mobilised, combined and adapted ideas from these traditions for a wide variety of purposes. As well as the work in philosophy and literary theory presented here for the first time in English (the essays are taken from Manfred Frank, *Das Sagbare und das Unsagbare. Studien zur deutsch-französischen Hermeneutik und Text-theorie*, Erweiterte Neuausgabe (first edition 1980), Frankfurt am Main: Suhrkamp, 1989), he has written major works on: the problem of time in early German Romantic philosophy and literature (*Das Problem 'Zeit' in der deutschen Romantik. Zeitbewußtsein und Bewußtsein von Zeitlichkeit in der frühromantischen Philosophie und in Tiecks Dichtung*, Paderborn, Munich, Vienna and Zurich: Schöningh,

---

[3] For a – in more ways than one – particularly crude example of this approach, see T.J. Reed's reply to my 'The Presence of Literary Theory in German Studies', in *Oxford German Studies* 20/21, 1992.

1990 (first published 1972): this was his PhD dissertation); Schelling's critique of Hegel (*Der unendliche Mangel an Sein. Schellings Hegelkritik und die Anfänge der Marxschen Dialektik*, Frankfurt am Main: Suhrkamp, 1975); Schleiermacher's hermeneutics (*Das Individuelle-Allgemeine. Textstrukturierung und -interpretation nach Schleiermacher*, Frankfurt am Main: Suhrkamp, 1977); themes in modern German and European literature such as the 'endless journey' (*Die unendliche Fahrt. Ein Motiv und sein Text*, Frankfurt am Main: Suhrkamp, 1979; *Kaltes Herz. Unendliche Fahrt. Neue Mythologie. Motivuntersuchungen zur Pathogenese der Moderne*, Frankfurt am Main: Suhrkamp, 1989); mythology in modernity (*Der kommende Gott. Vorlesungen über die Neue Mythologie I*, Frankfurt am Main: Suhrkamp, 1982; *Gott im Exil. Vorlesungen über die Neue Mythologie II*, Frankfurt am Main: Suhrkamp, 1988); post-structuralism (*Was Ist Neostrukturalismus?*, Frankfurt am Main: Suhrkamp, 1984, English translation: *What is Neostructuralism?*, trans. Sabine Wilke and Richard Gray, Minneapolis: University of Minnesota Press, 1989); the philosophical question of individuality (*Die Unhintergehbarkeit von Individualität. Reflexionen über Subjekt, Person und Individuum aus Anlaß ihrer 'postmodernen' Toterklärung*, Frankfurt am Main: Suhrkamp, 1986); Lyotard and Habermas on the question of argument (*Die Grenzen der Verständigung. Ein Geistergespräch zwischen Lyotard und Habermas*, Frankfurt am Main: Suhrkamp, 1988); early German Romantic aesthetics (*Einführung in die frühromantische Ästhetik*, Frankfurt am Main: Suhrkamp, 1989); the philosophy of time (*Zeitbewußtsein*, Pfullingen: Neske, 1990); and style in philosophy (*Stil in der Philosophie*, Stuttgart: Reclam, 1992). He has also produced an edition of Ludwig Tieck's *Phantasus*, perhaps the most densely allusive text in early German Romantic literature (*Ludwig Tieck, Phantasus*, Frankfurt am Main: Deutscher Klassiker Verlag, 1985), and new editions of Schleiermacher's *Hermeneutik und Kritik* ('Hermeneutics and Criticism') (Frankfurt am Main: Suhrkamp, 1977) and Schelling's 1841-2 lectures on the *Philosophie der Offenbarung* ('Philosophy of Revelation') (Frankfurt am Main: Suhrkamp, 1977). One aspect of Frank's most recent work consists of a continuing engagement with that side of the contemporary analytical philosophy of mind (Roderick Chisholm, Hector-Neri Castañeda, John Perry, Thomas Nagel, etc.) which, in contrast to contemporary physicalist accounts of the subject in analytical philosophy, shares key arguments with the post-Kantian philosophical tradition of reflection on subjectivity (*Selbstbewußtsein und Selbsterkenntnis. Essays zur analytischen Philosophie der Subjektivität*, Stuttgart: Reclam, 1991; *Selbstbewußtseinstheorien von Fichte bis Sartre*, Frankfurt am Main: Suhrkamp, 1991; *Analytische Theorien des Selbstbewußtseins*, Frankfurt am Main: Suhrkamp, 1994). Frank is also engaged in an ongoing project to rewrite and assess the history of German Romantic philosophy (see 'Philosophische Grundfragen der Frühromantik' in *Athenäum* 4. Jahrgang, Paderborn, Munich, Vienna and Zurich: Schöningh, 1994).

Throughout his work Frank has been concerned to combine ideas from different theoretical traditions. After focusing initially on an agenda still largely set by the dominant historical and hermeneutic philosophical tradition in Germany, he soon became concerned to increase communication between German theory and contemporary French thought – this was one reason for his move to Geneva. Having in some ways become disappointed by the failure of many French thinkers to engage in serious dialogue with other traditions, he has recently been concerned, increasingly successfully, to promote dialogue between the concerns of German Idealism and Romanticism, and contemporary American analytical philosophy.

The essays in this volume deal with figures like Derrida and Lacan (and many others) who are familiar to those working in literary theory, with the analytical philosophy of John Searle, and with figures from the past, like Schleiermacher, who have been largely ignored by literary theorists, let alone by analytical philosophers. To facilitate access to the selection of Frank's work translated here, I want, instead of rehearsing the arguments of the essays, to give a brief account of some of the philosophical heritage upon which this work is based, relating it to contemporary theoretical concerns. This heritage has remained largely unknown in the English-speaking world.[4] Had it been better known, some of

---

[4] For an account of some aspects of it see Bowie, *Aesthetics and Subjectivity: from Kant to Nietzsche*, Manchester: Manchester University Press, 1990, reprinted 1993; *Schelling and Modern European Philosophy: An Introduction*, London: Routledge, 1993; *From Romanticism to Critical Theory. The Philosophy of German Literary Theory*, London: Routledge, 1997. The only major work of Frank's previously to be translated is *Was Ist Neostrukturalismus?*.

the more questionable positions in the literary theory that emerged with post-structuralism might never have gained the dominance they did in some circles, and key debates in analytical philosophy would have gained a vital new dimension.

In the new afterword to the republished edition of his doctoral dissertation, *Das Problem 'Zeit' in der deutschen Romantik* ('The Problem of "Time" in German Romanticism'), Frank remarks: 'In retrospect I am aware that the ... seeds of all my later publications were sown here and that, even when on the most apparently distant thematic paths, I was always and still am engaged in an inner dialogue with early Romanticism (including Solger and Schleiermacher)' (Frank, *Das Problem 'Zeit'*, pp. 499–500).[5] Why, then, should the philosophy of Friedrich Schlegel, Novalis (Friedrich von Hardenberg), Karl Wilhelm Ferdinand Solger, Friedrich Daniel Ernst Schleiermacher, and Friedrich Wilhelm Joseph Schelling, which has not played a significant role in the English-speaking world since the time of the English Romantics – if it played any role at all[6] – have become so important for a contemporary philosopher writing on questions of interpretation? The simple reason is that the insights of early German Romantic philosophy already prefigure many of the arguments raised by literary theorists against received assumptions both in literary criticism and in certain influential areas of hermeneutic and analytical philosophy. The further reason is that some of the arguments of the Romantics, as Frank was probably the first to show in a convincing manner, are demonstrably superior to those in influential areas of contemporary literary theory and analytical philosophy.

---

[5] The stress on '*early* German Romantic philosophy' is to distinguish the cosmopolitan and rational nature of this philosophy from later nationalist and reactionary versions of Romanticism, of the kind that appear, say, in the worst aspects of Richard Wagner, or in the early Nietzsche.

[6] Schleiermacher's influence as a theologian, as opposed to his influence as a philosopher, has, of course, been considerable; Schelling has had far more indirect influence, for example via the effect of his early and late work on Nietzsche, and on American pragmatism, than has usually been realised (see Bowie, *Schelling*; F.W.J. von Schelling, *On the History of Modern Philosophy*, translation and introduction by Andrew Bowie, Cambridge: Cambridge University Press, 1994). On the whole, though, the main Romantic philosophers have never been taken as seriously as Hegel, not least because some of their key texts were not published until this century, some appearing only after the Second World War. The contents of these texts did, though, filter through to a wide audience via lecture notes and word of mouth.

The major points of theoretical orientation in the literary theory associated with French structuralism and post-structuralism have been the linguistics of Ferdinand de Saussure, and certain aspects of the tradition of German philosophy inaugurated by Kant, that are continued in the work of Hegel, Nietzsche, Husserl and Heidegger. The vital aspect of this tradition for literary theory is the rejection of what Hilary Putnam has termed 'metaphysical realism'. 'Metaphysical realism' presupposes an ultimately knowable 'ready-made world' which pre-exists our descriptions of it, and which it is the task of the natural sciences to describe.[7] The sciences are seen in metaphysical realism as aiming at an 'absolute picture', a true representation of the world in itself. Frank rejects the 'metaphysical realist' view, but he does so, as we shall see, in often unfamiliar ways. One way of approaching his work is to see how each of the central figures in the accounts of post-Kantian philosophy upon which much literary theory has relied has a counterpart in Frank's revision of the history of philosophy. In place of Hegel, the representative of a totalising 'metaphysics of presence', Frank concentrates on the arguments of Schlegel, Novalis and the Schelling of the Hegel-critique, which challenge the very basis of Hegel's thinking;[8] in place of Nietzsche's anti-metaphysical hermeneutics, Frank concentrates on a new interpretation of Schleiermacher's startlingly radical hermeneutics; Husserl and Heidegger play a less important role in his work than does Sartre, who is read in terms of his parallels with Fichte and Romanticism. Frank's work is not least important, then, because it leads to a new understanding of the history of philosophy, in which many of the assumptions about the nature of modern philosophy in both literary theory and analytical philosophy are shown to be questionable. Underlying Frank's attention to these neglected figures is a vital assumption about the course of modern philosophy, the explication of which will form the basis of this introduction.

---

[7] Aspects of the work of both Hegel and Husserl can be understood in realist terms, but the influential aspects of their work for literary theory are not the metaphysical realist aspects.

[8] On Schelling's critique of Hegel see Frank, *Der unendliche Mangel an Sein*; Bowie, *Schelling*; Schelling, *On the History of Modern Philosophy*.

The crucial moment in modern philosophy for Frank is what he terms the 'becoming non-transparent of the Absolute for reflection, from which both the turn towards aestheticism and to the philosophy of language emerged in early Romanticism, in one and the same movement' (Frank, *Stil in der Philosophie*, p. 65; see also Frank, *Einführung in die frühromantische Ästhetik*, 'Philosophische Grundfragen der Frühromantik'). To understand what is meant by the perhaps rather opaque terms in which Frank couches this assertion we need, then, to look at the relationship of positions in early German Romantic and Idealist philosophy to some of the main philosophical influences on recent theory.

SUBVERSIONS OF THE SUBJECT

It is a commonplace both within literary theory and – although the issue is couched in less emphatic terms – in much analytical philosophy that the self-conscious I has been 'subverted' by the fact that the language it speaks is, initially at least, external to it. One version of this subversion is the source of the idea of the 'death of the author'. The issue of the subject and language is, though, highly complex. Habermas refers to the 'paradigm of subjectivity', in which the truth about the object is regarded as based upon the constitutive role of the thinking subject, and he assumes that this is the dominant paradigm in modern European philosophy from Descartes onwards. The move away from this paradigm towards a paradigm based on language as the medium of intersubjectivity is, however, not necessarily the liberation from the aporias of modernity as which it is often presented.

One particular link of analytical philosophy to structuralism and post-structuralism can suggest why. At the beginning of analytical philosophy Frege's 'driving of thoughts out of consciousness' is directed, as is the early Russell's critique of Idealism, against any role of the activity of consciousness in the establishing of truth, in Frege's case in the name of a Platonic 'third realm' of timeless truths, and in Russell's case in the name of the absolute certainty of particular empirical propositions in the sciences. Truth in this view resides in language, in the form of what Bernard Bolzano had termed 'objective representations', not in the contingencies of the minds of its users.[9] That truth cannot just depend on the contingencies of my subjective experience is unexceptional: the real question is how self-consciousness is to be understood in relation to intersubjectively constituted truth and meaning. The nihilistic implications of the positivist view that developed from the early analytical conception, in which only verifiable scientific propositions are deemed worthy of truth status and all forms of intuitive human wisdom are rejected, is a reminder that the exclusion of the subject in modern philosophy can take very questionable forms. Not all of these forms chime with the suggestion in some literary theory that this exclusion is a liberation which enables the 'free play' of textual meaning, as opposed to locating and fixing meaning in terms of its origin in the subject. A radically externalist view of language is, for example, perfectly compatible with the worst kinds of behaviourism. It is against the tendency towards a disguised positivism which is often present in literary theory and which still plays a significant role in many areas of analytical philosophy that Frank's defence of a philosophy of subjectivity is directed.

What, then, is the real point of the move away from the 'paradigm of subjectivity' in parts of two major modern Western philosophical traditions? One answer lies in the way meaning relates to the subject *qua* language user. Barthes claims: 'Linguistically, the author is never more than the instance writing, just as *I* is nothing other than the instance saying *I*' (Lodge, *Modern Criticism and Theory*, p. 169). In much analytical philosophy self-consciousness becomes reduced, in a related manner, to the ability to apply the rules governing the use of the word 'I' correctly. Self-consciousness must in these terms be understood propositionally, and thus intersubjectively, via the rules for converting deictic expressions between the 'he' and the 'I' perspectives, which allow us to identify a person, including ourselves. It is therefore not to be understood via the epistemological problems concerning the

[9] As J. Alberto Coffa, *The Semantic Tradition from Kant to Carnap*, Cambridge: Cambridge University Press, 1991 shows, this idea, which is the essential idea that initiates what Coffa terms the 'semantic tradition', was already developed by Bolzano in the first half of the nineteenth century. See Bowie, *From Romanticism to Critical Theory*, chapter 5, which shows that Schleiermacher employs the same notion, though to different ends.

'intuitive' nature of self-knowledge or 'inner evidence' (see Ernst Tugendhat, *Einführung in die sprachanalytische Philosophie*, Frankfurt am Main: Suhrkamp, 1976, English translation: *Traditional and Analytical Philosophy*, trans. P.A. Gorner, Cambridge: Cambridge University Press, 1982; Tugendhat, *Selbstbewußtsein und Selbstbestimmung*, Frankfurt am Main: Suhrkamp, 1979, English translation: *Self-Consciousness and Self-Determination*, trans. Paul Stern, Cambridge, Mass.: MIT Press, 1986).[10] Because communicable meanings, which rely on intersubjective rules for the use of language, cannot be assumed to be constituted in the interiority of consciousness, the subject supposedly ceases to play any active role in the constitution of meaning at all. As Frank will suggest, however, this approach does not explain how the individual subject relates to intersubjectively constituted meanings, not least because it gives no way of explaining new initiatives of meaning of the kind that are most obviously apparent, of course, in literature.

The attempts to remove the subject from the centre of philosophy are most convincing when they are seen as a result of problems inherent in the notion of 'representation', which is where the problems with metaphysical realism become most obvious. Richard Rorty captured the essence of these problems in his critique of the notion of the mind as the more or less adequate mirror of external reality in *Philosophy and the Mirror of Nature*.[11] The basis of Rorty's conception is, along with the work of the later Wittgenstein, the account of 'Western metaphysics' developed by Heidegger from the late 1920s onwards. Heidegger saw Descartes as the initiator of a process of 'subjectification', in which the truth of the world comes to be located in the representation of the world to itself by the self-conscious subject. The simple problem with the notion of the 'I' as the locus of the true representations of objects, as

[10] The basic idea is derived from the later Wittgenstein's rejection of the notion of a private language; the question for Frank is whether the referent of the term 'I' can be understood as being of the same status as other kinds of referent (see, in particular, Frank, *Selbstbewußtsein und Selbsterkenntnis*, and below).

[11] Rorty suggests that most analytical philosophy must also be understood in terms of representation: '"Analytic" philosophy is one more variant of Kantian philosophy, a variant marked principally by thinking of representation as linguistic rather than mental, and of philosophy of language rather than "transcendental critique", or psychology, as the discipline which exhibits the "foundations of knowledge"' (Richard Rorty, *Philosophy and the Mirror of Nature*, Oxford: Blackwell, 1980, p. 8).

the 'mirror of nature', is, though, that there is no place from which the representation and its object can be compared. Judging the adequacy of a representation requires a position from which both the object and its representation can be apprehended. This position is, however, bought at the price of a regress, because the position from which the adequate representation is established must itself be an adequate representation of the relationship between representation and object, and so on. One perceived way out of this dilemma is to change the relationship of the 'I' to truth and meaning, by locating truth and meaning intersubjectively, in the forms which make communication possible, as Habermas does in the wake of Heidegger and Wittgenstein. At the same time, as opposed to the dominant assumptions in much analytical philosophy, which still aims at a version of a representationalist theory, true propositions are no longer seen by Heidegger, Rorty and Habermas as corresponding to a ready-made reality, because this merely repeats the problem of representation in another form.[12] The crucial question, then, is how this change in the conception of the 'I' is understood: Frank's work is not least important for the way it shows that the critique of representation is not coextensive with the critique of subjectivity as the basis of the intelligibility of language.

The fundamental move in the decentring of the subject takes place, then, when the Cartesian 'I', which is supposed to be transparent to itself in the immediate act of reflecting upon itself in the *cogito*, gives way to an 'I' that is subjected to its dependence on the language through which it speaks. Nietzsche suggested in this connection that the 'subject' is really a function of the subject–predicate structure of language itself. From Nietzsche to Wittgenstein, Heidegger, Habermas, Derrida, Lacan and many others the 'I' is no longer seen as 'present to itself' in relation to an opposed world of objects which it attempts to represent, because its very status as 'I' depends upon a language which originates in the world, not in the interiority of consciousness. The further correlate of these positions, as we have already seen, is that the question of self-consciousness ceases to be the central issue for philosophy,

---

[12] For the critique of the older analytical position see Putnam, *Realism and Reason. Philosophical Papers Volume* iii, Cambridge: Cambridge University Press, 1983 in particular, and any of his more recent work.

because the problems posed by self-consciousness are now located in the *inter*subjective realm of language, rather than the *intra*subjective space of consciousness. It is the way in which this further move against the subject is carried out which Frank questions, with consequences that affect many positions in analytical philosophy, the theory of communicative action, hermeneutics and literary theory.

FICHTE'S INSIGHT: RESTORING THE SUBJECT

The initial theoretical impulse for Frank's questioning came from the initiator of what has been called the 'Heidelberg School', Dieter Henrich, who was perhaps his most influential teacher. In a seminal essay on J.G. Fichte, *Fichtes ursprüngliche Einsicht* (Frankfurt am Main: Klostermann, 1967, English translation in Christensen, D. (ed.), *Contemporary German Philosophy. Vol. 1*, University Park, Pa.: Pennsylvania University Press, 1982), the implications of which he has been developing ever since, Henrich suggested a way of approaching the issue of self-consciousness in modern philosophy which offered an alternative to the dominant perspectives deriving from both Heidegger and analytical philosophy. By following up this alternative approach as it is manifested in the philosophy of German Idealism and Romanticism, Frank arrives at arguments which avoid some of the implausible consequences of the notion of the subversion of the subject while not regressing to the notion of the wholly self-transparent subject of the Cartesian tradition.

A lot of work in literary theory has actually shown little serious awareness that the major theoretical questions about the interpretation of texts involve issues that form the very substance of modern European philosophy, as opposed to the idea that they involve a completely new beginning beyond what both Heidegger and Derrida term the 'language of metaphysics'. In consequence, the extent to which the understanding of subjectivity in literary theory has depended upon the contentious story of modern philosophy told by Heidegger is often ignored. The aim of Henrich's revaluation of Fichte is to demonstrate the existence of an important alternative conception of the subject in modern philosophy. This conception severs the link between self-consciousness and self-preservation, in which the subject is ultimately understood as that which preserves itself against what would deprive it of its existence. Henrich sees this link as beginning with Hobbes and its essential consequence as the notion of the subject as lord over internal and external nature which Heidegger regarded as characteristic of Western metaphysics. Using Fichte to open up such an alternative conception might, however, seem perverse: Fichte is generally known as the philosopher of a subject whose power, like that of the God of the ontological proof, is wholly contained within itself, as *causa sui*. Importantly, the parallel of such an understanding of Fichte's conception with conceptions questioned by literary theory is easy to suggest: the author as absolute authority over the meanings of his or her own text plays a similar role to God in the ontological proof, and to Fichte's 'self-positing' subject.

What, though, makes Fichte's arguments so significant for Henrich, and, by extension, for Frank? Fichte arrives at his initial conception of the subject via the realisation that Kant's transcendental subject – the prior condition of possibility of objective knowledge – cannot ground its account of its own existence, which is just assumed by Kant as a 'fact'. Fichte argues that the 'I' cannot be an object of knowledge, because, *qua* subject, it is itself the necessarily prior condition of the very possibility of the world's intelligibility and thus of the objectivity of knowledge. Objectivity is established for Kant in judgements, in which the subject synthesises recurrent appearances given to it from the world of nature by subsuming them under categories and concepts. The vital point is that the 'I' cannot be subject to anything else in the manner of the causally determined nature which is its object of knowledge, because if it were the freedom evident in practical reason and in the 'I''s ability to step back from itself and reflect upon itself in philosophy would become incomprehensible. The centre of Fichte's philosophy is therefore an emphatic notion of freedom, which gives the subject a status that is inherently immune to description in terms of what can be said about the world of knowable objects. It is this conception of freedom which is, of course, the source of the hyperbolic aspect of Fichte, which regards the object world as 'posited' by the 'I'. The fundamental fact about the 'I' is, then, that in some sense it cannot, even in its purely cognitive operations, be objectified.[13] In Heidegger's view Fichte's 'I' is one of the culminations of Western metaphysics, which reaches its apotheosis in Nietzsche's theory of the 'will to power', the motivating ground of the appearing world that mirrors itself to itself in all the conflicting manifestations of the object world, including in the 'subject' itself. Heidegger links this conception to the growing dominance of nature by modern science and technology. Henrich, on the other hand, wants to show that there is another side to Fichte, one still connected to a conception of the freedom of the subject, which is not susceptible to the account given by Heidegger. It is this conception which leads in the direction that has been essential to much of Frank's work.

The central issue here is 'reflection', in which the 'I' splits itself into an objective and a subjective self, a self that is thought about and a self that does the thinking.[14] In line with Heidegger this act is seen by Lacan, Derrida and others as the founding moment in modern metaphysics. Henrich summarises this conception of the subject in Kant's predecessors as follows:

> they held that the essence of the Self (*Ich*) is reflection. This theory begins by assuming a subject of thinking and emphasises that this subject stands in a constant relationship to itself. It then goes on to assert that this relationship is a result of the subject's making itself into its own object; in other words the activity of representing, which is originally related to objects, is turned back on itself and in this way produces the unique case of an identity between the activity and the result of the activity. (Henrich, *Contemporary German Philosophy*, p. 19)

This structure of reflection is clearly the basic structure of a subject

[13] What is often forgotten is that the object world for Fichte is the world of knowledge constituted by the spontaneous aspect of the subject in judgements, as it is in Kant, not the world of immediate unconceptualised sensory data given in receptivity (see also John McDowell, *Mind and World*, Cambridge, Mass., and London: Harvard University Press, 1994, who makes much the same point, and Bowie, 'John McDowell's *Mind and World*, and Early Romantic Epistemology', in *Revue internationale de philosophie* issue on 'Romantic Philosophy', Autumn 1996). For a good interpretation of how Fichte can be understood without entailing some of the more bizarre arguments attributed to him concerning the absolute status of the 'I', see Frederick Neuhouser, *Fichte's Theory of Subjectivity*, Cambridge: Cambridge University Press, 1989. See also Bowie, *Aesthetics and Subjectivity* for a more detailed account of the move from Kant to Fichte. Those familiar with the Sartre of *Being and Nothingness* should recognise the proximity of Fichte's argument to Sartre's view of the subject.

[14] For a brilliant critique of Descartes' version of this issue see Schelling, *On the History of Modern Philosophy*, pp. 42–61.

which is understood to be 'present to itself'. Derrida, in line with Heidegger, seems to regard this as the only notion of the subject in Western metaphysics. Fichte's 'insight' was into the consequences of the inherent circularity of this model of the subject. *Some* sense of the identity of reflector and reflected is evidently fundamental to self-consciousness, otherwise I would have no way of thinking about my thoughts as *my* thoughts. It was this fact which led Descartes to make the reflexive identity of the self the one point of absolute certainty, the *fundamentum inconcussum*, which escapes the problems involved in knowledge of the unreliable world of appearances. The problem Fichte shows comes about when the whole structure of self-consciousness is to be explained in terms of the 'I' reflecting upon itself.[15]

Frank, following Fichte, often uses the metaphor of looking in a mirror to show why reflection is an inadequate model for the explanation of self-consciousness. If I look in a mirror in order to see myself as an object I will only recognise myself, as opposed to a random object or person, if I am already aware that it is myself that I am to look at *before* the reflection. The external image in the object world cannot itself provide the criterion which allows me to see the reflected *object* as myself, as the *subject* that is looking at the image. Sidney Shoemaker sums this idea up in the dictum that: 'Perceptual self-knowledge presupposes non-perceptual self-knowledge, so not all self-knowledge can be perceptual' (Sidney Shoemaker and Richard Swinburne, *Personal Identity*, Oxford: Blackwell, 1984, p. 105). The idea is underlined by the fact that I am capable of seeing what is really myself as not myself, as in the famous story of the philosopher Ernst Mach, who saw a 'shabby pedagogue' climbing on to a tram in the mirror at the end of the tram, only to realise that this was actually himself. Instead of the model of reflection being able to explain the nature of self-consciousness, it must either presuppose the phenomenon it is supposed to be explaining, or it would have to deny the existence of the phenomenon itself, which would be incoherent.

---

[15] For the textual evidence of Fichte's questioning of the reflection model see Bowie, *Aesthetics and Subjectivity*, chapter 3. On the whole question of 'reflection' see Rodolphe Gasché, *The Tain of the Mirror. Derrida and the Philosophy of Reflection*, Cambridge, Mass., and London: Harvard University Press, 1986, and my critique in Bowie, *Schelling*.

The detailed consequences of this insight for Fichte cannot concern us here, but one point is fundamental. Fichte is led to the realisation that his initial attempt to suggest that the subject is that which 'posits' itself, because it is the only case of the immediate identity of subject and object, must give way to a conception in which the subject depends, as Henrich puts it, on

an active ground existing prior to the active Self (*Ich*), a ground which explains the equiprimordial unity of the factors in the Self [the self as subject and as object], but is not itself present in the Self. The term 'Self' refers not to this ground, but only to its result. For 'Self' means to be for oneself. However, the Self does not focus explicitly on what makes its unity possible, even though this latter is its source. (Henrich, *Contemporary German Philosophy*, p. 30)

The crucial factor is that Fichte undermines the structure of reflexive self-presence, which entails a split between two aspects of oneself, by showing the dependence of that structure on a necessarily prior unity which cannot be accounted for in reflexive terms.

We can, therefore, only understand the nature of self-consciousness by realising that, unlike in the case of knowledge of states of affairs, where we can synthesise concept and intuition in seeing the initially indeterminate object determinately as 'x', the self's relation to itself cannot depend on such a synthesis, because it must already be familiar with itself for reflexive self-identification to be possible at all. This is summarised in Frank's recent contentions, with regard to the analytical philosophy of mind, that 'all knowledge (of something) is propositional' – because it has truth-value potential (Fregean '*Bedeutung*') – 'except of that which is present in *self*-consciousness' (Frank, *Selbstbewußtsein und Selbsterkenntnis*, p. 408), and that 'Knowledge of myself *as* of myself does not depend on classification. But it also does not depend on identification [on ascribing a mental predicate to a singular term which stands for myself, so that 'I know that I ϕ'] – for how should I identify an object which *could* not be anything but myself?' (*ibid.*, p. 407). The fact is that propositions can be false and identifications can be mistaken: this cannot be the case in relation to my immediate self-consciousness. The self, then, always already presupposes its own ground in any reflexive act. This dependence of self-consciousness upon a ground which transcends its reflexive acts will recur in important ways in Frank's account of the 'becoming non-transparent of the Absolute for reflection' in Romanticism.

We might by now seem to be rather far from the concerns of literary theory. It should, though, be clear that the Fichtean insight into the problem of self-consciousness is not taken account of in the critiques of 'self-presence' that Derrida and others see as the central issue in the deconstruction of Western metaphysics. This deconstruction can, as we saw above, be understood in terms of the subversion of the author's function as the transparent origin of the meaning that is to be recovered in interpreting the texts of that author.[16] It is the relationship of Fichte's argument to Hegel's philosophy of 'absolute reflection' which can most readily make manifest the link of the issues in Fichte to deconstruction. 'Absolute reflection' is, of course, one of the most frequent targets of post-structuralist attempts to deconstruct metaphysics.

At the end of his essay on Fichte Henrich suggests that Hegel failed to see the problem which Fichte had revealed: 'Hegel conceives the unity of opposites only dialectically, in terms of what results from their opposition. However, the phenomenon of the Self requires that this unity be interpreted as original and primordial' (Henrich, *Contemporary German Philosophy*, p. 52). Hegel's system is completed by the subject's realisation, at the end of its development, of its identity with what initially seemed other to it, the object world, via the explication of the 'identity of identity and difference'. The truth of the world turns out at the end to be the world's thinking itself – hence Hegel's dictum that the 'substance is subject'. In Hegel's 'absolute Idea' thought and the world are shown to reflect each other in the moving structure of what he terms *Geist* ('spirit' or 'mind'), which has the structure of '*self-reflection*': in the same way as the object only becomes determinate via its relation to the subject, the subject can only come to its own truth via its relation to the objects with which it engages.[17]

---

[16] See also Derrida's remarks about the kind of interpretation, which he wishes to avoid, that: 'seeks to decipher, dreams of deciphering a truth or an origin that escapes the play and the order of the sign, and lives the necessity of interpretation like an exile' (Jacques Derrida, *L'écriture et la différence*, Paris: Points, 1967 p. 427).

[17] This conception has recently received an interesting contemporary revival in McDowell, *Mind and World*: see Bowie, 'John McDowell's *Mind and World*', for a view of McDowell from the Romantic perspective.

Derrida suggests that in Hegel: 'The concept as absolute subjectivity thinks itself, it is for itself and next to itself, it has no outside and collects up, while effacing them, its time and its difference into its self-presence' (Jacques Derrida, *Marges de la philosophie*, Paris: Minuit, 1972, p. 60). Fichte's insight can be used to show that the structure of self-presence depends upon an *initial* grounding unity which cannot appear in reflection and which cannot, therefore, as Hegel thinks it can, be only a result of the subject's 'collecting up' of its differing moments into 'self-presence' at the *end* of the system.[18] Fichte's idea thereby suggests a different account of the metaphysics of subjectivity, which, because it is not dependent on self-presence, escapes Derrida's fundamental objection. This different account informs key aspects of the Romantic philosophy which is Frank's central point of orientation, for which, along with Kant and F.H. Jacobi, Fichte was the crucial influence.

THE ROMANTIC ABSOLUTE

The roots of early Romantic philosophy have yet to be adequately understood: for too long Romantic philosophy has been interpreted in the light of Hegel's and Kierkegaard's critiques, which obscured many of its most significant insights.[19] It is evident from recent work by Frank, Henrich and others that the basis of Fichte's 'insight' was already implicit in other areas of late eighteenth-century German philosophy. One constellation is increasingly clear in this respect, which sheds remarkable light on subsequent philosophy. In the 1780s, during what became known as the 'Pantheism controversy', a controversy over the theological implications of Spinoza's determinist understanding of nature, Jacobi claimed in discussing Spinoza's notion that 'all determination is negation' that 'we remain, as long as we grasp things conceptually [*begreifen*], in a chain of *conditioned conditions*' (in Heinrich Scholz (ed.), *Die Hauptschriften zum Pantheismusstreit zwischen Jacobi und Mendelssohn*, Berlin: Reuther and Reichard, 1916, p. 276; see Birgit

---

[18] It is, as Frank has shown, Schelling who first explicitly uses this structure against Hegel (see Frank, *Der unendliche Mangel*; Bowie, *Schelling*; and 'The Schellingian Alternative', *Bulletin of the Hegel Society of Great Britain*, 30, Autumn 1994).

[19] E.g. in Hegel's *Aesthetics*, and in Kierkegaard's *Concept of Irony* and *Either/Or*.

Sandkaulen-Bock, *Ausgang vom Unbedingten. Über den Anfang in der Philosophie Schellings*, Göttingen: Vandenhoeck and Ruprecht, 1990; Andrew Bowie, *From Romanticism to Critical Theory*, and 'Re-thinking the History of the Subject: Jacobi, Schelling and Heidegger', in Simon Critchley and Peter Dews (eds.), *Deconstructive Subjectivities*, New York: SUNY Press, 1996). There is therefore no way of arriving at a conception of that which is 'unconditioned', the '*Unbedingte*', the ground of what we try to understand by reason. There can be no further condition of this ground, which Jacobi terms '*Seyn*', 'being'. 'Being' cannot be an object of knowledge, because that would make it relative to a condition: it is 'that which cannot be explained: the indissoluble, the immediate, the simple' (ed. Scholz, *Die Hauptschriften*, p. 90). For Jacobi this ground – which he interpreted theologically – was what prevented acceptance of the 'nihilist' conception of modern science inherent in Spinoza's reduction of knowledge to the principle of sufficient reason, which leads to the 'chain of *conditioned conditions*'.

Even without the theological consequences he draws from it the structure of Jacobi's argument – which was well known to the key thinkers of the time, from Kant to the Romantics – prefigures at the level of ontology the structure of Fichte's insight into the need for a non-reflexive ground in self-consciousness. The identity of each moment in self-consciousness depends on its not being the other moments, but that is not enough to ground *self*-consciousness, which must be able to connect the differing moments on the basis of an identity which does not appear in reflection. In an analogous manner each particular truth that is arrived at via application of the principle of sufficient reason leads into a chain which makes the particular truth relative to other truths, leaving the question unanswered as to the relationship of the whole, which gives rise to the particular truths, to its relative parts. Schelling sees one consequence of this when he asks:

how can a series of cognitions be knowledge when no point of that series is anything absolute/unconditioned [*etwas Unbedingtes*]; the single link in the chain has a value, but it has it via another link, which in turn has it via another link, etc., into infinity; the value of each single element is therefore conditioned by an infinite series, which itself is not any thing [*ein Unding*] and will never really be. (Friedrich Wilhelm Joseph

Schelling's *Sämmtliche Werke*, ed. K.F.A. Schelling, I Division vols. I–x, II Division vols. I–IV, Stuttgart: Cotta 1856–61, I/IV p. 343)

What is meant by the '*Unding*' corresponds to Derrida's 'transcendental signified', and Schelling's development of the structure in question is one source of Heidegger's conception of 'ontological difference', the difference between the fact that things in the world are disclosed at all, and determinate propositions about specific entities (see Bowie, *Schelling*).

The structure Jacobi identifies and which Schelling adopts underlies a whole series of issues in modern philosophy which also recur in literary theory (see Bowie, *From Romanticism to Critical Theory*). The Spinozist structure of negation recurs in Saussure's conception of the sign, in which the signifier depends for its determinacy upon other signifiers, there being no positive terms in language. Derrida radicalises this thought, and thereby echoes Jacobi's insight, when he claims that the signifier can never, therefore, be present as itself because it is inseparably linked to the temporally occurring traces of other signifiers, which defer any final meaning in the process of *différance*: 'philosophy lives *in* and *from différance*, blinding itself to the *same* which is not the identical. The same is precisely *différance* (with an *a*) as the detour and equivocal passage from one different element (*différent*) to the other' (Derrida, *Marges*, p. 18). Just how Derrida's '*same*' is to be understood is the vital question, though it should already be clear that its structural role is much the same as that of the '*Unbedingte*' in Jacobi and Schelling, or, in some interpretations, of Heidegger's '*Sein*'. The basic idea of the Romantic tradition of which Derrida forms a part is that philosophy cannot claim to establish the nature of the relationship of thought or language to the world, thus to have access to a 'transcendental signified' which would be the ground that rendered that relationship finally transparent.[20]

---

[20] This tradition is not merely an abstract construction on the basis of a structure which is coincidentally repeated in a series of otherwise disparate thinkers. Its historical basis is the following: Jacobi's insight was developed, with the help of Hölderlin, by Schelling in his critique of the early Fichte and also later used in his critique of Hegel. Schelling's Hegel-critique has extensive parallels in the work of Heidegger who, though he does not discuss it, was clearly familiar with it; the critique also was central for the work of Franz Rosenzweig, who, along with Heidegger, was a major influence on Levinas, who, also along with Heidegger, was one of Derrida's most significant influences. On this see Bowie, *Schelling*, and *From Romanticism to Critical Theory*.

Frank's work connects the Romantic development of this idea to the attempt to understand subjectivity in the manner implied by Fichte's insight, and considers a whole range of subsequent theories in the light of the results. A crucial factor which differentiates Romantic philosophy from post-structuralism is that, while involving conceptual structures which parallel aspects of post-structuralism, Romantic philosophy also sustains conceptions of the subject which are not open to the critique of Hegelian self-presence we considered above. The power of the Romantic conception becomes apparent when it is realised how many motifs from Romantic philosophy have re-emerged in the most diverse areas of contemporary philosophy. Before looking at some of Frank's use of the insights of Romantic philosophy it is, therefore, worth briefly indicating one contemporary example of the recurrence of a central issue in that philosophy.[21] The underlying issue is the problem of the 'Absolute' we have just seen revealed in Jacobi's critique of Spinoza.

In Hegelian 'absolute idealism', as we saw, the opposition between subject and object leads to the overcoming of the relative and changing status of particular knowledge via the revelation that subject and object are the necessary complement of each other in the structure of *Geist*, which culminates in the 'absolute Idea'. Contemporary notions of the Absolute, on the other hand, tend to be 'materialist' or 'physicalist' conceptions,[22] in which the results of physics are the absolute point of reference. This absolute basis is supposed to move us beyond the relativity of our culturally bound conceptions of the world. For such a strong conception of physics to hold, though, it must be maintained that scientific investigation, as Hilary Putnam puts it, 'converges to a single true theory, a single explanatory picture of the universe' (Hilary Putnam, *Realism with a*

---

[21] Other examples are the recurrence of ideas from Romantic hermeneutics in the work of Donald Davidson, Hilary Putnam and others (see Andrew Bowie, 'Truth, Language and Art: Benjamin, Davidson and Heidegger', in Graham Bartram (ed.), *New Comparison* 18, 1995; and *From Romanticism to Critical Theory*); the concern in the philosophy of mind with the problem of whether self-consciousness has a propositional structure (see Frank, *Selbstbewußtsein und Selbsterkenntnis*); the parallels of 'anomalous monism' with Schelling's version of the Absolute in his identity theory (see Frank, *Selbstbewußtsein und Selbsterkenntnis*, Bowie, *Schelling*).

[22] In the period of the Romantics such positions, like that of Spinoza, were usually referred to as 'realism': many of the contemporary objections to physicalism were repeated in the Romantic period against 'realist' conceptions.

Human Face, Cambridge, Mass., and London: Harvard University Press, 1990, p. 170), which is the view put forward by Bernard Williams. The very notion of an absolute *conception* of the world is problematic, though, for reasons which were central to the Romantic tradition. Putnam claims against Williams, and in line with the Romantic tradition: 'It cannot be the case that scientific knowledge (future fundamental physics) is absolute and nothing else is; for fundamental physics cannot explain the possibility of *referring to* or *stating* anything, including fundamental physics itself' (*ibid.*, p. 176). The reasons for the failure of such an account of an absolute conception to give an account of intentionality are precisely what leads one back to the problems which concerned the Romantics.

Frank has shown that questions about the structure of the Absolute are fundamental to Romantic philosophy:

> two incompatible demands are contained in the thought of the Absolute: in order really to be absolute it must exist in itself, i.e. without any relation to an other; on the other hand the Absolute as the highest principle of philosophy must be thought of as self-conscious [Putnam would say it must involve 'intentionality'] (consequently as dependent on consciousness). (Frank, *Einführung in die frühromantische Ästhetik*, p. 239)

The very structure of an absolute *conception* inherently involves problems of circularity, as various strands of modern philosophy have shown. Any attempt to encompass a totality must either adopt a perspective outside the totality, and thus include the totality in itself as only a relative totality, or face the problem that totalities cannot describe themselves as totalities, because the description would then have to include a description of the description and so on *ad infinitum*. The claim that a particular kind of explanation is converging to the absolute conception must *already* know what that conception is, as otherwise it would have no way of recognising that the true conception had been reached. But what sort of knowledge would that be, given that it must be immediately available from the outset, as it would otherwise itself be relative to other knowledge, and therefore not absolute? This is, as Frank shows, exactly the objection Schelling made against Hegel's conception of the Absolute, which claimed not to presuppose anything and yet to be able to arrive at the absolute Idea (see Frank, *Der unendliche Mangel*, Bowie, *Schelling*). In this light any conception of an Absolute might appear doomed to failure, and only relative conceptions of reason would seem possible. In a Nietzschean perspective, of the kind familiar in much literary theory, this would mean, though, that no conception of reason is possible at all, and there can only be relative perspectives. Putnam denies this by claiming that 'The very fact that we speak of our different conceptions as conceptions of *rationality* posits a *Grenzbegriff*, a limit-concept of the ideal truth' (Hilary Putnam, *Reason, Truth and History*, Cambridge: Cambridge University Press, 1981, p. 216). Romantic philosophy is concerned precisely with the nature of this *Grenzbegriff*, which relates to what Romantic philosophers mean by the 'Absolute'. This leads Romantic philosophy to the question of aesthetics and Frank to his version of many of the issues that have been central to literary theory and which are now beginning to play a role in analytical philosophy.

In *Das Problem 'Zeit' in der deutschen Romantik* Frank considers Romantic philosophy to be perhaps the most apt philosophy for explaining the 'paradigm of modernity'. Unlike the Heideggerian paradigm, in which the subject dominates its Other, as Heidegger thinks it does in Descartes or in Hegel, Frank's idea of this paradigm, although it depends on the subject, is significantly two-edged: 'The insight which precedes all other experiences: only to be via oneself and only to be able to preserve oneself via oneself, is indissolubly linked in self-consciousness with the "feeling" that one cannot ground oneself via oneself' (Frank, *Das Problem 'Zeit'*, p. 19). The sense of the subject's dependence comes about because the *fact* of the existence of self-consciousness cannot be grasped in the subject's reflection upon itself, which, as we saw, always depends upon what cannot appear in reflection and must precede reflection. As Novalis puts it in 1795–6, in his 'Fichte-Studies': 'What reflection *finds*, *seems* already *to be there*' (Novalis, *Das philosophisch-theoretische Werk*, p. 17). This dependence becomes most apparent in the inescapable temporal structure of self-consciousness. Instead of self-consciousness being, as it is in Kant, the condition of possibility of time, Friedrich Schlegel and Novalis see it as being itself inherently temporal. The very nature of self-consciousness depends on the loss of the past and the lack of what will be in the future, which means the subject's present is seen as a 'gap' which tries to fill itself by linking these negations of itself into a totality. Frank cites Schlegel: 'In the same way as we cannot grasp ourselves, as we only appear to ourselves as a piece of ourselves, we cannot be a product of ourselves' (in Frank, *Das Problem 'Zeit'*, p. 65). However, despite its inability to grasp the total structure of itself because of the nature of temporality, self-consciousness must yet be constituted on the basis of a unity which is the necessary foundation of its *awareness* of its own divided nature – what Schlegel terms its 'striving' and what Schelling will later refer to as a 'lack of being'. A sense of lack can only be felt by that which has a sense of the completion that would overcome that lack. This ground of unity, Frank maintains, is the location of the sense of the Absolute which is manifested in art.

It might seem from what has been said so far that the Romantic Absolute simply repeats the problems of Hegel's idealism, in so far as the negative status of particular moments, their necessary relation to an Other as the condition of their own being, is the basis of the Absolute as the totality which encompasses these relations. The easiest way to understand both the difference between these positions and the reasons for Frank's championing of the Romantic understanding of the Absolute against Hegel, is to consider the role of art in each. In Hegel art is the 'sensuous appearing of the Idea', a lower stage of the development of *Geist* that is overcome when art is comprehended in philosophy. Art is still tied to the transient world of the senses and is therefore only a relative triumph over the transience of that world. The truth contained in art must be explicated in philosophy, which itself does not require the sensuous medium that art requires, because philosophical truth emerges through the insight into the reasons why any finite, sensuous aspect of the appearing world must negate itself. For Hegel it is philosophy that is able to explicate the absolute truth contained in the disappearance of finite particulars, in the 'concept'.[23] However, well before Hegel had developed his system, and

---

[23] The growth of a plant from seed to flower, in which each stage negates the preceding stage but also depends upon that stage, which is used as a metaphor of the concept in the *Phenomenology of Spirit*, helps explain what Hegel means.

had asserted that art is a subordinate medium of truth, Novalis, Schlegel and the younger Schelling had, precisely because of the problem posed by the explication of the Absolute within any philosophical system, given art a status above philosophy.

Frank has suggested that Romantic philosophy is, *avant la lettre*, 'Hegelianism without a crowning conclusion' (Frank, *Einführung in die frühromantische Ästhetik*, p. 228). The Romantics do not exclude the question of the Absolute from philosophy, rather they understand the relationship of philosophy to the Absolute in a different way from Hegel (see Bowie, *Aesthetics and Subjectivity*, pp. 194–8). Consider the following from Friedrich Schlegel's lectures on *Transcendentalphilosophie* of 1800–1, at which Hegel was probably present in the audience: 'Truth arises when opposed errors neutralise each other. Absolute truth cannot be admitted; and this is the testimony for the freedom of thought and of spirit. If absolute truth were found then the business of spirit would be completed and it would have to cease to be, since it only exists in activity' (Friedrich Schlegel, *Transcendentalphilosophie*, ed. Michael Elsässer, Hamburg: Meiner, 1991, p. 93). The only approach to the highest truth will, therefore, not be via a positive assertion which eventually determines what that truth is, but rather via a mode of assertion which cannot finally be made determinate. Friedrich Schlegel terms this mode 'irony', and regards it as intrinsically connected to art.

Irony is normally understood as the determinate negation of what is asserted in a proposition: 'That was good', asserted ironically, means it was not good. Romantic irony requires the negation of any assertion, but not in favour of a determinate contrary assertion, because all determinate assertions, as Jacobi already suggested in his notion of 'conditioned conditions', are relative to other assertions, and thus cannot be definitive. Hegel's system is ironic to the extent to which it does not rely on a prior basis which is posited at the outset: that is the point of his treatment of the notion of 'being' at the beginning of the *Logic*, where he tries to show that 'being' and 'nothing' are equivalently 'negative' because they are both indeterminate. The 'negation of the negation' means that any particular moment is always dependent for its identity upon other equally dependent moments. Hegel, though, restores the positive Absolute at the end, as a pure affirmation,

the 'absolute Idea', which is the result of the final negation of
the negation (see Frank, *Einführung in die frühromantische Ästhetik*,
pp. 307–8). It is the destruction of irony in the absolute Idea which
the Romantic position will not allow. Frank describes Romantic
irony as:

> the negation (*Aufhebung*) of the particular as particular in such a way that
> the conditions of finitude are at the same time respected (the particular is
> able to appear) and denied (the particular is negated). In this way the
> Romantic artistic device of irony reveals itself as the only conceivable
> solution of the contradiction involved in making that which is at the same
> time finite and infinite appear *within* finitude. (Frank, *Einführung in die
> frühromantische Ästhetik*, p. 311)

Irony is, then, understood as the essence of art. The work of art,
such as a piece of music, manifests itself as a finite object of the
understanding, which can be determined in scientific terms, as
wavelengths, frequencies and durations of pitch, but which, as
music, can never be finally determined. Music is also dependent
upon time to be itself: each note must give way to subsequent
notes, which both negate it and give it its significance. Most
crucially, subsuming music into concepts does not reveal what
makes it aesthetically significant (see Bowie, *Aesthetics and Subjectivity*, chapter 2 and chapter 7): any attempt to do so reveals a deficit
in conceptuality of the kind suggested by Romantic irony. If a
conceptual description could replace the music itself then the
music would become redundant, but this is precisely what aesthetic experience shows is not possible.

Why, though, does Frank still use the apparently discredited
metaphysical term 'the Absolute' in this context, instead of asserting, as post-structuralism does, for example, that the inherent
temporality and differentiation involved in all forms of articulation, whether aesthetic or not, means that meaning cannot be
either 'foreclosed' by or 're-appropriated' in interpretation, and
therefore that talk of 'the Absolute' has become indefensible?
Frank denies that the intersubjective identity of meaning required
for a philosophically articulated conception of the Absolute can
ever finally be known to be established: that is one point of his
reviving Schelling's critique of Hegel and other aspects of Roman-

tic hermeneutics. The reasons for Frank's retention of the notion of the Absolute relate to his refusal to renounce a rational conception of truth in favour of the Nietzschean attempt to subvert the idea of truth in the name of its being grounded in the 'Will to power', as well as to his refusal to subordinate the subject to language in the manner characteristic of literary theory, Gadamerian hermeneutics and many versions of analytical semantics.

Frank's position diverges from the post-structuralist attempt to make the subject an 'effect' of differential articulation in his demonstration, via his interpretation of the Romantic Absolute and subsequent related arguments in modern philosophy, that differentiality is a necessary, but not a *sufficient* condition of subjectivity. The meaningfulness of the differential marks in which language is manifested cannot be explained without involving the consciousness which renders those marks intelligible as language, as opposed to their being just natural phenomena. The reification which ensues from making the subject the 'effect' (Derrida) of the text is countered in Frank's insistence on a ground in self-consciousness that allows difference – which *is* evidently a necessary condition of meaning – to be registered *as* significant difference. This ground cannot itself appear, but without it the very nature of subjectivity becomes incomprehensible. The failure of the ground to appear in reflection, and thus to be subsumable into a concept, is what links subjectivity to the significance of art in Romantic philosophy.

The Romantic understanding of art develops Kant's argument in the *Critique of Judgement* that what appears in art is, *qua* object of conceptually determinable knowledge, not what is aesthetically significant: it is just moving air waves, marks on surfaces, etc. But the fact that what appears points to what cannot appear means

there can be no intuition [*Anschauung*] of the Highest, but it does not simply mean for this reason (as complacent common-sense would like impatiently to conclude) that the Highest does not exist at all. It exists as that which, in the divisions and fragmentations of our world of the understanding, yet creates that unity, without which contradiction and difference could not be shown as such. (Frank, *Einführung in die frühromantische Ästhetik*, p. 340)

In the same way the essence of the subject is not manifested in a particular moment or fixed insight into its identity but in 'longing', which inherently moves the subject beyond any coincidence with itself. 'Longing' must, though, as we have seen, be grounded in a unity that is the condition of division. It is, Frank maintains, in the engagement with art that we can understand the nature of the unity which makes contradiction manifest as contradiction. One of his most striking contentions is, then, that art is inherently linked to the subject's relationship to truth.

ART AND TRUTH

Frank's defence of the subject in the face of its subjection to 'tradition', '*différance*', the 'symbolic order', language games, etc., is a defence of the active role of self-consciousness in understanding and language use, a defence of the capacity to mean something which the linguistic code or existing linguistic praxes cannot contain and which therefore cannot be contained within a philosophy that tries to circumscribe the sayable. Those aspects of signification which cannot be exhausted by analysis of language as a repeatable rule-bound code connect the philosophy of language to aesthetics, as the realm of that which cannot be subsumed into concepts. Although it is clear that the subject's understanding requires intersubjective rules of language, and that much that happens in communication simply follows the rules, the fact that meaning is continually shifting requires an account of those shifts which does not fall prey to the reifications evident in the metaphors concerning language and the subject that abound in contemporary philosophy from positivism to Gadamer and Derrida.

Frank's emphasis on the philosophical significance of art locates him in the – Romantic-derived – tradition which in this century is particularly associated with Adorno, Heidegger and Gadamer. This tradition has given rise to a tension which underlies many of the differences between analytical and European philosophy, the tension between conceptions of language as the medium of propositional assertion and as the medium of 'world-disclosure', the basis of which we already encountered above in relation to Heidegger's notion of ontological difference (on this see Bowie,

Schelling, and *From Romanticism to Critical Theory*; Charles Taylor, *Human Agency and Language*, Cambridge: Cambridge University Press, 1985, and *Philosophical Arguments*, Cambridge, Mass., and London: Harvard University Press, 1995). Frank's work offers a new way of understanding this tension. Like Gadamer in *Truth and Method*, Frank thinks that the significance of art lies in its relationship to a conception of truth, but he sees this relationship in a different manner from Gadamer. Gadamer's account of the truth of art relies on the assumption that Kant, in line with the Cartesian tradition of subjectivity, had 'subjectified' aesthetics, reducing the status of art to the level of the judgements of individual taste of its recipients and thereby excluding it from any kind of wider claim to truth. For Gadamer it is Heidegger's move away from a philosophy of subjectivity which allows us to understand how the recipients of art are transformed by their experience of the work of art, which 'discloses' the world in new ways. This experience is 'of' the work in the 'subjective', not the 'objective' genitive. Language, Gadamer claims, is '*ichlos*' ('self-less'), and 'being that can be understood is language' (Hans-Georg Gadamer, *Wahrheit und Methode*, Tübingen: J.C.B. Mohr, 1975, p. 450, English translation: *Truth and Method*, revised translation by Joel Weinsheimer and Donald G. Marshall, New York: Seabury Press, 1989). Understanding is the involvement of the individual in the happening of intersubjective 'tradition'. Tradition is manifest in the continuing life of the art-work, in its changing interpretations through history, a life which transcends that of its interpreters: 'The "subject" of the experience of art, that which remains and persists, is not the subjectivity of the person who experiences it, but the work of art itself' (Gadamer, *Wahrheit und Methode*, p. 98). Gadamer's position therefore subscribes in its own way to the subordination of the subject to language we examined above.

In Frank's view, however, Gadamer retains an essentially Hegelian conception of a world which reflects itself in language, in the form of what Gadamer terms the 'self-interpretation of being'. This makes language into the equivalent of Hegel's *Geist*, because the individual subject only makes sense to the extent to which its meanings are part of an overall process, in which the part is a self-reflection of the whole. Frank suggests that in Gadamer: 'The being of the Other *qua* Other is lost. As the appearing to itself of the same it is appropriated in the subjectless subjectivism of effective history' (Frank, *Das Individuelle-Allgemeine*, p. 33). Against this Hegelian conception of the Other Frank insists on a 'Sartrean' sense – which he already finds in the work of Schleiermacher – of the irreducibility of the relationship of self and Other to reflection, which is what sustains a role for the individual in interpretation.[24]

One reason that Gadamer's view has been influential in the English-speaking world is because it supports the critique of representation that is central to literary theory. Interpretation for Gadamer is not the attempt at an adequate presentation of the inherent 'ready-made' meaning of the object to be interpreted, but a 'fusion of horizons' between text and interpreter. His understanding of art is grounded in his understanding of 'play', or 'game' (*Spiel*), in which the participant corresponds to a happening whose rule-dependency means that it is constituted outside of what the participant may think while playing the game. 'Play' is the 'mode of being of the art-work itself' (Gadamer, *Wahrheit und Methode*, p. 97), and there is a 'primacy of the game in relation to the consciousness of the player' (*ibid.*, p. 100). This notion of the game points to an informative link between two influential theories in modern philosophy, which can clarify the reasons for Frank's opposition to the elimination of the subject from the question of meaning.

It is not difficult to see Gadamer's view of understanding art as closely analogous to Wittgenstein's notion of the 'language game', which is taken up by Habermas, Rorty and others as part of the move away from the paradigm of subjectivity. The common factor here, as we have seen, is the elimination of the subject, in the name of what cannot be subordinated to the subject, because the subject depends upon it. Without the rules of language there could be no way for the subject to articulate meaning to others. Albrecht Wellmer has criticised Frank's position precisely on the basis of a Wittgensteinian conception of 'meaning', which

points to the concept of the rule, or of the *manner* of use . . . If one assumes [as Frank does] that linguistic signs only gain their own particular sense

---

[24] Frank's critique of Gadamer also takes up motifs from Schelling's critique of Hegel, which formed the basis of his *Der unendliche Mangel an Sein* (see also Frank, *Das Individuelle-Allgemeine*, p. 33, Bowie, *Schelling*).

via an act of interpretation, then one secretly is again making 'meaning' [*das 'Meinen'*, with the sense of subjective 'opinion'] into the source of meanings [*Bedeutungen*]; it then appears incomprehensible how what *I* mean [*meine*] should be able to be understood by an *other*; indeed it seems incomprehensible how I should understand it myself. (Albrecht Wellmer, *Zur Dialektik von Moderne und Postmoderne*, Frankfurt am Main: Suhrkamp, 1985, p. 83)

The crucial issue is what is meant by 'understanding' and how it relates to 'meaning', which Wellmer thinks is defined by intersubjectively agreed use within the rules of a language game.

Rorty, who adopts a similar Wittgensteinian position to that of Wellmer, insists that he belongs among 'those for whom language is a tool rather than a medium, and for whom a concept is just the regular use of a mark or noise' (Richard Rorty, *Essays on Heidegger and Others. Philosophical Papers Volume Two*, Cambridge: Cambridge University Press, 1991, p. 126), there being nothing useful to be said about what is 'subpropositional'. However, Rorty's minimalist conception of the 'mark' leaves unexplained how we understand that a mark is being *used*, as opposed to its just occurring as a random physical event like an involuntary burp or its being analogous to an animal cry. Furthermore, even understanding that the recurrence of a mark is its use does not seem enough to explain how an already familiar mark can be used to mean something new in completely unfamiliar and unrepeatable contexts, such as, most vividly, in a modernist literary text. In his essay on 'Non-reductive physicalism', which tries to make the subject merely the concatenation of a 'web of beliefs' (without telling us who or what is doing the believing), Rorty claims that the creativeness evident in art is just a special case of the 'ability of the human organism to utter meaningless sentences – that is, sentences which do not fit into old language games, and serve as occasions for modifying those language-games and creating new ones. This ability is exercised constantly in every area of culture and daily life' (Richard Rorty, *Objectivity, Relativism, and Truth: Philosophical Papers Volume One*, Cambridge: Cambridge University Press, 1991, p. 125). Rorty thereby makes a strict demarcation between 'meaning', which is the function of 'old language games' and is the condition of 'argument' – 'playing sentences using old words off against each other' (*ibid.*, p.124) – and metaphor, which is therefore, as Donald Davidson maintains, 'meaningless' because, unlike in literal usage, there is no definitive way of establishing its truth-conditions. Frank's point is, though, that the 'meaninglessness' of metaphor is still significant because subjects have the ability to *make* sense, to disclose the world in new ways, *not* just to play language games. Even in 'argument' an aspect of this must come into play, because there can never be the certainty that playing a language game from one subject's perspective is the same as playing it from another subject's perspective. Unless a clear line of demarcation between meaning and metaphor can be drawn, which would seem to require the sort of metaphysical conception which Rorty elsewhere exhorts us to abjure, the role of the subject in understanding cannot simply be eliminated.

Frank therefore maintains that 'Something is understood in the emphatic sense only when the leap is made from the universal system (from the code, the convention, the type) into the individual style of a historically situated subject. Only via this leap does the universal schema achieve its individual sense' (Frank, *Das Sagbare und das Unsagbare*, p. 553). It is undeniable that at the level of syntax and pragmatics the rules of usage are largely fixed, but innovation at the level of 'style', which is evident, for example, in new metaphors and in new syntactic and other rhythms, is vital to the creation of new meaning. Wellmer thinks Frank's claim that there is no way of finally controlling the relationship of the subject's uses of a word or an utterance to the ever different situations in which that same word or utterance is used is irrelevant to the question of meaning, which Wellmer, like Rorty, explains in terms of 'a *plurality* of the situations of use of a linguistic sign' (Wellmer, *Zur Dialektik*, p. 82). He claims that 'The philosophical decentring of the subject', which he characterises in terms of Wittgenstein's theory of linguistic praxis as participation in language games, implies the 'discovery of a common world within reason and within the subject which has already been disclosed' (*ibid.*, pp. 83–4), which manifests itself in the rule-bound praxis of everyday language.

The vital question here is the nature of this 'world disclosure', which Wellmer sees as necessarily constituted at the level of the 'general', of the language into which we are socialised and which we use to regulate interpersonal exchange.[25] The crucial issue here, exemplified in the difference between Wellmer and Frank, is the relationship of world-disclosure of all kinds, in cognitive and other kinds of truth claims, to aesthetics and subjectivity. As has already been suggested, in the Romantic tradition the idea of thought as the representation of a pre-existing reality makes little sense when considered in relation to art, which is significant because it discloses the world, not because it duplicates or mirrors it. Following the Romantics, in his essay *The Origin of the Work of Art*, Heidegger links art's capacity for revealing new aspects of the world to the question of truth, in the manner subsequently adopted by Gadamer. For Heidegger the truth that is disclosed in a proposition does not consist in that proposition's correspondence to a direct intuition of reality, but rather in its expressing a state of affairs in which something is *understood* 'as something'. It is in this dimension of understanding that the aesthetic aspect of our relationship to language becomes most apparent.

Frank sees the disclosure referred to by Wellmer and Heidegger as inherently still linked to the individual subject, not as a happening which is always already intersubjectively constituted in the rules of a linguistic community or in language as the 'house of being'. Rules only exist because of the recursive praxes of the members of a community, but the point is that those praxes are not stable, so it becomes hard to suggest exactly where the rules are really located without slipping into a Platonist 'regulism' (see Robert Brandom, *Making it Explicit*, Cambridge, Mass., and London: Harvard University Press, 1994). The crucial epistemological point here is that if Wellmer is to refute Frank's insistence on the role of the subject in world-disclosure he must settle the problem of self-consciousness via the semantics of the – intersubjective – terms which we use to discuss self-consciousness, so as to make our understanding of the terms for self-consciousness be wholly defined by the use made of them. But, as Frank has argued in relation

---

[25] Wellmer does not deny, of course, that meanings change, but he sees this only at the level of the general acceptability of a new use, which defines 'meaning', not in terms of the generation of such new use.

to Ernst Tugendhat – another representative of a Wittgensteinian approach to the issue of language and the subject – this means that there would have to be a demonstration of 'semantic symmetry', the postulated identity of the sense of a word from the 'I' and the 's/he' perspective, including, of course, the sense of the word 'I' itself, such that one could *know* that the presupposition of semantic identity is fulfilled (see Frank, *Die Unhintergehbarkeit von Individualität*, in particular). This identity, though, cannot be demonstrated, for the reasons suggested in relation to the critique of representation: there is no location from which it could be established. It has to be presupposed. Pragmatically this may not be important: in every-day usage language usually 'works' in Wittgenstein's and Well-mer's sense. However, Frank's point is that the failure of 'semantic symmetry' to be more than a postulate that is continually tested in real communication is significant because of the continual trans-formation of sense in the process of intersubjective communica-tion, which necessarily points to an *a*symmetry: 'it is only *because of* epistemic asymmetry [between individual subjects] that there are shifts in meaning (and progress in knowledge)' (Frank, *Die Unhinter-gehbarkeit von Individualität*, p. 88). Wellmer, then, gives no way of understanding how it is that semantic innovation can result within *any* area of communication.

The key figure in Frank's alternative to the conception of meaning as rule-following is Schleiermacher, who holds together the sense of language as inherently general and rule-based, with-out which communication would be impossible, with a conception that is able to account for the transformation of meaning, which must, for lack of a convincing alternative, take place at the level of the individual language user. Without the interpretative activity of the individual subject in relation to the notionally stable linguistic code the potential for meaning-transformation becomes inexplic-able. Frank argues via Schleiermacher that the

dependence of self-consciousness on language . . . does not mean that each speaker, in speaking, does not permanently displace, distort, draw new limits for the codification of signs – including unconsciously – according to their own individual way of disclosing the world (i.e. chang-ing conventions that have been learnt by applying them), or that they *cannot* do this (a structural possibility is not limited by naming cases in which a change has not taken place: it is a question of whether change *can* take place). (Frank, *Das Sagbare und das Unsagbare*, p. 104)

This position, the defence of which informs the essays translated here, is another result of the basic insight of Romantic philosophy into the lack of an Archimedean point from which intersubjective certainty can be established. Reflection on the philosophy of language here coincides with an awareness of an aesthetic potential in *all* language use. The very fact that literary texts are made up of the same linguistic elements as any other texts can suggest how the difference of literary from other texts cannot be based on the idea of linguistic usage which is different in principle from other usage: which language would be used to draw the line between the two?[26]

Interestingly, it is not even clear whether Wittgenstein's own position is exhausted by Wellmer's understanding of meaning as use, as the following passage from the *Philosophical Investigations* can suggest:

We speak of understanding a sentence in the sense in which it can be replaced by another sentence which says the same thing; but also in the sense in which it cannot be replaced by another sentence. (As little as a musical theme can be replaced by another theme).

In the first case the thought of a sentence is what is common to differing sentences; in the second something that only these words in these positions express. (Understanding a poem). (Ludwig Wittgenstein, *Philosophische Untersuchungen*, Frankfurt am Main: Suhrkamp, 1971, p. 227)

The second of these kinds of understanding – Wittgenstein insists that his concept of understanding must involve *both* kinds – involves a form of aesthetic judgement, because there is no possible concept of the thought of the poem which could express the same as the poem expresses, in the same way as there is not in the case of a musical theme. Indeed, Wittgenstein claims, 'Understanding a sentence in language is much more related to understanding a

---

[26] The literary is therefore constituted at the level of aesthetic judgement, not as a radically other kind of language. Once this is admitted Terry Eagleton's dismissal in *Literary Theory* of the very notion of literature can be shown to be based on the scientist assumption that the literary must be identifiable via a concept that clearly delineates it from non-literature. 'There can', though, as Schleiermacher argues, 'be no concept of a style' (Schleiermacher, *Hermeneutik und Kritik*, p. 172), so the literary is a possibility in all language use.

theme in music than one thinks' (*ibid.*, p. 226). Wittgenstein's assertion relates to another aspect of Schleiermacher's development of Romantic philosophy, which suggests a further way of understanding Frank's contentions.

In the *Critique of Pure Reason* Kant characterised judgement as the subject's 'capacity to subsume under rules'. He realises, though, that there cannot be rules for the application of the rule to the particular case, as this would lead to an infinite regress of rules for applying rules. Judgement must therefore depend upon the prior 'schematising' capacity of the subject, which gives an initial coherence to experience before it is subsumed into judgements (see David Bell, 'The Art of Judgement', *Mind* 96, 1987).[27] Schleiermacher seizes on the fact that the nature of this schematisation does not remain constant, which is evident in shifts in the way the world is interpreted, and links the schema to language. Wittgenstein's reflection on the two ways of understanding reintroduces the Kantian distinction between judgements of particulars based on a pre-existing general rule ('determining judgements') and judgements based on trying to establish a rule in relation to the particular ('reflective judgements'), which Kant introduced in the *Critique of Judgement* as part of the attempt to overcome the problem of the regress of rules.

The initial point is that there can be no rules for Wittgenstein's second kind of understanding. More importantly, as Schleiermacher showed, the distinction of one kind of judgement from the other can never be finally articulated, and depends upon the role of the interpreting subject, because there are no a priori rules for applying rules, even in determining judgement. For Schleiermacher the application of the pre-existing concept to an intuition depends upon the prior contextual understanding of a state of affairs which cannot be derived from a rule, and which is therefore inherently open to revision. This, Schleiermacher claimed, made hermeneutics a universal task, even for the natural sciences: 'The

---

[27] Bell refers to this capacity as a 'rule governed spontaneity'. On this topic, which has become a major issue in analytical philosophy, see Brandom, *Making It Explicit*; Bowie, *From Romanticism to Critical Theory*, and 'The Meaning of the Hermeneutic Tradition in Contemporary Philosophy', in Anthony O'Hear (ed.), *'Verstehen' and Humane Understanding*, Publications of the Royal Institute of Philosophy, Cambridge: Cambridge University Press, 1996.

complete task of hermeneutics is to be regarded as a work of art, but not as though the carrying out of the task ended in a work of art, but in as much as the activity has the *character* of art, since the application is not given with the rules' (Schleiermacher, *Hermeneutik und Kritik*, p. 81). As Frank puts it: 'For Schleiermacher the aesthetic situation has simply become epistemically general' (Frank, *Einführung in die frühromantische Ästhetik*, p. 69), because the line between the two kinds of judgement can itself only be drawn by another judgement, so there is no final criterion for any kind of judgement which would make it immune to revision.

Once the notion of truth as representation is abandoned all truth must be established in real processes of communication, there being no possible court of appeal outside that process. In Frank's conception this links the aesthetic to the consensus theory of truth. What, though, distinguishes Frank's position from that of Habermas' consensus theory, the most influential version of such a conception of truth in recent European philosophy? The differences between Habermas and Frank are important because they highlight fundamental alternatives in contemporary theory. Habermas' consensus-oriented theory of communicative action has in recent times frequently been contrasted with Lyotard's 'agonistic' position in *Le différend* and other texts (e.g. by Rorty, *Essays on Heidegger*, pp. 164–76). Frank has himself devoted a highly polemical book to the relationship of Lyotard to Habermas (Frank, *Die Grenzen der Verständigung*), in which he expressly favours Habermas. He sees Lyotard's characterisation of the '*différend*', the discursive conflict which is totally undecidable because a 'universal rule of judgement between heterogeneous types of discourse is lacking' (Jean-François Lyotard, *Le différend*, Paris: Minuit, 1983, p. 9, English translation: *The Differend: Phrases in Dispute*, trans. Georges van Den Abbeele, Manchester: Manchester University Press), as incoherent, because even the putative awareness of the undecidability of a discursive conflict must rely on more than Lyotard's definition of the *différend* will allow. Without some identification that is shared by both partners of what is at issue in a dispute one cannot claim to be involved in a dispute at all, irresolvable or not.

For Lyotard the 'rules' of a 'regime of discourse' supposedly prevent someone located in one discourse moving between incommensurable 'regimes', so that Nazis and liberals could never communicate about, let alone agree on, essentially contested issues. The fact is, though, that it is precisely because Lyotard formulates the whole issue of validity in terms of the incommensurability of 'regimes' of rules that he generates so many aporias: the assumption that the rules of a discourse or a language game finally determine the actual interpretative praxes of those 'located' within it (which is itself a questionable metaphor) is pure Platonism. If we cannot claim there is a final foundation for the employment of rules the obvious conclusion, given the fact of continuing, sometimes successful, communication, is that there is, as Frank suggests, no reason to see rules as the final criterion of meaning.[28] In this sense there is no reason to accept the necessity of irreconcilable regimes of discourse, as opposed to the ever present fact of conflicting but potentially revisable beliefs held by real individuals: Nazis, after all, do sometimes become good liberals. The conflicting regimes of the *différend* are, therefore, the regulist's, not the Schleiermacherian hermeneuticist's theoretical problem.

Frank's rejection of Lyotard's position is based on his insistence on retaining the Romantic notion of the Absolute: without the orientation towards the consensus which is the condition of possibility of contradiction there can be no way of even showing how differing utterances contradict each other. In this connection Frank cites another fundamental insight of Fichte's:

Everything which is opposed to something is the same as what it is opposed to in one characteristic = X; and: everything the same is opposed to what it is the same as in one respect = X. Such a characteristic = X is the ground, in the first case the ground of *relation*, in the second the ground of *difference*; for identifying [*gleichsetzen*] or comparing [*vergleichen*] what is opposed is called relating; opposing what has been identified is *differentiating* them. (J.G. Fichte, *Werke 1*, Berlin: de Gruyter, 1971, p. 111)

Lyotard's position is, in this light, essentially an incoherent version of the problem encountered in aesthetic judgement. Aesthetic judgement, as we saw, comes into play because there is no rule for the application of rules, which means the activity of interpretation

---

[28] Davidson, incidentally, agrees. He maintains that language has no 'rules in any strict sense' (in E. Lepore (ed.), *Truth and Interpretation*, Oxford: Blackwell, 1984, p. 446).

is inescapable even in cognitive judgements. As such there cannot be any final guarantee that agreement has been definitively reached in *any* realm. Frank regards this as the fundamental situation in modern philosophy, and thus not as a manifestation of a new 'postmodern' situation with all the – sometimes ludicrous – implications Lyotard tries to draw from this supposed situation.

While sharing Habermas' concern with the necessary orientation towards truth which is inherent within the very structure of communicative action, Frank's opposition to the post-Wittgensteinian conception of subjectivity does, however, lead him to question other aspects of Habermas' position, in ways which, rather paradoxically, sometimes bring him closer to the arguments of Derrida and others, of which he is often critical in other respects (see Robert Holub, *Crossing Borders: Reception Theory, Poststructuralism, Deconstruction*, Madison: University of Wisconsin Press, 1992). The insights of Romantic aesthetics make Frank suspicious of the strict division between truth as a 'validity claim which we connect to statements when we assert them' (Habermas), and truth as the world-disclosure which becomes evident to us in the experience of the work of art. This does, though, raise some highly controversial issues.

Habermas has, in many ways justifiably, warned against 'an abdication of problem-solving philosophical thinking before the poetic power of language, literature and art' (Jürgen Habermas, *Texte und Kontexte*, Frankfurt am Main: Suhrkamp, 1991, p. 90). Like Rorty, Habermas thinks that separating the discourses of problem-solving from language as 'world-disclosure' enables one not to confuse 'argument' with writing a new vocabulary that changes the language game altogether. Frank offers the following alternative conception, based on the links of the 'poetic' function of language to his conception of the subject:

The creation of sense and the changing of sense belongs in the division of labour to the 'poetic function' of all utterances; the measuring out of the spaces of propositional truths and normatively correct prescriptions belongs more to philosophy. But that does not prevent the latter from working in a space of comprehensibility which is opened up by the former. Literature (*Dichtung*) is not indifferent to truth in the sense that it first of all makes possible the distribution of truth-values in linguistic contexts; but it does not necessarily partake of truth in the narrower sense of this term, namely as propositional truth. My thesis is, of course, that propositional truth is founded in truth-*qua*-comprehensibility; this thesis can without doubt exist together with a concept of 'formal semantics' which has been revised in a contextualist direction. (Frank, *Stil in der Philosophie*, pp. 72–3)

Although one way of understanding this passage – which is clearly influenced by Heidegger as well as by the Romantics – brings Frank close to what Habermas has termed Derrida's tendency to make the 'problem-solving capacity of language disappear behind its world-creating capacity' (Jürgen Habermas, *Der philosophische Diskurs*, p. 241), the congruence of Frank's remarks with Putnam's worries about Habermas' position can suggest a different perspective.

Putnam claims that one cannot, as Habermas tries to,

achieve a correct conception of rationality by pasting together a positivistic account of rationality in the 'nomothetic' sciences and a vague account of rationality in the 'ideographic' sciences. A better approach would be to begin by recognizing that interpretation, in the very wide sense of the term, and value are involved in our notions of rationality in every area. (Hilary Putnam, *Realism and Reason*, p. 300)

Against Habermas' tendency to think he can create a theory which would be able to draw a definitive line between the criticisable claims to validity of philosophy and the sciences, and 'literature', in the sense of 'world-disclosing' forms of language, Frank insists that what Habermas would consign to the aesthetic can itself be vital in problem-solving. However, Frank differs from Putnam, who in this respect is closer to Wittgenstein, in giving an emphatic role to the individual subject in the process of interpretation, thus in the orientation of his philosophy away from a dominant concern with the publicly testable results of the natural sciences.[29] The recent reminders of the importance of aesthetics in modern philosophy that have arisen in sometimes questionable forms in literary theory are revealed in Frank's work as dependent upon a repressed part of the philosophical discourse of modernity, thus as a part of the discourse of reason, not as the signs of a new postmodern era.

[29] Putnam himself, though, seems to be more and more suspicious of the scientistic orientation of much contemporary philosophy.

At the same time Frank questions positions in modern philosophy which fail to take account of those creative and irreducible aspects of the individual subject which, although never subsumable into a theory of rationality, yet belong to our understanding of the possibilities of reason.

Frank's positions are, while posing crucial challenges to much received wisdom in contemporary philosophy, evidently not unproblematic. His emphatic defence of the role of the subject in the constitution of meaning may run the risk of entailing a kind of solipsism in relation to meaning. It is also not clear whether practical questions of truth, meaning and validity are really affected in the last analysis by consideration of the role of the individual subject in the constitution of truth. The Sartrean aspect of Frank's account of subjectivity involves a concentration upon the epistemological aspect of the 'I' in a manner which renders crucial aspects of intersubjectivity hard to explain. Any developmental account of subjectivity will, for example, necessarily involve more concern with intersubjective phenomena like identification, intuitive understanding, love etc., than is apparent in the strictly epistemological account upon which Frank focuses (see Roger Frie, 'Subjectivity and Intersubjectivity in the Work of Sartre, Binswanger, Lacan and Habermas', PhD dissertation, University of Cambridge, 1994, forthcoming Rowman and Littlefield, 1997). Reflections on subjectivity from the perspective of analytical philosophy might question whether the notion of the non-reflexive 'familiarity' of the subject with itself does not involve a semantic problem, in so far as any term that can be used to describe what is in question seems necessarily to have a reflexive element, even though the logic of Frank's argument demands that all traces of reflexivity in that which is always already 'familiar' with itself be eliminated. From another perspective, the phenomenology of actual language use, where our reflexive control of our utterances seems at least limited, points to the ways in which we are indeed 'spoken' by the language we have learned in familiar social contexts, rather than to any creative initiatives. Such initiatives are perhaps more apparent at the level of our ability spontaneously to interpret ever new situations in terms of 'background knowledge' than to generate new forms of language. Despite such possible objections, there is in Frank's position a clear sense of a vital intuition, the intuition that any theory of understanding which does not take account of the way in which meanings are only ever constituted by inherently individual acts of understanding entails the attempt to repress the kind of contingency that makes us human. These issues are evidently far from settled and the success of subsequent debate will depend upon a widening of philosophical horizons that prevents the narrowness of focus which still dominates many strands of contemporary philosophy. Perhaps the most important lesson to be learned from Frank by contemporary philosophers and other theorists lies, therefore, in his openness to dialogue – and argument – with other intellectual traditions than his own.

CHAPTER I

The text and its style: Schleiermacher's theory of language

For at least three decades, the cultural academic disciplines have seen a flourishing and proliferation of theories which in one way or another orient themselves via the theme of language. Whether this occurs in the different varieties of analytical philosophy, structural semiology or existentialist hermeneutics – what is common to them all is their attempt to revise, by means of linguistic theory, the modern paradigm of 'transcendental consciousness' or 'subjectivity'. Before suggesting possible motives for this change of paradigm, I would like to point to an apparently contingent fact, namely that the shared concern with this paradigm has by no means drawn together the strands I have mentioned in a unity of discussion and cohesiveness of research. Certainly in Germany – and the same is true of the Scandinavian countries and the United States – there have been fruitful discussions between positions of analytical philosophy and of phenomenological hermeneutics. But the few, timorous attempts to initiate a discussion between representatives of these two movements and French post-structuralist semiologists[1] have met with almost no response. More recently, the initial polemics and resistance typified by Alfred Schmidt's *Geschichte und Struktur* (Munich, 1971) have given way to a first

---

[1] My respect for the representatives of this direction of thought calls for a distinction to be made between them and those befuddled opponents of enlightenment (allegedly) following in Foucault's footsteps and above all the intellectual Calibans of the 'Anti-Oedipus', whose garbled 'discourses' one can hardly study without experiencing the sort of pleasure that Schopenhauer felt when reading Hegel. (See my essay, 'Die Welt als Wunsch und Repräsentation', in *Das Sagbare und das Unsagbare. Studien zur deutsch-französischen Hermeneutik und Texttheorie*, new expanded edn. (Frankfurt am Main, 1990), pp. 561ff.) Certainly it is necessary to extend the theory of psychosis to pathological phenomena in society: that this need not itself be done 'en style de psychose' or 'en psychose' is demonstrated by Sartre in his lucid analysis of 'objective neurosis' in the fourth part of his *Flaubert*.

hesitant, then curious and finally almost totally positive receptiveness to the ideas, strange and impossible to ignore, which come pouring in, in an ever-growing tide – and generally in dubious translations – from France. But as far as I can see the divide in scientific standards which previously more or less followed the national boundaries has simply moved into Germany, without any effective attempts being made to mediate between the divergent methodological options. The effect of the methodological split is of course most visibly mirrored in the inconsistent methods used in literary studies, which have long been dependent on the impetus of new ideas from related disciplines, notably from philosophy and sociology, since their exponents find themselves incapable of independently laying down a satisfactory theoretical basis. German studies in particular offer a striking instance of the general experience that the march of time is not necessarily accompanied by an advance in insight. In this discipline, as Ernst Robert Curtius said about literary criticism, there is Romanticism and there are beginnings. Ironically, this gives German studies the advantage that in the extremity of their need they can legitimately look back and draw upon the rich resource of the fundamental work done by the Romantics, without thereby manifesting a merely archaeological interest in acquiring knowledge. I want to try to show how relevant the philological approach of Schleiermacher in particular has remained, and how well he lends himself to getting the dialogue moving between structuralist positions, and hermeneutic positions and positions in analytical philosophy.

Before I start, I want to attempt to guess why there has been this failure to bring about discussion precisely with the contemporary French theoreticians. If the differences between on the one hand the analytical approaches based on methodological discipline and on the other those of existentialist hermeneutics which seek to base scientific hypotheses on irreducible effective-historical communication processes – if these differences can be cleared up, as is shown by the examples of Apel, Taylor, von Wright or Toulmin, then this is because they are all, if you will allow me this simplification for the sake of brevity, committed to a 'semantistic' perspective. They are concerned either to explain the process of understanding meaning or to examine the validity of judgements concerning the meaning of utterances. The question of *How to Do Things with Words* is, despite its choice of methodology, not fundamentally irreconcilable with the question of how linguistic worldviews are built up and how they determine the meaning horizon of the language participants fitted into them. Even where the category of the subject is no longer considered appropriate to explain the *Meaning of Meaning*, what is attempted is a reformulation of the classical critique of reason as a critique of meaning. To investigate the meaning of human utterances is clearly even more fundamental than to investigate their rationality. Here it has been perfectly possible to link up with neo-Kantian traditions (for instance that of Cassirer) in which the restrictively logical meaning of the transcendental synthesis was extended to include the activities of the capacity to symbolise in general and the capacity for language in particular. And if – especially since Wittgenstein – the symbolic forms are thought of as regulatory apparatuses which determine the concrete actions of denoting and of investing with meaning, and even have the power autonomously to bring about extensions of and changes to the lexico-syntactical repertoire, they are thereby also deemed to have the capability of spontaneity and reflection which were traditionally thought of as essential characteristics of subjectivity. Viewed from this kind of perspective, the English Channel, which has often, metonymically, been held accountable for the division between Anglo-Saxon and continental philosophy, has not really had the effect of 'splitting the discourse': after all, the premises and methods of analytical philosophy too are based on the paradigm of reflection which has dominated continental metaphysics ever since Parmenides.

This at any rate is the objection which both analytical and in the broadest sense hermeneutic theory must expect to encounter as soon as they take on the challenge of contemporary French semiology. Derrida, for instance, has claimed to see the same premises at work in Paul Ricoeur's hermeneutics and in Austin's and Searle's speech-act theory (and incidentally also in Foucault's 'archaeology'),[2] surreptitiously welding the disagreeing positions into the unity of a *single* scientific formation. According to Derrida, they are

[2] Jacques Derrida, 'Avoir l'oreille de la philosophie', interview with Lucette Finas, in *Ecarts. Quatre essais à propos de Jacques Derrida* (Paris, 1973).

unanimous in suggesting that consciousness, speech or 'discourse' have in principle access to the meaning of the utterances that are made, even if these – as elements in social orders – may at first be concealed from the individual and need to be brought back by means of what Merleau-Ponty called 'archaeological' reconstruction. For Parmenides' *noein*, the thinking perception of what is in its being, only creates *meaning* if something positive, and not nothing (μὴ ὄν), is given. That which does not exist simply *is* not, and thus has no presence, no truth which could be repeated in the same form, and is not a possible object of a necessarily *general* knowledge. Friedrich Schlegel called Parmenides' nothing an '*emptiness* which seeks to be filled', indeed 'a gap in existence' which – itself invisible – gives the visible its determinacy.[3] Within the framework of a structure the only things that are visible, objective, significant, and so are also capable of being reduplicated and generalised, are the signs and their relationships with one another (the mass of the codifiable). The gap as such evades the eye of knowledge, although it is precisely the gap that installed the positive terms in their function as signs, i.e. as units of expression of meaning. For, as Saussure had shown, the way that the identity of the signs is created and they are fitted into the economy of a structured system is that very definite cuts are made in the unarticulated mass of the material of signifiers (whose meaningfulness he characterises as 'en soi nulle' – nothing in itself), and that through these cuts the individual blocks are split off from one another and are precisely thereby invested with profile, contour, individuality, in short, with 'differential characteristics'. Only after the work of differentiation and of the formation of intervals between the 'full and positive terms' has been concluded[4] (and strictly speaking it continues unceasingly, with every new use of a sign), can the 'distinctness' of the signs as a synthesis of intelligible meanings and material substrates of expression be completed. To put it differently, it is only through the subtraction, as it were, of the work of differentiation from the completed structure of signifiers that this structure changes from being a meaninglessly furrowed material into a

---

[3] Friedrich Schlegel, *Kritische Ausgabe seiner Schriften*, ed. Ernst Behler (Munich, Paderborn and Vienna, 1958–), vol. XII, p. 192.

[4] Jacques Derrida, *Positions* (Paris, 1972), p. 38ff.

subdivided order of signs which are capable of conveying meaning – an old insight, most famously expressed by Spinoza in the words, 'Omnis determinatio est negatio' (Every determination is a nega- tion) and perpetuated in Sartre's formulation, 'That which is not is the reason for the determinacy of that which is.'[5]

However, making this link with Spinoza, Hegel or Sartre does not get us any further. For them, negation remains in the inter- mediate space between two positions, for whose benefit it works and cancels itself out, whereas the offence committed by Derrida or Lacan against 'semanticism' in the understanding of meaning consists of an insistence on a negation that cannot be dialectically cancelled out, which splits the meaning away from itself without permitting it to return to itself. When Gadamer speaks of the 'speculative structure' of language,[6] this is intended to suggest that the two elements in the process of communication 'are mirrored in each other' and thus are essentially similar in nature: in the process of the effective-historical consciousness one mind is always speak- ing to another mind or, to put it in a more pointed fashion, the context of meaning of one tradition is speaking *to itself* in the form of an understanding which is open to this tradition. In this way, in both Gadamer and Ricoeur – and in all information and com- munication theories – effective-historical hermeneutics becomes linked with the paradigm of reflection, for which the alienation of consciousness from itself can be only one stage on the path of its constant return into itself. There is, however, as Derrida empha- sises, an alterity of quite another order, which is necessarily ne- glected in such conceptions. After all, within the order of a linguis- tic world-view every element, even before it is able to comprehend itself as what it is, carries within itself the trace of all other elements of the structure of signifiers, i.e. it acquires its identity-as-meaning precisely not through its specular reference to itself or to an indestructible core of *truth* but through its unreserved externalisa- tion to that which is other than itself: 'An interval', says Derrida, 'must split it away from what it is not, so that it can be itself.'[7] Thus the meaning that is to be understood is not based on a continuum

[5] Jean-Paul Sartre, *L'être et le néant* (Paris, 1943), p. 130.
[6] *Wahrheit und Methode*, 2nd edn. (Tübingen, 1965), pp. 432ff.
[7] *Marges de la philosophie* (Paris, 1972), p. 13.

entirely made up of meaning like itself, but on something which is itself not meaningful. The immediate transparency of the meaning is already clouded in its very origin; and if one were to call meaning the sayable, one would have to call its origin silence, as for instance Mallarmé does.

The trouble is that this is also true of reflection itself – that is, of the basic theorem of the modern period by which philosophy thought that it had proved its claim to be rigorously scientific. For one can *neither* think of reflection without presupposing simple self-conscious identity (otherwise the one element in the relation-ship cannot be certain of seeing in the other *itself* and not another); *nor* can one ignore the fact that this identity is not directly present to itself but must call upon the other – the other element in the relationship – to bear witness to its sameness to itself. Hölderlin already demonstrated the aporia in this form. Fichte, to whom he refers, admittedly discovered that the witness of the other was vouched for by the pre-reflexive knowledge of one's own identity. But Fichte too became entangled in a circular argument. On the one hand, he explains in the *Wissenschaftslehre nova methodo* (of 1798), the determinacy of the idea of 'I' (the *concept* of it) is bound to the *difference* between at least two expressions which are distinguished from each other ('You think "I" and thus you do not think everything else, you do not think "not-I" '). On the other hand this split between the two elements must also be got round by means of an immediate *intuition* of their *non*-separation, for otherwise the other is no longer the same as the One, and the indispensable identity of the thought 'I' is lost.[8]

So there is no way round this: the condition of possibility of the 'I' is that it gives itself to the other. This giving of itself now of course splits the self into two parts, even though retrospectively it may well deny its differential basis. Nevertheless the path of the reflected one to itself as the one reflecting is barred, by the irremovable externality of a signifier. 'A speaking', Derrida says, 'has preceded my self-consciousness'.[9]

This thesis – and this brings me to the real subject of my lecture

---

[8] See also J.G. Fichte, '*Wissenschaftslehre 1798 (nova methodo)*' in Hans Jacob (ed.), *Nachgelassene Schriften* (Berlin, 1937), vol. II, pp. 355ff.

[9] *La dissémination* (Paris, 1972).

– is prefigured in Schleiermacher's *Glaubenslehre* (Doctrine of Faith) and his *Dialektik*. He was the first, to my knowledge, to draw conclusions relating to the theory of signs from the failure of the reflection model, which result in the project of his *Hermeneutics*. That he nevertheless did not give up the theorem of a meaning-creating subject – albeit a semiologically demoted one – is what makes his position so attractive in the context of the current debate about methods in linguistic and literary studies.

In the works I have mentioned, Schleiermacher shows that the concept of the 'subject' seems ill-suited to serve as a philosophical starting-point: even in the highest of all syntheses, that of willing and thinking, it exists as a relation, that is, as a virtual divergence of things that refer to each other. That the subject nevertheless has a knowledge of the sameness of the related things is an achievement whose real ground it cannot attribute to itself. The cognitive ground of self-consciousness – its immediate being-transparent-to-itself – thus becomes peculiarly delayed in relation to the ground of its being. The absolute inwardness of this feeling of identity, says Schleiermacher, comes into being 'only *in* the subject', but is not brought about '*by* the subject'.[10]

Thus the subject has an awareness of the unity which prevails within it, and recognises at the same time that it cannot be the originator of this knowledge. It is familiar with itself only because it reads the characteristic mark of its 'transcendental determinacy'[11] as a pointer to an identity which 'supplements' the 'defect' written into reflection (*Dial O*, p. 287; pp. 290, 295–6). This is, in broad outline, the outcome of 'the analysis of self-consciousness in relation to the co-positedness of an Other' (*Gl*, p. 24), which in its religious attitude causes it to give up wishing to try to recuperate (*einholen*) the ground of its uncontrollable *determinedness* as itself.

Schleiermacher speaks of a 'crisis of the subject': this occurs as soon as the subject can no longer create the truth in which it has its

---

[10] *Der christliche Glaube*, 7th edn, newly edited on the basis of the second edition and a critical examination of the text by Martin Redeker (Berlin, 1960), vol. I, § 3, p. 3. (My italics, MF) (Henceforth cited in the text as *Gl* with the number of the paragraph and section, or in the case of marginal comments the page number.)

[11] F.D.E. Schleiermacher, *Dialektik*, ed. Rudolf Odebrecht, for the Prussian Academy of Sciences, on the basis of previously unpublished material (Leipzig, 1942, reprinted Darmstadt, 1976), p. 290 (cited as *Dial O*).

existence but can only bear witness to it. Because 'its power is broken' (*Gl*, p. 27) in the face of the facticity of uncontrollable self-mediation, there is no longer a possibility of its being seen as the location of a truth which is trans-historically present to itself and which contains, wrapped up in itself, all the facts of the historical world, and releases them in deductive steps.

This theoretical premise prevents Schleiermacher from using a whole range of strategies of argument which are typical of idealistic philosophy. Above all, reference to the instance of self-consciousness no longer offers an assurance of the possession of an 'absolute' truth present to itself in a trans-historical perspective. On the contrary, this truth escapes from it, because it is tied to the relationship (and thus to time) and is defined as a 'general consciousness of finitude' (*Gl*, § 8,2), i.e. as the consciousness of a 'dependence' which is 'absolute' with regard to its being-at-all and relative with regard to its 'being in the world' (*Gl*, § 4,2; cp. §§ 3–5).

The reflection of the crisis of the subject has consequences for hermeneutics: since '[its] power is broken' (*Gl*, p. 27) in the face of the facticity of uncontrollable self-mediation, there is no longer any question of its being the point from which one might by a monologic process of deduction reach judgements independent of individual experiences about what exists in the historical world. Rather, the transcendence of the ground of knowledge forces the subject to prove the validity of the evidence of its cognitions in the field of communication between persons. This is the task of dialectics, which Schleiermacher defines as the 'setting out of the principles for a discussion conducted in the adequate manner in the domain of pure thought'.[12] The goal of dialectics is 'knowledge', i.e. bringing the theory to a state of 'unchangeability and universality' (*HuK*, p. 414). There must be consensus between the partners in a discourse as to the orientation to this goal; for without the 'presupposition' of an ideal of knowledge (however unattainable)

---

[12] Schleiermacher, *Hermeneutik und Kritik. Mit einem Anhang sprachphilosophischer Texte Schleiermachers*, ed. M. Frank (Frankfurt am Main, 1977) (cited in the text as *HuK*), p. 412. See also Schleiermacher, *Hermeneutik*, ed. Heinz Kimmerle (Heidelberg, 1959). This edition assembles in a critical form all Schleiermacher's notes, including early handwritten ones, and remains indispensable for the serious student.

there would be, given the insoluble differences between the opinions confronting one another and the inadequacy of a 'truth'
controlling the conversation from above, no guarantee of the
intersubjectivity of the agreements reached in any discourse.

A further presupposition of dialectics implied in the postulate of
the ideal unity of knowledge is the sameness of the object to which
divergent predicates are ascribed. This alone makes possible the
clash between 'contradictions' which are to be resolved by dialectics (*HuK*, pp. 426ff.) The dispute between these cannot of course
be decided 'objectively' (i.e. by an external instance), since a
decision as to whether mutually incompatible judgements are or
are not correct in relation to a 'being' (A) intended as the same, or
to a particular section of being (A'), cannot be made simply by
exclusion. The lack of a trans-subjective criterion for the 'true'
predication of something that exists forces the participants in the
discussion to include in the formulation of their possible consensus
every predicate that is honestly acknowledged to apply to it, i.e. to
admit that the object of the judgement is not indifferent to the
individual interpretations which the totality of subjects forms of it.
The predicated sphere constantly expands with the expression of
views. The recognition of the relativity of one's own point of view
in itself represents as it were the breakthrough to truth: this does
not mean an ability positively to fix a material statement (this
would precisely be relative, because it would rest upon a provi-
sional consensus and would in fact turn into untruth as soon as it
claimed to exhaust the possible meaning of being), but takes the
form of a movement, which totalises every individual insight and is
incapable of ever being completed, towards truth.

Now the concept of a simultaneous relativity and universality of
the interpretation of being, by which a group of subjects defines
itself as this particular 'community of thought' (*HuK*, p. 417), has
the structure of a language, i.e. of a both historically 'empirical'
and 'speculative' apparatus of categories which make communication possible (*HuK*, pp. 234, 467). There is no community of
thought which has not *ipso facto* recorded its dialectical consensus
in the grammar of a 'linguistic circle' (*HuK*, pp. 420ff.), i.e. codified
it as a context of involvements or signs through which it effects its
synthesis as a society; for the 'idea', according to Schleiermacher,

is nothing but the immediate self-illumination of 'action' (cp. *Dial O*, p. 70). It is as a result of its dependence on specific grammars that dialectics shares in the particularities and disinformations of the historical world (specific traditions, historically or biograph- ically induced understandings of oneself which are reflected in the conventions of speech and are internalised at the same time as the conventions are acquired as so many practices). Dialectics can never wholly free itself from this dependence, since the truth constituted by it can never advance beyond the status of a single and historical interpretation of being, based on intersubjective agreement. For this reason it voluntarily renounces 'any claim to general validity' (*HuK*, pp. 422, 424) (in the sense of an objectivity independent of subjects) and acknowledges that 'the individual character of a language' determines not only the formation of the ideas of the individuals socialised in it but 'also [has an influence on] the way in which every other language is understood' (*HuK*, p. 421). The irreducible non-generalness or 'relativity of thought' (*HuK*, p. 410) points dialectics towards the 'art of interpretation' or 'hermeneutics'. This looks at linguistic utterances chiefly from the point of view of the way in which individuality asserts itself; whereas the aspect emphasised by dialectics is the fact that even the most private utterance of meaning takes place partly with a view to an 'idea of knowledge' common to all thinkers, and must be composed in language partly for the sake of its possible com- municability: 'It is clear from this that both [hermeneutics and dialectics] only come into being together' (*HuK*, p. 411).

Thus it is a consequence inherent in the system that provides the framework within which Schleiermacher's hermeneutic theory of language will develop: the transcendence of being over the mean- ing through which every linguistic community both reveals and conceals it immediately forces one to recognise the concept of an individuality which cannot simply be regarded as a deduction from or something subsumed under the semantico-syntactical system. After all, there cannot, from one end of the historical universe to the other, be a universality whose economy is un- limited and whose structure does not preserve the unity of this particular movement which the crochet needle of an individual disclosure of meaning performs at this historical point in time upon the thread of which it is woven. This being so, individuality is never (in Schleiermacher) merely implied by a universal context of signs but is always also its boundary and the potential challenge to that context by the subjects who in the *use* of signs also bring into play their 'individuality' as a 'non-transferable' quality. There cannot be a 'universal language', if only because 'communication [by means of it] [is] itself . . . subject to the individual languages' (*HuK*, p. 461): Schleiermacher recognises the non-individual universal for what it is, a scientistic utopia. There is in principle an opposition between on the one hand the 'use of reason . . . with the character of identity' coded in the language and as 'language' – the subject of dialectics/grammar – and on the other 'cognition . . . with the character of particularity, i.e. of non-transferability' (*HuK*, p. 361) – the concern of hermeneutics/rhetoric. The latter cannot simply be absorbed by the former, just as the former never prescribes an absolutely definite 'linguistic usage'. It is a mistake to believe that language speaks by itself, as some structuralists, following poetic symbolism and Heidegger, have said (talk of the autonomy of language is revealed to be a metaphor which hypostasises the signifier into an objective force). Language never provides the 'interpretant' which would individualise the meaning of its signs in a particular situation (as C.S. Peirce has shown). Nor of course does individual meaning – because of its non-communicability – of its own accord achieve communication, i.e. the way of being of a linguistic sign, because 'language as a general system for denoting things' (*HuK*, p. 458) provides 'the mediation for the communality of thought' (*HuK*, pp. 76–7). It could only achieve communication if it were to make use of those 'ideas . . . for which its language already has designations' (*HuK*, p. 78) and to limit its ability to individualise to the symbolic over-determination of the codified sign (which is not, however, itself subject once again to rules) which belongs to 'style' (cp. *HuK*, p. 168).

Now Schleiermacher maintains that every linguistic utterance (*Rede* – speech or discourse) is doubly marked. On the one hand it manifests the 'system' (*HuK*, pp. 458ff., 364, 380) or the 'totality of the language' (*HuK*, p. 78), which identically prescribes for the language participants the syntax and semantics of their discourses (the 'grammar'): 'the language . . . [determines] the thinking of all individuals . . . if one regards the individual human being only as a location for the language' (*HuK*, p. 79; cp. 78). On the other hand, however, 'the language [only comes into being] . . . through speaking' (*HuK*, pp. 78–9), because (1) it has its origin in totalised meaning-disclosing initiatives by the speakers and (2) each individual 'does a share of the work in language: for in part he brings forth new things in it . . . in part he preserves what he repeats and transmits' (*HuK*, p. 167).

The first aspect – and it is immediately clear that the difference between the two can only be defined in terms of a function 'predominating' or 'receding' – is represented by 'grammar' (as the system which formally determines the mass of the uses of language, but which is nevertheless only virtual), the second by 'rhetoric' as the general doctrine of the art of discourse (*HuK*, p. 76), which does not mean that rhetoric is defined as applying only to artistic (artificial) discourse.

This 'dual relationship' (*HuK*, p. 77) in whose electrical field 'discourse' is placed, obeys a dialectics whose law still remains obscure. For one thing, the mechanism which reveals that the sign encoded in a linguistic system is nonetheless a function of a 'non-transferable' project of meaning (and thus makes the historicity of taxonomies comprehensible) is not understood; for another, it has not been shown how individual thinking, given that in some ways it evades the 'linguistic law', is nevertheless supposed to be capable of being formulated in language.

As far as the thesis of the irreducible linguisticality of thought is concerned, it is opposed by the classical view that the linguistic sign is only the external re-presentation of something internal that is also able to perceive itself in an authentic manner without the detour via the signifier, indeed perhaps *only* without that detour. On the basis of such thinking the theoreticians of a rationalist universal grammar assumed that empirical languages, in their combination of words to form sentences, reflected more or less completely the ideal judgement-syntheses of a timeless order of ideas (logic). One can analogously interpret Kant's apparatus of categories and principles as the plan of a transcendental semantics whose repertoire is still accessible to itself before it is externalised to signifiers, and which only turns towards the world of the senses in a second step – via a system of schemata of experience. To this view Schleiermacher makes the objection (which he had analogously made against Fichte) that even the non-sensuous idea, if it is to be 'clear', that is, distinct (cp. *HuK*, pp. 77, 367) must be inscribed into an oppositive structure of the type of a language; for 'everything that is a concept derives from opposition'.[13] The meaning of 'ideas' or intelligible 'principles' can also only acquire a profile by means of a 'system . . . [of] determinate distinguishing of the significant units' (*HuK*, p. 365). And the difference between a (non-sensuous) idea and a discourse (conducted through the defile of the signifier) is reduced to the unimportant difference between an audible and a silent use of signs (*HuK*, p. 77; cp. *Sämtliche Werke* III/9, 126, 703).[14] The point of this astonishing thesis (which Saussure did no more than develop in greater depth) is that if any thinking takes place at all (i.e. if distinct meanings – or linguistic values (*HuK*, pp. 107, 135, 137, 141) – are coherently linked together), this presupposes the 'totality of the language' (*HuK*, p. 77) as a differential system (cp. *HuK*, pp. 144, 466), by which an identical schematisation of the experience of the 'world' (cp. *Gl*, § 42) of a community of speakers, and thus communication as a *fait social* (social fact – Saussure) is guaranteed from the outset.

This brings us to the second problem that requires clarification: does not the 'subversion of the subject by the signifier' (Lacan) imply the loss of its individuality? And if that were not the case, where could the intermediate element be found that would keep the dialectic of 'linguistic law' and 'linguistic usage'[15] in flux without on the one hand reducing thought to an executive organ of the structure or on the other hand detaching it from its connection to language?

Now an important supporting argument for the claim to universality made by Schleiermacher's hermeneutics (*HuK*, p. 75) is the

---

[13] See also *Monologen*: 'Denn nur durch Entgegensezung wird das Einzelne erkannt (For the individual is recognised only by opposition)'. In: Schleiermacher, *Kleinere Schriften und Predigten 1800–1820*, ed. H. Gerdes and E. Hirsch (Berlin, 1970), vol. I, p. 38.

[14] Friedrich Schleiermacher, *Sämtliche Werke* (Berlin, 1834–64).

[15] *HuK*, p. 79.

demonstration that no possible linguistic utterance (level of rhetoric) delivers up its meaning, i.e. is 'understood', merely on the
basis of a purely grammatical reconstruction: 'As a modification of
language, too, it is not understood unless it is understood as a fact
of the mind [of thought], because in this lies the basis of all
influence of the individual on the language, which itself comes into
being through speech' (*HuK*, p. 79). Thus the reconstruction of a
grammatical sequence and of the elements of meaning chained
together in it becomes a hermeneutic operation 'only with the
determination of [their] meaning'; this determination comes
about only '*by means of* those elements'[16] but is not also brought
about *by* them. If one admits that the individual 'meaning' perpetually also describes anew the unity of the codified 'linguistic values'
by virtue of their sensitivity to context (i.e. of the effect of the
'immediate surroundings'[17]), then it becomes necessary to redefine
the concept of 'language' in the differential between grammatical
and rhetorical function.

Following the Kantian tradition, Schleiermacher calls the scope
allotted to the unity of the meaning of a linguistic sign (*HuK*, pp.
104, 106), between the strict identity of the concept (its unity as a
linguistic value or paradigm) and the variability of its always
particular combinations and applications, individual each time, in
the syntagmatic unit of discourse, a 'schema'. The (empirical)
schema is the 'unity in the determination of sensuousness' (Kant,
Kritik der reinen Vernunft (*Critique of Pure Reason*), A 140/B 179) aimed
at from the side of intuition. Its origin in the resources of the
capacity for intuition (of the imagination) makes possible the
production of synthetic acts whose noematic correlate, regardless
of its unified organisation, remains in principle open to new
initiatives of constitution on the part of subjects. The unity of a
'linguistic value' differentialised in the web of the language is
obviously of this nature. The meaning of a sign cannot be said to
have the universality of a pure concept, for no single one of its
applications could ever correspond to it in its entirety (moreover, it
is not clear what transformation would be supposed to be able to
enlarge the extension of something that exists universally). Nor

---

[16] *Hermeneutik*, p. 154. (My italics, MF.)   [17] *Ibid.*, p. 65.

could it be a single intuition (it would not be communicable). The only thing that could be considered is to make the material of intuition uniform in such a way that the determination of its noema takes place in anticipation of a concept without, however, submitting to the guardianship of the concept once and for all. A change in the synthesis of the imagination modifies in an instant the extension of the corresponding schema. It is, Schleiermacher says, an intuition that is 'shiftable within certain boundaries'[18] and is in that way akin to Wittgenstein's 'language game', which is defined as a 'concept with blurred edges'.[19] The guideline for the admissibility of the usage of a word is thus offered to the participants in a language in the *intuition of the rule*[20] which the designatory competence of the speakers follows in order to produce the appropriate verbal schema in the flexible unity of its meaning relationships, which vary according to context.

Incidentally, Schleiermacher by no means confines discussion of the schema to single terms ('subject concepts'), but considers that all categorematic expressions, including the 'predicate-concepts', are capable of schematisation (*Dial O*, pp. 340ff.). He sees a 'floating unity' mediating between the two. Accordingly, he regards the 'unity of meaning' not as an exclusively semantic problem but equally as a 'structural' one,[21] and discusses it in his lectures at length and with extraordinary astuteness. Basically he is prevented by the ingenious discovery of the law of the double determinacy of any discourse – in relation to the 'total linguistic domain' by means of paradigmatic exclusion,[22] and in relation to its 'immediate context' by means of syntagmatic 'determination' (*HuK*, pp. 101ff. and 116–17) – from making an abstractive separation between semantics and syntactics: just as paradigmatic selection establishes the identical meaning of the word (its 'linguistic value') in all contexts, so syntagmatic determination tests out the

---

[18] *Ibid.*, pp. 47, 57ff., see also *HuK*, pp. 106, 109, 437.

[19] Ludwig Wittgenstein, *Philosophische Untersuchungen*, (Frankfurt am Main, 1971), p. 50 (= § 71).

[20] 'Anschauung der Regel (intuition of the rule)' is the expression used by Schelling (*Sämtliche Werke*, ed. K.F.A. Schelling (Stuttgart, 1856–61), part I, vol. III, p. 508), who in some other respects too laid the foundations for Schleiermacher's transference of Kantian schematism to the designatory acts of language.

[21] *Hermeneutik*, pp. 60, 93.   [22] *Ibid.*, p. 42.

range of its implications, singular in each instance, in specific contexts (the 'local values' of the schema (*HuK*, pp. 195ff., 141ff.)). The two operations are interrelated: the lexical paradigm is never anything but an abstraction produced by comparison and differentiation from the wealth of its uses which vary according to context; conversely, the syntagmatic linking presupposes the linguistic value as something that has yet to be modified by the immediate surroundings.

The essence of all concepts of predicates and of subjects is thus 'a floating unity between the general and the particular' (*Dial O*, p. 342), between distinctness and changeability, between concept and judgement, between the intellectual and the organic function or whatever terms Schleiermacher uses to express this dialectical relation.

This 'language schema' theory, which is worked out with great astuteness and does not sidestep any detail, means that Schleiermacher is now able to give a plausible explanation of both the relationship between linguistic structure and linguistic change and that between normal and metaphorical use of language.

For just as the terms in a language do not absorb their predicates (recruited from intuition and accorded to them by judgement) into themselves once and for all, but remain modifiable in their substance through changes on the part of the organic function (their unity of meaning is defined in relation to the judgements passed on them, which are a priori incapable of being completed), so the linguistic system in general must be regarded as an unstable, i.e. historically open 'parasemic context' [23] (Saussure), the worldview of which changes according to interpretative judgements by individuals and never attains the manner of being of a foundational Idea which can shake off interpretation and comment from the outside. While each individual communication presupposes the unity of the world as the noematic correlate with reference to which the messages are exchanged, this unity is only the inert reflex of that schematic unity of discourse as a totality by means of which a particular society seals its practical synthesis. 'The identical construction of thought set down in language' thus offers 'no

---

[23] 'Parasemic' means placing *seme* (sign) next to (*parà*) *seme* and so determining it.

complete guarantee of the correctness of thought' (*HuK*, p. 460); and 'every communication about external objects is a constant continuation of the experiment to see whether all people construct identically' (*HuK*, p. 460).

Language is thus an individual universal. It exists as a universal system only on the basis of agreements between its speakers which could in principle be revoked, and changes its total meaning with every act of speech and at every moment, at least if this semantic innovation succeeds in making the breakthrough into the grammatical repertoire, as constantly happens in the course of acts in conversation. Saussure described this phenomenon of 'analogical' or 'parasemic transformation' in a manner wholly in accord with Schleiermacher's thinking and thereby contradicted the deductionism on which his supposedly orthodox pupils wanted to base the relationship between *langue* and *parole*: there is a 'creative activity' which is indeterminable (or at least not determinable by something which is purely potential like the *langue*), indeed there is an 'individual liberty' on the part of the speakers which manifests itself in 'incessant, daily creations in the language (*langue*)' and could not be conceived of as such if one could anticipate it on the basis of the *langue*.[24]

For Schleiermacher this meaning-creating potential of language appears in its pure form in poetic discourse.[25] For the metaphorical nature of the symbolic use of language undermines the conventionalised meanings (schemata) of the words by means of a carefully calculated semantic shock (cp. *HuK*, p. 143) which issues a challenge to the reader's 'free productivity in the language' (*HuK*, p. 405f.). As the usual ('literal') meaning of the term (the 'schema' in the strict sense) is revoked (cp. *HuK*, p. 105f.), the offer of a new description (what Mary B. Hesse has called 're-assignment') of its intention (an

[24] 'In the "langue" there are thus always two sides which correspond to one another: it is $\frac{\text{social}}{\text{individual}}$.

If one therefore considers the sphere where the "langue" lives, there will always be the individual "langue" and the social "langue". (Forms and grammars exist only socially, but the changes originate with an individual)' (F. de Saussure, *Cours de linguistique générale*, ed. R. Engler, (Wiesbaden, 1974), vol. II, p. 28).

[25] 'Accordingly poetry would be an extension and new creation in language. But . . . the possibility of this is already originally inherent in language, but of course it is always only in the poetic that it becomes visible, whether in a pure form or indirectly' (*HuK*, p. 405).

'image', says Schleiermacher) appears and with it the possibility of a new vision of the designated state of affairs which, according to Schleiermacher, is a hermeneutic function of speech (the 'correct' objectification corresponds to grammatical correctness and the contentfulness inscribed in it by means of schemata of experience). If the image, which is at first still absolutely singular (*HuK*, pp. 407–8), is taken possession of by the recipient of the discourse, then it has ceased to be exclusive or private and exists as a virtually universal schema or as a rule of linguistic usage (among others) in the totality of the language (cp. *HuK*, p. 410f., n. 2, para. 2).

Here the fundamental argument in Schleiermacher's theory of language comes into view, the one whose effective history has without any doubt been interrupted by the worst misunderstandings: the theorem of divination.

Its original location is not (as suggested by Gadamer and with him most exegetes of Schleiermacher) in the historical dimension of the bridging of the temporal gap between the interpreter and the material to be interpreted, and it cannot in any instance be equated with 'empathy' (a term which is not to be found in Schleiermacher's works). 'Divination' appears in the context of a theory of 'style' (*HuK*, p. 168). (In what follows I will confine myself to the linguistic dimension.) By 'style' Schleiermacher means the 'treatment of language' with reference to how the speaker brings 'his own particular way of understanding the object . . . into the use and thus also into his treatment of language' (*HuK*, p. 168). It should be noted that he is speaking here of an event that is essentially identical with metaphorical 're-description', because the stylistic modification challenges the general schematism of the language by means of a 'thought' of the speaker's which to begin with is still uncommunicable. The poetic 'image' which overlays the general schema is after all 'defined as something altogether unique' and thus *ipso facto* as 'something . . . against which language is irrational' (*HuK*, p. 408). Poetry – but it is only an extreme form of everyday language use – has something to give in the medium of the language 'which cannot really be given through language, for language always gives only the general' (*HuK*, p. 401). Nevertheless, the speaker who acts poetically in the true sense of the word (that is, producing new meaning) forces upon the language his individuality (which is not yet codified and in this sense is indeed inexpressible) (*HuK*, p. 401); and he does this 'by the way in which he weaves [the words] together' (*HuK*, p. 401). The style's 'individual manner of combining' elements, which can *ex negativo* give an intimation of 'the essence of individuality' (*HuK*, p. 370) is quite distinct from the combination of the words according to a syntactical rule (see for instance *HuK*, p. 171, section 5). The sentence or discourse as something to which universal regularities are applied (be these of a generic, social or grammatical kind) is an 'object of grammatical interpretation' (*ibid.*) and appeals only to 'language as a general concept', i.e. as the transcendental apparatus for the production of all 'necessary forms for subject, predicate and syntax' (*HuK*, p. 171). These, however, Schleiermacher continues, 'are not positive means of explanation' of the actual treatment of language (of the style), 'but only negative ones, because what is contrary to them . . . [cannot] be understood at all' (*HuK*, pp. 171–2). Thus syntax, semantics and (in so far as it formulates rules itself) pragmatics do constitute the *conditiones sine quibus non* of the use of language; but this in itself does not make any of these instances the *causa per quam* of the individual combination through which the free thought of the speaking subject manifests itself in its 'individuality' which can never be necessitated and thus can also never be wholly schematised. It 'cannot be constructed a priori' (*HuK*, p. 172). Indeed, 'in terms of grammar one cannot sum up any individuality at all in a concept . . . There can be no concept of a style' (*HuK*, p. 172).[26] This is why all models which try to subject style to a generative apparatus, as a rule-led or multiply-coded procedure, are doomed to failure. Not because style brings an extra-verbal quality into play or is contrary to some existing rule (Schleiermacher actually says that the rule is a precondition for style), but simply because it is style that instals the universal signs in the particular meaning in whose light they, in this unique combination (which is opposed to all others and even to all others that can be analytically paraphrased), are bathed. *Post festum* (when

---

[26] See also *Die christliche Sitte*, 2nd edn, ed. L. Jonas (Berlin, 1884), p. 572: 'The individual can never be wholly resolved into concepts; one can perceive it only in intuition. But it can therefore also never be constructed a priori, but is always merely recognised.'

the 'sense' (Sinn) has been understood, i.e has become 'reference' (Bedeutung)), one recognises their rule by abstraction: it too has no necessitating power with regard to future speech acts.[27] In each individual project of meaning, says Schleiermacher, 'there remains something that cannot be described . . . that can only be called harmony' (*HuK*, p. 177). This harmony is not a characteristic of any sign, or indeed of all signs and the laws according to which they are linked together, but something like the synthetic unity of their invisible scansions or like the effect of those differential *brisures* (Derrida) at the joints of their articulation, by means of which they are revealed as impermanent schemata and reminded of their unlosable ability always to express things other than what they mean in this particular context.[28]

But then it becomes impossible to characterise the 'complete understanding of style' (*HuK*, p. 168) in terms oriented towards the metaphor of decoding: there is no continuous transition from the system to its application,[29] because the possibility can never be excluded that the signs used have semantically re-interpreted the codified totality of the language (which assigns to each signifier its and only its signified). A meaning which is only created in the act

---

[27] Thus one can comprehend the style of an individual and give the rules for it; but one cannot from this make a law for its (future) action: every rule has an index of obsoleteness and of transience. Incidentally, Schleiermacher regarded divination, through which the peculiar quality of an individual style beyond the generality of discourse is 'guessed', as 'the feminine strength of human knowledge' (*HuK*, p. 169), while the comparative approach is a 'masculine [talent]'. In the lectures on psychology (*Psychologie*, ed. L. George (Berlin, 1862)) he stresses that there is no 'qualitative inequality' between the sexes but that there is a 'difference in the intellectual functions', such that it is easier for the male consciousness to replace 'the individual . . . with general conceptions', while the 'virtuosity (of the woman)' shows itself 'in the original grasping of the individual . . . in the form of subjective consciousness' (pp. 298–9; see also pp. 556–7). Both of these capabilities possess 'the same dignity'; but the hermeneutic talent definitely requires a highly developed capacity for the 'construction' of a totality of meaning from the individual style, and 'from the state of chaos the whole intellectual power is in action already in the establishing of the individual, if it is to be correct, because precisely in this way the intrinsic forms corresponding to the division of being are presupposed' (*Psychologie*, p. 557). In declaring the comprehension of the individual in its uniqueness to be the main requirement of understanding, Schleiermacher has in his hermeneutic theory (as also in many other of his writings) paid a tribute to women which has not received sufficient attention.

[28] See also Jacques Lacan, *Ecrits* (Paris, 1966), p. 505.

[29] That this is true even of systems such as that of mathematics has been shown by Gilles-Gaston Granger in his *Essai d'une philosophie du style* (Paris, 1968), to which far too little attention has been paid.

of speaking (a 'creative act' (*HuK*, p. 325)) – i.e. a meaning which is defined only at the moment of speech as the appropriate interpretation of its chain of signifiers – cannot be described using the means available to the very repertoire whose sphere it has moved beyond. (This objection applies especially to the hermeneutic conservatism of E.D. Hirsch's genre theory in *Validity in Interpretation*.) Therefore the 'comparative method', which assesses the new description of the meaning of a sentence by comparing it with the usual meaning of the signs used, will be able to extract the core of their individual meaning *as* something unique only on the circular premise that 'divination' has previously inventively disclosed it as something as yet uncommunicable (*HuK*, pp. 169–70, § 6).

In Schleiermacher's language the term 'divination' stands precisely for the insight that language systems in themselves never provide a determinate interpretant for the actual use of language and that individual meaning (on this side of the codified semantics/syntax of the chain of signs transporting it) cannot in principle be deduced on the basis of *discovery procedures* of the deduction/decoding type.

To attempt to arrive at a description of style by means of the differential method of determination by comparison and opposition must inevitably lead to an infinite regress ('then it would go back into infinity' (*HuK*, p. 176)): what has been made commensurable by means of 'comparison' cannot, analytically, be what is 'new' (*HuK*, p. 167), cannot be what is still incomparable in a speech that is heard; unless a conjectural hypothesis ('divination') had previously, by an imaginative leap or an originary 'guess' (*HuK*, p. 318) made its meaning, the author's individual way of combining elements, commensurable or differentiable (cf. *HuK*, p. 326).

Decisive proof of the everyday reality of such divination is provided by the way in which children learn language. They must literally 'understand in an original way';[30] for 'they do not yet have the language [thus they also do not have any rules to apply], but must first seek it . . . They have as yet no points of comparison, but must acquire them gradually as a basis for a comparative

---

[30] *Hermeneutik*, p. 61.

procedure which, admittedly, does develop with surprising rapid-
ity' (*HuK*, p. 326). However, the decisive question, and the point on
which all code models of speech fail, is 'how do they fix the first
thing?' (*ibid.*). That is to say, how do they make the leap from the
merely potential capability of language to the realisation of a
meaning which becomes known to them only in the act of guessing
itself – for this is what 'divining' means? It is only possible to
answer this question by recognising 'the same divinatory boldness'
(*HuK*, p. 327) which even when we have left childhood behind
enables us, though to a lesser degree, to understand meaning.

The recognition that the universality of semiological systems[31] –
a thesis for which Schleiermacher after all helped to lay the
foundation[32] – does not close that gap of *'différance'* in which,
according to Derrida, something like sense and meaning are first
formed – the recognition that every spoken word, then, is veiled in
a silence which *ipso facto* escapes the precepts of the code, and
which Mallarmé calls 'condition et délice de la lecture [the condition and delight of reading]'[33] – seems to me to be the almost
forgotten insight to which Schleiermacher's theory of language
can once again give us access. The fact that Schleiermacher's
theory has been more thoroughly distorted by its effective history
than is the case with most Romantic theoretical texts, indeed that
Schleiermacher's own utterances crop up almost like trouble-
makers in the levelled landscape of modern linguistic and literary
studies, strengthens the suspicion that the model offered by Romanticism still remains relevant in a wholly different sense than
merely that its riches are to this day not fully known, let alone
exhausted.

[31] It was, incidentally, Schleiermacher who introduced into the terminology of our subject
both the concept of structure and that of understanding meaning, in the specific sense in
which they are used today; cp. *HuK*, p. 139 and *Hermeneutik*, p. 60.

The 'exceptional importance' and anticipatory significance of this concept of structure
above all (which covers both grammatical and textual structures) was already pointed out
by Joachim Wach (*Das Verstehen. Grundzüge einer Geschichte der hermeneutischen Theorie im 19.
Jahrhundert*, 3 vols. (Tübingen, 1926), vol. 1, p. 133f.)
[32] See also *Hermeneutik*, pp. 38, 56.
[33] Stéphane Mallarmé, *Œuvres complètes*, ed. H. Mondor and G. Aubry, 3rd edn (Biblio-
thèque de la Pléiade, Paris, 1965), p. 310.

CHAPTER 2

What is a literary text and what does it mean to understand it?

PREMISES

The interpretation of texts is the daily bread of anyone who deals with literature, whether as a subject of study or simply for pleasure. To find in a text just 'words, words, words', as Hamlet mockingly suggests, is clearly not enough: to discover its meaning requires an additional effort which was described in Romantic hermeneutics as an *art*, as 'the art of understanding rightly the discourse of another' (Schleiermacher, *Hermeneutik und Kritik. Mit einem Anhang sprachphilosophischer Texte Schleiermachers*, ed. M. Frank, (Frankfurt am Main, 1977) (cited in the text as *HuK*), pp. 75, 8off.). In contrast to the rationalistic maxim, put forward for instance by the champions of the hermeneutics of the Enlightenment, that interpretation of a text becomes necessary only when a discourse or piece of writing is not self-explanatory – when, for instance, it contains statements that are contrary to reason, is expressed in a language or by symbols that are no longer understood, or presupposes historical knowledge – Schleiermacher demanded, in the early decades of the nineteenth century, that a hermeneutic approach be universally applied. Not only the incomprehensible but also the seemingly self-explanatory, he claimed, needs an initial methodological distancing. This is what 'stricter practice' demands: it 'is based on the assumption that misunderstanding arises spontaneously and that on every point understanding must be willed and searched for' (*HuK*, p. 92).

This is the starting-point of modern hermeneutics ('hermeneutics' being defined as a theory of the art of, or theory of, interpretation). It is located at a meta-level from the business of interpreting a text: it is a reflection and a systematisation of a given conception of textual interpretation. We call post-Romantic hermeneutics modern where it adopts Schleiermacher's methodical doubt: nothing is self-explanatory, everything calls for the work of interpretation. One never knows from the outset what a passage of text is supposed to mean; indeed, it seems to be an attribute of a text that it admits of more than one meaning and that the simplicity of an utterance is no protection against a *conflict of interpretations* (Ricœur, *Le conflit des interprétations* (Paris, 1969)).

This scepticism towards one's own suppositions about meaning necessarily also extends to the rules by which texts are interpreted. If there is no system of signs valid for all epochs in the evolution of the human race, and consequently no unchanging view of the world, then it follows that there is no permanently valid set of rules for the elucidation of all texts of whatever period. The rules for understanding are themselves historical institutions, and they constantly alter with the manner in which texts are composed and with the world-view which is written into a text.

This is not to say that the conversion of world into text is an enterprise ungoverned by rules and that interpretation is a matter for the anarchic exercise of genius. Rather the interpreter must in each instance carefully seek to discover firstly *what* rules determine the grammar of a given text ('grammar' in the broadest sense of the word, as the totality of the socio-cultural codes of an age) and secondly according to what rules the author makes use of or changes that grammar in an individual way in his own text. The first aspect is the subject of 'grammatical' interpretation, the second that of 'technical' (or 'psychological') interpretation. Schleiermacher explains this exegetical division of labour as follows: 'Just as every discourse stands in a dual relationship, to the totality of the language and to the totality of the thinking of its author, so all understanding consists of the two elements of understanding the discourse as extracted from the language and understanding it as a fact within the thinker . . . Understanding is only present in the combination of these two elements (the grammatical and the psychological)' (*HuK*, pp. 76, 79).

This division into the two aspects is as valid now as it was in Schleiermacher's day, and the structure of this chapter is based on it. A general discussion of the term 'text' and of the thing that it designates, which is the subject of any interpretation, will be followed by a brief account of grammatical and of technical (textual) interpretation. There will be no outline of the history of literary hermeneutics: this is adequately covered by Wach, *Das Verstehen. Grundzüge einer Geschichte der hermeneutischen Theorie im 19. Jahrhundert*, 3 vols. (Tübingen, 1926); Gadamer, *Wahrheit und Methode* (Tübingen, 1960), cited as *WuM*; Dilthey, 'Die Entstehung der Hermeneutik', in *Gesammelte Schriften* (Stuttgart and Göttingen, 1961), vol. v, pp. 317–38, and 'Leben Schleiermachers', in *Gesammelte Schriften*, vol. II; Szondi, *Einführung in die literarische Hermeneutik* (Frankfurt am Main, 1975); see also Ebeling, 'Hermeneutik', in *RGG*, vol. III (1960), pp. 242–62; Frank, *Das Individuelle-Allgemeine. Textstrukturierung und Interpretation nach Schleiermacher* (Frankfurt am Main, 1977), et al. The method of textual interpretation which, if not originated by Schleiermacher (see Birus, 'Hermeneutische Wende', *Euphorion* 74 (1980), pp. 213–22), certainly became established as a result of the history of his influence, will be examined exclusively with reference to contemporary theories of interpretation and most particularly in the context of a discussion of the structural and the meaning-oriented (technical) conceptions of interpretation. One can best do justice to a historic achievement if, instead of consigning it to the archives, one demonstrates its continuing relevance, focusing not on the historic contribution itself but on what has followed from it.

First of all, some remarks on the use of the terms 'text', 'understanding' and 'interpreting'.

Though the word 'text' derives etymologically from Latin and there are numerous instances of its use in ancient times (e.g. Quintilian, *Institutio oratoria* 9, 4, 13; 9, 4, 17; Augustine, *Confessions*, 7, 21, 27), only nowadays has it become a technical term used in literary theory to signify the lowest common denominator for the object of all conceivable interpretations. In this broad sense, 'text' is the name given in the first instance to all utterances of whatever kind, whether articulated in a natural or a technical form of language, whether spoken or non-verbal, provided that they are made with the intention of communication (Titzmann, *Stukturelle Textanalyse* (Munich, 1977), p. 10). When confined to linguistic utterances, 'text' may be defined, as for instance in S.J. Schmidt's *Texttheorie*, as 'all utterances by communicating partners which are linguistic and function communicatively . . . and in which "textuality" or "textual form" are the means by which they manifest themselves, or the structure through which they are realised. If communication takes place at all it does so by means of text and in the form of text' (*Texttheorie* (Munich, 1973), p. 144). Understood in this way, 'textuality' means a context of meaning which is developed by means of 'games of communicative action' (*ibid.*, pp. 43ff.). It will be necessary to consider whether this very broad definition is of use in the study of literature.

I will from now on use the terms 'textual exegesis' (*Textauslegung*) and 'textual interpretation' (*Textinterpretation*) synonymously, and distinguish both from 'understanding'. Successful understanding is clearly a precondition for the task of exegesis, and the two are not the same thing. Up to the eighteenth century (and in some contemporary works too) one finds a distinction being made between 'subtilitas intelligendi' and 'subtilitas explicandi' (Ernesti, *Institutio Interpretis Novi Testamenti* (Leipzig, 1761), chapter 1, section 4), i.e. the separation of the 'art of *understanding*' and the 'art of *expounding*' that understanding, for instance to 'a third party' (*HuK*, p. 75). The exegesis of a text apparently does not consist merely in understanding it correctly, but also in presenting this understanding in articulated discourse. We will examine whether this distinction can be upheld in practice, and in particular whether it is true that 'silent understanding' does not by itself transform and historicise the original meaning, but that (as is assumed for instance by Hirsch, *Validity in Interpretation* (New Haven, 1967) (cited as *VI*), pp. 166ff., 171ff.), this is achieved only by the explicit articulation of that meaning in a discourse of one's own (which could then in its turn be interpreted). Even at this stage, however, it seems clear that literary hermeneutics is concerned first and foremost with 'correct understanding'.

TEXTUALITY AND LITERARICITY
Literality and literaricity of the text

What *is* a text? And what tendency inherent in the meaning of that word leads us at once to associate it with 'the literary'?

These are the questions upon which the first part of this article will concentrate. For it is surely remarkable that when we are promised an 'interpretation of a text' we immediately think of an interpretation of a piece of literary writing rather than, say, of looking something up in a railway timetable, even though, in a famous poem written in the 1960s, H. M. Enzensberger did ironically urge us to read not odes but timetables: 'They are more precise' (*Gedichte* (Frankfurt am Main, 1962), p. 29).

Certainly they are more precise than the many and by no means unanimous definitions by which contemporary linguistic and literary theorists try to enlighten us on the essential nature of a 'text'. In his examination of the semantic field of *texte* and *écriture* in 'post-structuralist' French literary studies (*'Texte' und 'Ecriture' in den französischen Literaturwissenschaften nach dem Strukturalismus* (Bonn, 1976)), Richard Brütting has been able to show that the meaning of the word 'text' has undergone more rapid and more frequent changes in the last fifteen years than in decades of its previous history. This of course demonstrates not only, as one might suppose, the questionable nature but also the *topicality of the concept of a text*. So long as a subject is still being researched, its terms are still open, its definitions are in a state of flux. Only that which is fluid has a future; anything that has been de*fin*ed is, as the word itself denotes, completed and finished with.

Consulting the dictionaries of the major European languages, one finds that the earliest meaning of the word 'text' (from Latin *textus*, something woven or plaited) is the Scripture, or a passage from it, as distinct from any exegesis, gloss or sermon which follows. Alongside this meaning German has its own, earlier use of the word, distinguishing 'text' from 'song'. But in both cases 'text' denotes something like the original form of expression of a piece of writing as distinct from its various possible transpositions into speech, commentary or song.

Before venturing too hastily into the frozen terminological

wastes of modern definitions of a text, it is as well to be equipped
with a heuristic compass which not only points reliably to the
North Pole of theory but also, with its south-pointing needle,
indicates the milder zones of everyday language. For if it is true
that the technical language of scholarship ultimately rests on the
language of everyday speech, then it makes sense to begin by
seeing what can be learned from the everyday use of the word
'text'.

We normally speak of a *text* when we mean a discourse which is
cast in written form, makes connected sense, and is generally, as I
have said, literary.

Each of these disparate characteristics may in itself seem appropriate and even necessary, but the connection between them is not
immediately clear. Let us first single out – since one has to start
somewhere – the *written form as a characteristic* of a text. In contrast to
the usage, of which I gave a few random samples above, practised
by some schools of textual linguistics – it would be more accurate
to call this, as the French do, 'linguistique du discours' – wherever
a text is referred to in the context of literary studies the written
form seems to be an indispensable characteristic (cf. Ricœur,
'Qu'est-ce qu'un texte', in R. Bubner et al. (eds.), *Hermeneutik und
Dialektik* (Tübingen, 1970), vol. I, pp. 181–200, and 'Philosophische
und theologische Hermeneutik', in R. Bubner and E. Jüngel (eds.),
Metapher (Munich, 1976), pp. 24–45; Kurz, 'Hermeneutische Aspekte der Textlinguistik', *Archiv für das Studium der neueren Sprachen
und Literaturen*, vol. 214, 139th year (1977), pp. 262–80).

This can be justified, for instance by a further excursion into
everyday language and etymology. When referring collectively to
the body of work left by an author, we speak in German of his
Schriften ('writings'). Only writings, not spoken words, have
authors; and these works should ideally be not only written down
but also literary in character.

By this criterion Alma Mahler-Werfel, for instance, would not
count as an author, for her book on Mahler is, as Ernst Polak
wrote to Werfel in July 1939, 'a book that was *spoken* on to the
page ['ein hingesprochenes Buch'], the living expression of a
person' – and therefore not a text, not 'written literature' (Dieter
Sulzer (ed.), 'Der Nachlaß von Ernst Polak im Deutschen Litera-

turarchiv', *Jahrbuch der Deutschen Schillergesellschaft* 23 (1979), pp. 514–48, 526).

This, then, is a further instance of how the terms 'text' and 'literature' are semantically intertwined. For *Text* in German is the terminological successor to the previously more common expression *Schrift* (writing), with which, for instance in present-day France, it is still linked – in contradistinction to *discours*, which is not written and has no author (see Foucault, 'Was ist ein Autor', in *Schriften zur Literatur* (Munich, 1974), pp. 8–31, and *L'ordre du discours* (Paris, 1971)). The other connection, namely that between 'text' and 'literature', can also be clarified by etymology. For 'literature' – deriving from the Latin *littera*, a letter of the alphabet – points us towards the semantic field of writing. The writer, the *Literat*, or, as he has been called in German since the seventeenth century, the '*Schrift*steller' is, in contrast to the orator or reciter, a virtuoso of the *written* word. He shares this characteristic with the *Dichter* (poet or literary writer), for the etymology of the loan-word *dichten* points to the Latin *dictare*, meaning to dictate something that is to be *written down*. Just as *Illiterat*, now used in German to mean a person ignorant in literary matters, originally meant someone unable to read or write, so up to the seventeenth century *dichten*, as well as referring to the act of devising or inventing, also meant any form of expression in writing.

We have established, then, that there is a historical semantic connection between 'text' on the one hand and literature or *Dichtung* on the other, with writing forming the link between them. Could it be that the mere fact of being written is what gives the text its literary character? The schoolmaster Lämpel would rebut this notion: 'It's not the ABC alone that lifts a man to greater heights . . . A rational being does not only practise reading and writing.' Very true. To say that writing – taking that word in a broad sense to mean any permanent form of expression (Hofmannsthal, 'Das Schrifttum als geistiger Raum der Nation', in B. Schoeller and J. Beyer-Ahlert (eds.), *Gesammelte Werke, Reden und Aufsätze* (Frankfurt am Main, 1980) (cited as *GW*), vol. III, p. 24), is a necessary precondition for literary utterance is not to see in it the positive source of literary culture.

Nevertheless, scholars in the field of literary studies ought at this point to recognise the great extent to which they confine their interpretations to written texts. They hardly deal at all with essentially spoken language – with folk tales, folk songs, the language of the disco generation, etc. – until some Brothers Grimm or Ernest Bornemanns have collected them, written them down and had them published.

Now our opening definition stated not only that texts are writings but that they are written *discourses* – sequences of articulated word-symbols going beyond the boundaries of the sentence. Hegel underlined this by referring to the 'speaking work of art' ('redendes Kunstwerk'), and dismissed the role of the letters on the page as 'external' or 'only incidental' (*Ästhetik*, ed. F. Bassenge (Berlin, 1955), pp. 87ff.).

Now speech – unlike language, which exists only as a capability – is an *act*, or rather a series of acts: something that happens, something real but transient. This characteristic – of existing at a particular point in time – seems to mark the one difference between text and speech: the act of utterance is manifested in a substance of expression which in the one is vocalised and transitory, in the other written and permanent ('verba volant, scripta manent').

But is it really true that a text merely reproduces the orally articulated signs in a different medium? Does it not perhaps add something to verbal utterance? Let us, to make sure, use the example of the statement to examine this supposition.

A statement is a simple speech act and consists, as everyone knows, of a single activity, namely predication. Its content and its meaning reveal a particular aspect of the world; they say what is the case if the statement is correct. One might think that this would obviously also be true of the statements that form a written text. And yet it is only the statements contained in spoken utterance that have both a propositional content and a relation to reality (cf. Ricœur, 'Qu'est-ce qu'un texte').

To justify this last statement, since at first glance its truth is not at all self-evident, I will use an argument consisting of two steps.

Firstly, texts need not necessarily relate to the same world, the same historical frame of reference, as that in which the reader's mind has been formed. It is quite different with conversations between actual interlocutors, for there I can assume a shared world and the presence of a context for the utterance. In a text, on the other hand, the world that is being articulated may, in the most extreme case, have vanished, like the mysterious culture of that Antarctic people whose indecipherable hieroglyphics puzzle Poe's character Pym on the island of Tsalal. Michael Krüger, in his poem *Reginapoly*, speaks of 'ancient writing . . . older than the memory of words'. But even where comprehensible statements about facts of the historical world are concerned, I cannot simply check whether they are true: historical statements cannot be compared with the facts because those facts as such have passed away, that is to say that they are preserved only in texts which require interpretation. But even in a normal instance – and where do we draw the boundaries of what is normal? – the context and the world of the text are never unequivocally present. The communication situation between a text and the reader is not so much given as requiring to be created. (Textual linguisticians refer to the 'situational abstractness' of the text.)

Hegel urged us to consider the statement, written down last night, 'It is now night-time.' One might suppose that the truth of that statement 'cannot be diminished by its being written down'. But if we look at our piece of paper 'now', in broad daylight, we see 'that the truth has become hollow' (Hegel, *Phänomenologie des Geistes*, ed. J. Hoffmeister, 6th edn (Hamburg, 1952), p. 81).

In the poem *Plein Ciel* by the French poet Jules Supervielle we find a more charming allusion to this enigmatic phenomenon of a time discrepancy existing within the statement made in a text: *Me distinguez-vous, / Je suis celui qui / Parlait tout à l'heure, / Suis-je encore celui / Qui parle à présent, / Vous mêmes amis, / Etes-vous les mêmes? / L'un efface l'autre / Et change en montant (Choix de poèmes,* (Paris, 1947), p. 271).

But then – and this is the second stage of my argument – writing, even if it is contemporary, makes the text in some sense independent of the intentions of its creator. If he is alive he can instruct me as to his intentions. But leaving aside the fact that in poetic or fictional texts the fictive aspect creates a break between the intention and the text, any such instruction about what he has written has only the same claim to validity as have the interpretations produced by others.

Nor does it help to follow the path of so-called 'empirical reception studies' and replace the elusive intention of the author by an intersubjectively monitored survey of the 'concretisations' or 'processing' of the meaning of a text by the reading public. For Groeben's 'concretisation-amplitude' of a text will never lead to the discovery of its true *vouloir-dire*, because (1) given that Groeben's so-called 'interpretations' are paraphrases which depart from the language of the text, they are not 'positive data' but themselves require interpretation, and (2) the processing of the meaning of the text has not at any point in time been, nor will it ever be, complete (see Groeben, *Rezeptionsforschung als empirische Literaturwissenschaft* (Kronberg/Taunus, 1977)).

Is what the text says what the author meant?

Before deciding whether these two conclusions are over-hasty and possibly untenable, we must ask ourselves whether in principle 'textual interpretation' can be used at all as a means of finding out what an author meant by his text.

The view that it can is prevalent above all in Anglo-Saxon hermeneutics. Thus, to name but one, the American hermeneutist Eric Donald Hirsch Jr believes that he can invoke the authority of Schleiermacher and Boeckh when – in what he calls his 'modest and in the old-fashioned sense, philological effort to find out what an author meant' (in contrast to the search for the independent meaning – 'semantic autonomy' – of the text) – he largely reduces the hermeneutic task to the 'authorial meaning' aspect of it (*VI*, p. 57).

In fact this definition belongs not to the German intellectual tradition but to a scientistically reduced variety of the tradition of linguistic analysis within which – amongst many others – John R. Searle, the theoretician of the 'speech act', stands when he insists that normally (in 'standard discourse') only such utterances are communicated as 'precisely' (Searle, 'Reiterating the Differences: a Reply to Derrida', in *Glyph* 1 (1977) (cited as *R*), p. 202) 'represent' the intentions of the subjects involved in the conversation and thereby have at the same time the character of invariable and codified 'types': 'The author said what he meant' (*ibid.*, p. 201).

And therefore 'understanding the utterance consists in recognising the illocutionary intentions of the author and these intentions may be more or less perfectly realised by the words uttered' (*ibid.*, p. 202). What we have here is a scientistic concept of understanding a text, which Hirsch, following Emilio Betti, characterises as 'objective interpretation' (Hirsch, *VI*, pp. 209ff.). Betti – in an equally fictitious claim to be following Schleiermacher – had addressed the question of the 'epistemological preconditions for the possibility of objectivity in the process of interpretation' (*Die Hermeneutik als allgemeine Methodik der Geisteswissenschaften* (Tübingen, 1962) (cited as *HaM*), p. 38), that is, the question of the 'objectivity of the meaning which is to be found', which is (relatively) independent of the interpreter's attempt to establish the meaning (*ibid.*, p. 19; see also 53f.). By this both writers – following the classical 'correspondence' theory of truth ('truth exists where there is agreement between the thing and the view of it') – mean that the interpreter's attempt to establish the meaning is directed towards the original and 'autonomous' (Betti) meaning of the author's words, which expresses itself independently of the way in which it is meant on any particular occasion. 'Correctness', says Hirsch, 'implies a correspondence between the interpretation and the meaning reproduced by means of the text' (*VI*, p. 110). Betti had set up a 'canon of understanding *adequate to the meaning*', according to which 'the interpreter [should] strive to bring his own living actuality into the most inward correspondence with the impulse that comes from the object' (*HaM*, p. 53; *ibid.*, p. 43, he demands 'that the understanding arrived at should correspond to the underlying meaning of the text, as an objectification of mind, in a wholly adequate manner'). Where they find the pragmatic criterion or yardstick by which to measure this correspondence, and in particular what is meant by the 'objectivity' of an original meaning prior to its actualisation through interpretation, the objective interpreters do not reveal.

Briefly, Hirsch's concept is this: what is to be sought is – as I have said – the *mens dicentis*, in other words what was subjectively intended to be conveyed by the matter which is to be interpreted, i.e. the text to which the author has entrusted his meaning. But how is an author to communicate his subjective meaning without using the universal instrument of a *language* in the act of utterance?

The author's 'will' or 'intention', uttered and separated from himself, must therefore be realised in the objectivity of the available grammatical schemata. Hirsch calls this the 'verbal meaning', the neutral meaning of his utterance, which is self-identical and as such both independent of time and neutral in respect of prejudices, resulting from effective history, on the part of the interpreter. Hirsch distinguishes between the 'verbal meaning' and the 'significance' of the same utterance, by which he means 'any perceived relationship between construed verbal meaning and something else [e.g. the discursive formation of the interpreter's epoch or his personal experience of life]' (*VI*, p. 140; cp. Searle, 'Literal Meaning', *Erkenntnis* 13 (1978), pp. 207–24, *Ausdruck und Bedeutung* (Frankfurt am Main, 1982), *Expression and Meaning* (Cambridge, 1979); the *significance* of an utterance opens up an aspect which under the exegetical division of labour falls to literary criticism (*VI*, pp. 132, 136, 141, 143ff.). (For this, binding 'canons' can indeed be set up, but only ones that are of such general application as to be virtually useless, *ibid.*, p. 168.)

Whereas the 'significance' of an utterance may, he says, vary in the course of history, since it is a function of the 'historicity of all interpretations' (*ibid.*, p. 137) (and by 'interpretation' Hirsch means any reformulation of an author's utterance expressed in words different from his), the 'meaning' perceived by the understanding is 'dumb', with no temporal index, and capable of being repeated identically and with the same meaning (so much so that any exegetical reconstruction 'involves the notion of the repetition of the same' [Searle, *R*, p. 207]) and therefore does not offer itself as an object of hermeneutical dispute: only *interpretations* can be controversial, because they are presented in discrete discourses and reflect the subject-matter of *understanding* as it were in a wealth of aspects which, though different, are not therefore necessarily incompatible: the unity of what is understood is not broken up by this conflict of interpretations any more than the essential unity of Husserl's intentional object is destroyed by the large number of *noemata* in which it presents itself.

With this conception of understanding a text it is noticeable that returning to the 'authorial meaning', to what the author intended to say, did not, as one might at first have imagined, draw the interest of the interpreter towards the individuality as such of the author. Going back to the 'subject' followed from purely method-ological conclusions: firstly, a series of signs could not of itself (i.e. without being directed by an intention) have 'determinacy' (and if an utterance were semantically indeterminate, its meaning could not be 'objectively recognised'); secondly, there would be no objective criteria for the validity of an understanding if the mean-ing of the discourse that was to be interpreted was not identical with what the author intended by his utterance. (This is also the reason why within the framework of a programme of 'objective interpretation' no account is taken of the 'significance' – precisely the dimension of meaning of a text which only develops in the process of the reader's engagement with it and which therefore could not be reconstructed in its timeless semantic identity.)

This being so, an unintended convergence arises between Hirsch's 'theory of immanent meaning' and the 'theory of seman-tic autonomy' which he opposes (M. Peckham, 'Semantic Auton-omy and Immanent Meaning', *Genre* I,I (1968), pp. 190–4), be-cause he ascribes to 'authorial meaning' a semantic determinacy which excludes a priori all those meaning-implications which cannot be directly checked against the grammar-book, the dic-tionary and the pragmatic code. As M.C. Beardsley has objected ('Textual Meaning and Authorial Meaning', *Genre* II (1968), p. 172), there is a latent equivocation in the concept of the 'verbal meaning intended by the author': on the one hand it seems to mean the individual intention underlying the utterance of the person speaking or writing, yet on the other hand the individual can only say what the grammar of his language permits him to say. The authorial meaning therefore has in principle the status of an intention that is more than merely individual; it can be con-strued in a way that is unambiguous and adequate to the meaning by means of the identification, in conformity with the underlying grammar, of the signs used and an awareness of the pragmatic convention which governs the meaning with which they are used (Hirsch speaks of the 'genre' of the particular utterance or text). The concept of the genre is introduced in order to overcome a tendency to see the utterance as having only the function of making statements: thus it also includes forms representing other kinds of intention – requests, wishes, imperatives, symbolic uses of language etc. – in the spectrum of textual interpretation. In short, the 'entire complex system of shared experiences, usage traits, and meaning expectations which the speaker relies on . . . Understanding can occur only if the interpreter proceeds under the same system of expectations' (*VI*, p. 80). Now this does not mean that generic interpretation (a term taken from A. Boeckh) – because it takes account of the pragmatic signals in the text – does after all take account of the individual intention of the author in making the utterance: a genre is after all a linguistic *convention*; to be recognisable it has to obey rules that are supra-individual and as such are just as invariable, self-identical and 'objective' as the rules which determine the function of making a statement.

What instance determines the meaning of the text?

Before we decide if Hirsch is justified in claiming to follow Schleiermacher and Boeckh when he defines 'understanding a text' as the reconstruction of the author's intention in making the utterance, and before embarking on a general critique of his argument, we must see where his thesis stands *vis-à-vis* our earlier proposition that the (literary) text becomes separated not only from the world but also from the intentions of its author. For the truth of this assertion is not self-evident. Even while admitting that there are texts – like Brentano's *Waja, waja, kur libu, / Ich bin ich, und du bist du!* (*Werke in zwei Bänden*, ed. F. Kemp (Munich, 1972), vol. 1, p. 378) – in which raising the question of the author's intention provokes merriment rather than showing understanding, and even if one concedes, with Mendelssohn, that no text preserves its meaning unchanged even for one generation (*Jerusalem oder über religiöse Macht und Judentum* (Berlin, 1783), p. 31), one will still insist that the multiplicity of aspects which a literary work presents is not an argument against the semantic unity of its message.

Here are two illustrations of this, of the kind of which E.D. Hirsch approves. Kafka's story *Die Sorge des Hausvaters* ('The cares of a family man')[1] has been interpreted along biographical-

---

[1] The reference should be to *Das Urteil* ('The Judgement') (Editor's note).

psychoanalytical lines (the condemnation of a member of the family by the father), in terms of social emancipation (an act of self-liberation from the head of the household), or of reception theory (the text's attainment of independence from the intentions of its creator) (H. Binder (ed.), *Kafka-Handbuch*, (Stuttgart, 1979), vol. II, pp. 342ff.). A second example: F. Rastier has attempted three equally possible and equally valid interpretations of Mallarmé's sonnet *Salut (Rien, cette écume, vierge vers / A ne désigner que la coupe*, etc.). The meanings of the words interwoven in the poem point to the semantic sphere of the banquet, or of navigation, or of literature (U. Japp, *Hermeneutik* (Munich, 1977), pp. 79ff.). The conflict between these interpretations, which can all be supported from the text, does not disprove the identity of the textual meaning, so long as there is is merely a difference but no logical contradiction between them.

But what becomes, then, of the thesis advanced above that writing uncouples that which is written from the intentions of the author and thereby also from the meaning that he lends to his words? Did not Flaubert say, 'Madame Bovary, c'est moi'? (Sartre, *Critique de la raison dialectique* (Paris, 1960) (cited as *Crd*), p. 89). And did not Kafka write to Felice Bauer, 'The novel is me, my stories are me'? (Kafka, *Briefe an Felice und andere Korrespondenz aus der Verlobungszeit*, ed. E. Heller and J. Born (Frankfurt am Main, 1967), p. 226; on what follows see G. Kurz, *Traum-Schrecken* (Stuttgart, 1980), pp. 85ff.). Research has shown just how closely life and writing were connected precisely in Kafka's work. By means of arrangements of letters in his heroes' names which recall his own, or the appellative meaning of those names – *Gracchus* for instance has, like the Czech *kavka*, the meaning 'jackdaw' – he effectively placed his signature on his texts. Like himself, his characters suffer because of an excessively powerful father-figure, like him they are perpetual wanderers in search of an impossible salvation, like him they are bachelors, and so on.

On closer inspection, however, one discovers that not a single one of the aspects referred to is specific to Kafka's work. The father–son conflict has been a common theme in literature since the *Sturm und Drang* movement and is so especially in the texts of Kafka's expressionist contemporaries; the theme of the vain search

for salvation, the unending journey which simultaneously exists as
a text with no ending links Kafka's work (for instance in the story of
Jäger Gracchus – the hunter Gracchus) with the tradition of the
Flying Dutchman, the Wild Huntsman, the Drunken Ship and the
old metaphorical tradition which compares poetic creation to
navigation (*ingenii barca*) (M. Frank, *Die unendliche Fahrt. Ein Motiv
und sein Text* (Frankfurt am Main, 1979)); and the figure of the
bachelor is already present in the novels of Jean Paul, Tolstoy,
Dostoevsky, Gottfried Keller, Rilke, Wilde, Huysmans or Thomas
Mann. Parallels can similarly be found for writing one's own name
into the text; Marcel in the *Recherche* and Adalbert in *Adalbert's Fabel*
bear the first names of their authors, Proust and Chamisso. In
short, the intention in Kafka's way of writing, which appears to
aim at individuality, reveals itself as following the pattern of a
literary tradition and so cannot confirm an individual intention of
the author.

Perhaps all this is still not sufficient to justify the thesis of texts'
loss of meaning. What is decisive is the characteristic of the written
nature, the literality in the literal sense of the word, of poetic
utterances. Following Jacques Lacan, Roland Barthes spoke of a
'revolution' in the manner of being which affects the subject
uttering the discourse and its relationship with reality at the
moment of its being fitted into the symbolic order of a text: '*The one
who writes* (in the narrative) is not *the one who writes* (in life) and *the one
who writes* is not *the one who is*' ('Introduction à l'analyse structurale
des récits', *Communications* 8 (1966), 19/20). Marcel Proust had
similarly rejected Sainte-Beuve's equation of the author with the
work. The work, he says, 'is the product of a different "I" from that
which expresses itself in our habits, in society, in our vices' (*Contre
Sainte-Beuve*, ed. Pierre Clarac (Paris, 1971), p. 221f.). To these
somewhat speculative formulations I will add a more concrete
instance, the quarrel with the city of Lübeck in which the author of
Buddenbrooks became embroiled. Some respected citizens of that
Free Hanseatic City felt that the novel had portrayed them in an
unflattering manner. The author was compared to a certain Herr
Bilse, now forgotten, who had written a crude *roman à clef.* Thomas
Mann defended himself in a short essay, 'Bilse und ich' (1906). The
decisive sentence runs: 'Stupidity! If I have made a thing into a

sentence, what has the thing still to do with the sentence?' (*Altes und Neues* (Frankfurt am Main, 1953), p. 31).

Text as something communicated

That sounds over-subtle and like an excuse; and yet in a quite general way it strikes a blow against an approach to the study of literature according to which the meaning of a piece of writing continuously points back to the author's intention or to a real state of affairs in the historical world. But intentions and happenings in the world are not in themselves meaningful. They become so only when a subject who is capable of interpreting them articulates their meaning, that is to say, raises them to the level of a linguistic event. But the meaning that has been imparted immediately also slips away – as we were able to observe in the unintended consequence of Hirsch's argument – from the interpreting subject; for speech – and also the written text – are communicative events. 'A fact in our lives', Goethe says, 'is not valid in so far as it is true but in so far as it means something.' But the *meaning* of a spoken utterance and still more that of a written one is never determined only by the utterer but always also by the community within which the communication is made. A literature as an expression of the private is as unthinkable as a private language (Kurz, *Traum-Schrecken*, p. 86). One always writes, as Sartre says, 'for and through others' (*Situations* II (Paris, 1948), p. 93). In the understanding of its readers the text, even a biographical text, acquires a meaning which exceeds the memory of its origin.

And this is connected – somehow – with the literality of the text. For through the permanence of the signs used in writing, literature is able to surpass the individual intention of an author to a far greater degree than is the case with speech. This is why right into the seventeenth century 'dichten' could mean both 'to produce a piece of writing' and 'to invent something'. Strange as it may sound, a word – or, in E.D. Hirsch's terminology, a 'linguistic type' – cannot, strictly speaking, be written down. For a word, like any other sign, is made up of two parts: an imperceptible one, the meaning, and one perceptible by the senses, the expression. Now, *only* the expression can be written down, because only it belongs to the world of (graphic or acoustic) perception. Meaning, on the other hand, is, in the old poetological metaphor, 'unsayable' and cannot be captured in writing. Meaning, says Mallarmé, is 'what the discourse does not say'; 'the condition and pleasure of reading' (*Œuvres complètes*, ed. H. Mondor and G. Aubry [Paris, 1945], p. 310; cp. Derrida, *La dissémination* (Paris, 1972), p. 309). It therefore reveals itself only, but always in a new and different way, in the light of creative understanding, creative reading, which Schleiermacher called 'divination' (*HuK*, pp. 169–70). This never leads back to the semantic-pragmatic core of an 'authorial meaning', and this is not because of a whim or arbitrary wish on the part of the interpreter blithely to ignore what the author intended to say, but because the meaning of linguistic types only comes into play and becomes effective in the process of communication, that is, in the act of concretisation performed by the particular hearer. It is in this sense – and not as a declaration in favour of restoring an original *vouloir-dire* – that we should understand Schleiermacher's famous philosophical imperative (not invented but only quoted by him) that one must 'understand the discourse first as well as and then better than its originator' (*ibid.*, p. 94). The explanation of this principle which Schleiermacher gave in his lecture to the Academy, 'Über den Begriff der Hermeneutik' ('On the Concept of Hermeneutics' of 1828) makes it clear that understanding 'better' cannot mean understanding more truly or correctly but only differently and more richly. *Differently*, because 'aesthetic criticism' helps us to attain an 'enhanced understanding of the inner process of poets and other artists in language, of the whole procedure of composition' (*HuK*, p. 324). For the author, Schleiermacher continues, has no privileged access to the meaning of the utterances he produces, since it is only in the process of communication that meanings can be formed and prove effective. For this reason there may be much of which the author 'remain[s] unconscious . . . except insofar as he himself, by reflecting, becomes his own reader' (*ibid.*, p. 94). Even then he is not in a privileged position compared to any other reader of what he has written, for 'on the objective side he too has no other data than those that we have' (*ibid.*, p. 94). Any productive understanding may be considered *richer*, because in the course of reading it adds to one and the same material of expression new meaning which was not yet articulated in the original act of speech. This increase in meaning cannot, as Hirsch and Searle would like, be split away from the original 'meaning' of the authorial utterance and be relegated, under the label of 'significance', to the historical relativism of commenting-on-a-text; for the meaning of a text *is* nothing but what the readers realise in it (Iser, *Der Akt des Lesens* (Munich, 1976); Sartre, 'L'écriture et la publication', in *Obliques* 18–19 (Paris, 1979), p. 22). The only meaning that would be self-identical would be the meaning that has not been communicated; but this would be a *reductio ad absurdum* since it would then cease to qualify for the name of 'meaning'. This is what happens in Hirsch's fiction of a 'silent understanding', in which the reader/interpreter expresses the meanings of an authorial utterance 'in its own terms and not in foreign categories' (*VI*, p. 135), as though a text had meaning in itself, 'silently', before it enters into the communicative process.

Incidentally, the term 'divination', which Schleiermacher takes from theological tradition and uses to designate productivity in the understanding of a text, is quite usual in French. Proust, for instance, writes, 'In reading one divines, one creates' (*A la recherche du temps perdu*, ed. P. Clarac and A. Ferré (Paris, 1954), vol. III, p. 656). The term is also used for instance by Sartre (*L'idiot de la famille* (Paris, 1971), vol. I, pp. 56, 658) or by G.-G. Granger, who defines 'deviner' to mean 'not a conscious and explicit recognition, but being receptive to certain (stylistic) regularities transported by the message, which, however, are wholly independent of the macroscopic regularities on which general usage has to rely' (*Essai d'une philosophie du style* (Paris, 1968), p. 213).

At this point it seems possible to give a first summing-up. In the transition to written form, discourse suffers not only a transformation of its material of expression; the texts are also, in a way which can never be wholly controlled, released from their meanings and from the communicative context and the intentions of the author. Having been uttered and given external form, discourse moves *out* of its context of actuality and so also *out* of the domain where the producer has any power over it: it becomes de-actualised, unrealised. This certainly does not mean that one can ignore the conventions of language and normal linguistic usage if one wants

to be understood. But in conceding this one must not, on the other
hand, fall prey to the illusion cherished by the advocates of 'objective interpretation' that the grammar of a language is a self-
contained machine, timeless and static, whose sole task consists of
*en*coding and *de*coding identical 'meanings'. By underlining the
view that an intention can only be understood as a communicative
event, one cuts through the fetters of the static taxonomic model;
for communication is a historical *process* with an open, that is to say,
semantically unforeseeable outcome; the meanings of the words –
and therefore also the views about the world written into them by
the interlocutors – change in proportion as the conversation that
they conduct has substance and is not merely a 'chat about the
weather' (Schleiermacher, *HuK*, pp. 82-3). The discourse fixed in
writing – the text – merely makes this release of the meaning from
its previous synthesis with the signs a conscious release; to put it in
a rather striking way, it places the meaning at the reader's disposal.

Text as a paradigm of the poetic

Is it not this that makes us spontaneously inclined to associate the
world of the text with that of poetry – with the world of letters, of
literature? The sometimes magical character of poetry, by which,
as we tellingly say, it transports us away from reality (in order, of
course, to teach us to see reality differently) is only an *extreme* form
of those effects which arise from the imaginary of *any* text. The
most ordinary bit of paper can – like those left by Nietzsche and
Mallarmé – become the locus of hermeneutic revelations. Here
there are many kinds of transitions. Always, however, a part is
played by *writing*, which after all has since ancient times (for
instance by Hesiod or Aeschylus) been linked with the art of the
Muse. For it is only through the means that enables the expression
as such to be captured but the memory of its meaning to be set free
that texts can acquire more meaning and a different meaning from
that which they can acquire at *one* time, for *one* interpreter and in
accordance with *one* accepted norm of interpretation – even in
accordance with the grammar or the norm of interpretation which
are enshrined in the societal regulations and conventions of what
we read. For the relationship between words and their *meaning*,

Sartre says, is quite different in nature from the relationship between the grammatical *meaning* (*signification*) and its *expression* (*signifiant*). The *meaning* of a sentence or of a text is 'contained' in its conformity to linguistic usage as prescribed by grammar; whereas the *significance* is 'une lie indéfinie du texte' – an indefinite sediment, a deposit of yeast in the text which rises, causing meaning to develop, in consciousnesses other than those of the 'original reader' or the 'author', and allows something to be discovered in the words which was not put there (only) by the dictionary or the grammar or the author or previous readers: 'Such that one sees onself differently than one was when one was writing' (Sartre, 'L'écriture', pp. 25–6). And this change of meaning is 'not a risk, but on the contrary an *opportunity* for the work, if despite everything it produces a meaning in connection with the words, even if it is one that departs from *my* meaning . . . I regard this as an opportunity; for whatever I say about myself that is purely individual [for instance in *Les Mots*] acquires a far more comprehensive, almost general character, when and because [lorsque] it says something that *I* did *not* mean to say. It's an adventure of the book – a fine adventure' (*ibid.*, p. 27).

Here we have arrived at a formulation of the so-called reception theory (Iser, Jauss); Sartre anticipated it by his famous definition of reading as 'directed creation [création dirigée]' (*Situations II*, p. 95; *Que peut la littérature*, ed. Y. Buin (Paris, 1948), pp. 107–27), and developed it further in his book on Flaubert, but it can already be found in the works of the early Romantic theorists. That 'the act of creation is only an incomplete and abstract element in the production of a work' and 'that the action of writing demands that of reading as its dialectical correlate' (Sartre, *Situations II*, p. 93; see also Starobinski, *L'œil vivant II* (Paris, 1970), p. 16f.) already underlies Schleiermacher's definition of 'interpretation' as an 'art' (*HuK*, pp. 80-1); the main point being made is that all understanding is itself an act of creation, because the expressions in the text are not meaningful in themselves but only vouchsafe their meaning in the encounter with another subject which articulates them (afresh) and, in a way that cannot be controlled, alters, transfers, shifts their 'actual meaning'. Texts have the character neither of facts of experience (their 'meaning' is not perceived but produced by the imagination) nor of prescripts (one cannot condition a reading experience), but of 'appeals' (Sartre, Iser), which may freely be followed or contradicted.

Schiller already expressed a very similar view – with reference to the aesthetic – when he wrote to Körner (25 October 1794): 'The beautiful is not a concept relating to experience but rather an imperative' (similarly Novalis, *Schriften*, ed. P. Kluckhohn and R. Samuel (Stuttgart, 1968), vol. III, p. 413; Sartre, *Situations II*, p. 98). The idea is as familiar to Novalis as it was to the Jena circle as a whole: since 'literary creation [*Dichten*] is begetting' (Novalis, *Schriften*, vol. II (Stuttgart, 1965), p. 534), a poem will be judged rightly only by someone who is capable of 'himself creating the product that is to be criticised' (*ibid.*). In short, 'The true reader must be the extended author. He is merely the higher instance which receives the matter already prepared by the lower instance' (*ibid.*, p. 470). And Schleiermacher speaks quite generally of the work of art as 'something abstract, which accordingly . . . (is) nothing in itself, but . . . only (becomes) something through the relationships which the observer puts into it' (*Die christliche Sitte*, ed. L. Jonas, 2nd edn (Berlin, 1884), p. 682; see also p. 679).

The history of acts of communication and readings of text may destine an expression not merely to change but directly to revoke its original meaning: its outer shell lives on after its earlier meaning has become obsolete. An example of this is, as Seume caustically writes, the word 'Höflichkeit' (courtesy): it 'ought to come from "Hof" (court); but the word seems, like many others in life, to be the antiphrase of the meaning, and now "Hof" often means only a place where one finds no courtesy; just as "Gesetz" (law) is often the opposite of justice' (Seume, *Prosaische und poetische Werke* (Berlin, n.d.), vol. II, p. 11). This changeability of the meaning in relation to the expression can of course also be used for poetic effect. For a vivid example of this constant possibility of a change from writing to poetry one may think of Peter Handke's preservation in writing of a football team, *Die Aufstellung des 1. FC Nürnberg vom 27.1.1968* (The line-up of 1st FC Nuremberg of 27 January 1968), which perishes as a piece of the world but is resurrected as a poem.

TWO ADDITIONS: AESTHETIC EXPERIENCE AND TEXTUAL COHERENCE

Aesthetic and hermeneutic experience

Before we turn to the second task referred to in the title of this chapter, namely to the methods used for *interpreting* texts, it is worth once again recalling our opening definition. The text, we learned from the everyday use of the word, is a connected, written and usually literary discourse. We have now found some explanation for the association between written form and literature. Above all we know that because of their literality all texts are creations of a kind which need to be understood individually. Before the main features of this understanding are outlined, it must be admitted that the foregoing discussion of the definition of a text has left two gaps.

Firstly, it is surely legitimate to doubt whether what is actually poetic in and about a text is adequately explained by its multiplicity of meanings or, to use the terminology of Iser's reception hermeneutics, its 'polyfunctionality'. Polysemy too is, as Derrida in particular has pointed out, still a *semantic* quality of the text; and if the hermeneutic project – in a very broad sense – devotes itself to the task of decoding the semantics of a discourse by someone else (which, as we have said, need not mean the 'authorial meaning'), then it must be permissible to ask whether the aesthetic qualities of a text come within the scope of a (literary) hermeneutics at all (cp. Anz, *Die Bedeutung poetischer Rede* (Munich, 1979)).

Incidentally, polemics against hermeneutic attempts to reduce fictional texts to a discursive meaning are as old as the tradition of the 'apologias for poetry' (Sidney, Shelley); with the coming of modern poetry, however, they reached a new level of intensity which is clearly reflected in Susan Sontag's still absolutely topical essay *Against Interpretation* (New York, 1966): 'The old style of interpretation was insistent, but respectful; it erected another meaning on top of the literal one. The modern style of interpretation excavates, and as it excavates, destroys; it digs "behind" the text, to find a sub-text which is the true one . . . To understand *is* to interpret. And to interpret is to restate the phenomenon, in effect to find an equivalent for it.

'Thus, interpretation is not (as most people assume) an absolute value, a gesture of mind situated in some timeless realm of capabilities. Interpretation must itself be evaluated, within a historical view of human consciousness' (pp. 6–7).

Even after Gadamer (*WuM*, pp. 128ff.) and especially Jauss (*Ästhetische Erfahrung und literarische Hermeneutik*, vol. 1 (Munich, 1977)), who has made what so far remains the most penetrating study of this problem, there has still been a constant succession of attempts to include aesthetic experience within hermeneutic experience. And there are good reasons for this: hermeneutics as a doctrine of the art of understanding (or interpreting) was brought into being above all by the experience of the poetic, and has tried to deal with that experience using the tools of philological theory. It is true that – above all since Schleiermacher – the interpretation of poetic texts has no priority in principle, only one of degree, over the interpretation of non-poetic texts; and yet 'textual interpretation' is, rightly, generally associated with the interpretation of poetic (or sacred) texts. Jauss has been able to show that 'the productive, the receptive and the communicative activity' as set out in hermeneutic dialectic follows the triad of '*poesis, aisthesis* and *katharsis*' of classical poetics (*ibid.*, p. 8), and that it is difficult, if not impossible, to exclude from one's perception of the text the experience of its aesthetic commitments: for to understand an artistic text always means also to enjoy it as the work of art that it is ('*Selbstgenuss im Fremdgenuss*' – enjoyment of oneself in the enjoyment of something outside oneself – *ibid.*, p. 59); and it would indeed be questionable whether one could make a plausible case for the characteristic of certain hermeneutic readings, namely the experience of 'objectively binding meaning', if the 'communicative function of art' were excluded (*ibid.*, p. 158).

This opens up a complex of problems for hermeneutics to which I must at least draw attention. For in the name of the poetic, representatives of, in particular, contemporary French textual theory have criticised the project of hermeneutics for reducing the aesthetic qualities to those of meaning. The flaws of this *démarche* were demonstrated most impressively by Derrida in his response, which has attracted little attention in the German-speaking countries, to Richard's major interpretation of Mallarmé (Derrida, *La dissémination*, pp. 199–318). He calls Richard's analysis 'thematistic', since while doing full justice to the polysemy of Mallarmé's poems it does not abandon the dream that one might be able hermeneutically to master a theme as 'the sum, or rather the putting in one single perspective, of its diverse modulations' (Richard, *L'univers imaginaire de Mallarmé* (Paris, 1961), p. 28; Derrida, *La dissémination*, p. 282, quoted here from the English translation by Barbara Johnson, *Dissemination* (London, 1981), p. 250). 'This concession', comments Derrida, 'still allows for the hope, the "dream"', of reaching a sum and of determining a perspective, even if these are infinite. Such a sum or perspective would enable us to define, contain, and classify the different occurrences of a theme.

'To this we would oppose the following hypotheses: the sum is impossible to totalize but yet it is not exceeded by the infinite richness of a content of meaning or intention [*vouloir-dire*]; the perspective extends out of sight [so it goes beyond the distance that the eye can see – 'à perte de *vue*' –] but without entailing the depth of a horizon of meaning *before* or *within* which we can never have finished advancing. By taking into account that "laterality" Richard mentions in passing, but by going on to determine its law, we shall define the limit otherwise: through the angle and the intersection [*croisement*] of a re-mark [a re-marking of the poetic sign-mark] that folds the text back upon itself without any possibility of its fitting back over or into itself, without any reduction of its spacing [the crystal-lattice structure of the text]' (*La dissémination*, p. 282; Johnson, *Dissemination*, p. 250, insertions in square brackets by MF).

This passage seems obscure and is intended to be so, since it is taking a stand against the monopolising grip of an understanding that seeks to pin down meaning – that, like the hermeneutics of Ricœur (*De l'interprétation* (Paris, 1965) and *Le conflit des interprétations*), sees poetic expression just as the small detour which the (non-sensuous) meaning has to make in order to become identifiable (by the senses), in the spirit of the Aristotelian *metaphor*, which *re-presents* the idea, in itself non-sensuous – the *diánoia* – in a sensuous medium, that of discourse (*léxis*); the interpreter of the metaphor merely goes back along that path to reach its (true and non-sensuous) meaning (see M. Frank, 'Die Aufhebung der

Anschauung im Spiel der Metapher', in *Das Sagbare und das Unsag-bare. Studien zur deutsch-französischen Hermeneutik and Texttheorie*, ex-panded edn (Frankfurt am Main, 1990), pp. 213ff.). In this case the hermeneutic interpretation of texts follows the Western scheme of reflection. 'Reflection' is of course itself a metaphor. The word means reflecting back, mirroring. In the act of reflection the idea of a subject is mirrored in its truth, or – to put it differently – by means of a detour via an externalisation-of-itself-in-the-form-of-signs, the subject assigns its real meaning to itself. Formulations like this, such as 'reappropriation of the meaning', have been used for instance by Paul Ricœur to characterise the work of textual interpretation (Ricœur, *De l'interprétation* and *Le conflit des interpréta-tions*; see also M. Frank, *Das Individuelle-Allgemeine*, pp. 134ff.). Now if the language of poetry is defined by its use of metaphor, and if moreover metaphor involves two (chains of) signs and two mean-ings corresponding to one another (on the basis of an 'analogy' which mediates between them), then it is indeed tempting to characterise the business of textual interpretation roughly as fol-lows: the task of interpretation is to trace the figurative expression back to the literal expression, or – put more abstractly still – to find the *meaning* in the *expression*.

Derrida argues against this in the following way. If it is true that we only know the meaning after it has already been externalised in its expression, then we must redistribute the emphases. After all, we do not know the so-called original meaning (of the author, of the text) *before* it has been articulated; and so one cannot describe interpretation as an act of *re*appropriation, of recalling again or recognising again. For a thing can only be *re*cognised again if it has already been known; but Humboldt and Saussure have shown that we only get to know the meaning of an utterance through the work of the articulation of the material of expression itself. After all, we have no common yardstick for the (intelligible) meaning and its (sensuous) expression; the meaning is not the originator of the articulation, but its effect. This is also a valid objection to a hermeneutics of 'polysemy' as put forward by Ricœur or Richard, that is to say to the thesis that the unity of the meaning of a word is in the strict sense impossible to discover because it appears to me each time in a new light, depending on the other expressions to which I – as I read and interpret – relate it 'diacritically' (and 'laterally'), a process of linking and of differentiating which is by its nature inexhaustible. The word never appears in a pure lexical form but always in contextualisations, that are in principle unpredictable, which destroy its 'real meaning'. This was already emphasised by Schleiermacher (*HuK*, pp. 104ff.). Richard and Ricœur have basically not advanced beyond him. But they still think it possible to attain a global 'perspective' from which one might succeed more or less in bringing the transformations of the themes and leitmotifs in, for instance, Mallarmé's work, under control. There is no strictly 'mathematical order' of themes and complexes of meaning, but there is something in the nature of a concept 'with blurred edges' (Wittgenstein, *Philosophische Untersuchungen* (Frankfurt am Main, 1971), p. 50), which encompasses them and gives us an inkling of their continuity of meaning. Then interpretation or the thematic analysis of a text would consist of reducing its ambiguity, not completely, and certainly with extreme caution, but still as far as possible. And in this approach Derrida discovers the legacy of Plato and Aristotle, namely the idea that truth (for instance that of poetic *mimesis*) is broken up into its manifestation but that the philosopher or the textual interpreter gathers together the scattered parts (*légein* – German *lesen* – literally means to gather) and so restores the central meaning or the truth of the text.

While modern hermeneutic theories, for instance those of Ricœur or Gadamer, have indeed broken with Hegel's notion that in a long process of searching one can find what in the text of the world is the genuinely and timelessly 'true', they too nevertheless continue to adhere to the old reflection model which says that '*all understanding is ultimately an understanding of oneself*' (Gadamer, *WuM*, p. 246). Gadamer even writes that language (which he conceives of as a process of communication in which tradition and present are interchanged) has a 'speculative structure' (*ibid.*, pp. 432ff.). 'Speculative' means like a mirror: with every understanding *of* something the interpreter is *himself* mirrored in the thing *which* he is interpreting, or the other way round: he allows the thing that is interpreted to be mirrored in his interpretation-horizon. It is precisely from this hermeneutic narcissism that Derrida wants to release hermeneutics. And he does this, as I have suggested, by showing that expression is not only an instrument for the repossession of the (externalised) meaning by means of interpretation, but that it is a precondition for the possibility of this meaning. If this is the case then one may call all methods mistaken which regard the expressions in a text as emanations of a quasi-transcendental unity of meaning which gives the text a semantic identity.

It now becomes clear what Derrida wishes to designate by the artificial expression *re-marque*, namely the kind of movement of exegetical reflection which does not lead one back to an (imagined) original meaning but uncontrollably shifts, distorts and redefines it. The poetic, Derrida says, is at once *in* the text and *outside* the text, in exactly the same sense as when (Saussurean) 'differentiality' grounds the meaning of the signs in distinctions between the materials of expression and yet cannot be dissolved in the meaning of the signs articulated in this way. Thus a doubly marked discourse marks not only the function of the signs but always in addition (*de surcroît*) the differentiality which permits the signs to designate anything at all, i.e. to refer to a state of affairs (Derrida, *La dissémination*, p. 283), but which can certainly also, through a new differentiation of the elements in the text – by poetic means – wipe out or change the meaning of the signs, at all events split them from their original semantic allocations, as suggested by Mallarmé's metaphor of the 'folding or pleating of the text'. (Like reflection, the fold is a way of describing the movement of something back upon itself without coinciding with itself.) Reading in a way that takes account of this principle of the non-identity of the meanings split away from themselves and that refrains from enclosing them in in a vague horizon of meaning would be what Derrida calls 'disseminal reading'.

This is especially appropriate where the text reaches from the ambiguous to the uninterpretable (asemantic), as is the case with some examples of the Romantic, Symbolist or Dadaist lyric, or in concrete poetry: 'If', says Derrida, 'there is thus no thematic unity or overall meaning to reappropriate beyond the textual instances, no total message located in some imaginary order, intentionality or lived experience [*vécu*], then the text is no longer the expression or representation (felicitous or otherwise) of any *truth* that would come to diffract or assemble itself in the polysemy of literature. It is this hermeneutic concept of *polysemy* that must be replaced by *dissemination*' (*La dissémination*, p. 294; Johnson, *Dissemination*, p. 262).

This may be illustrated by an example from Mallarmé's *Alchemy of letters* (*Œuvres complètes*, pp. 398–9), parts of which Derrida quotes and comments on in a long footnote to 'La double séance' (*La dissémination*, pp. 294–7). Here Mallarmé has placed in a context a number of words which all contain the sound OR: dehORs, fantasmagORique, trésOR, hORizon, majORe, son OR, sonORe, s'honORe, signe OR, SignOR, décOR, licORne, nORd, autORe, encORe, etc. Derrida calls OR an ironic and precious expression (*signifiant*). Mallarmé's *Alchemy of Letters* exploits its sensuous, phonetic, graphic, logical, syntactical and economic possibilities. Derrida uses Mallarmé's meditation on the high sums whose value is raised to infinity simply by the addition of noughts, so that in the end the total amount leaves one as cold as if it were worth 'almost nothing' (Mallarmé, *Œuvres complètes*, p. 399; also p. 656), as the basis for a demonstration which aims to show that OR is not merely an ambiguous or not *completely* interpretable 'signifier' but actually one which is *un*interpretable or 'disseminal'. OR in French has three meanings: (1) 'gold', (2) temporal adverb ('now'), (3) logical conjunction ('so, consequently; yet, however'). To this extent it can be an object of (semantic) interpretation. If one were able, on top of that, to show that in Mallarmé's work *or* is a central sign, perhaps a cypher for poetry itself, then one would be close to giving *or* the status of 'the central meaning, the general theme' of that work. This cannot be done, however; for *or* is generally enclosed in other expressions – dehORs, trésOR, hORizon etc. – or transposed, as in zérOs, where it serves, so to speak, as the signature of the nought (o) which was talked about in the text entitled *Or*. OR is not (only) a sign but appears as a grapheme or a sound structure, according to what register Mallarmé's 'orchestration' chooses on a particular occasion. At all events one cannot simply 'read' this signifier, that is, construe it by means of the classical philological criteria for classification which draw a distinction between its semantic and its syntactical function (its 'gold' and its conjoining 'now, so, however'), between its content and its sound, its basic and its figurative meaning (metaphor or metonymy). For this reason, Derrida says, one cannot explain its mysterious occurrence in Mallarmé's text by hermeneutic methods, but only analyse its functioning by means of reflection on the orchestration. OR is a frequent epithet in connection with expressions from the semantic field of music: music is often golden or gold. But music is not a matter of semantics, just as, indeed, Mallarmé says of OR that it 'loses all meaning' (*Œuvres complètes*, p. 398). Derrida uses several examples to show how Mallarmé's syntax 'organises not only its polysemy, its polygraphy and its orchestral polyphony, but also, most particularly, its out-of-line ex-centricity and its brilliant suspension' (*La dissémination*, p. 295; Johnson, *Dissemination*, p. 263). Besides having a relationship with music – with the 'sounding silence' (Wagner), with the asemantic – *or* also always relates to the matter, to the actual order of the signs. In the *Triolets* there is a *Signor* ('Il Signor'), 'qui s'ign*or*e', and this expression is made to rhyme with 'signe, *or*' (Mallarmé, *Œuvres complètes*, p. 186). The 'sign of gold' fuses diverging complexes of meaning as it were in a musical way – not via a semantic analogy – through a similarity of sound in the signifiers, which brings to light the secret identity of the signifieds. Mallarmé also uses homophony in order, in *Igitur*, to connect *hora/heure* and *or* (*ibid.*, p. 751): *orfèvrerie* and *horlogerie* are fused in this way. A fusion also takes place between *lingot* (an ingot) and *lingua* (language) – and it is brought about by means of the expression 'l'antre do*ré* d'une glotte', where *glotte*, Latin *glossa*, means glottis, but in an early etymological stratum of French can also mean *lingot d'or* (ingot). *Littré* (*Dictionnaire de la langue française*) notes that an old etymology derived *lingot* directly from *lingua*. In addition, Mallarmé also fuses the meaning of *or* as a conjunction with that of *or* as a noun when in the first paragraph of *Igitur* (*Le Minuit*) he groups together the words *heure, or, orfèvrerie*, and then reads this grouping of words as 'le hasard infini des conjonctions'; *conjonctions* here can of course mean both the grammatical and the spatial conjunction, and it is further compared to *conjoncture* in the economic/astrological sense ('pareille conjoncture'). 'The hour [*l'heure*] has not disappeared through a mirror, nor has it buried itself in drapes, evoking furniture through its vacant sonority ['par sa vacante sonorité']. I remember that its gold ['son *or*'] was about to feign in absence some null ['nul/o'] jewel of reverie, something rich and useless that had survived, unless it was that upon the watery and starry complexity ['sur la complexité marine et stellaire'] of a work of gold the infinite accident of conjunctions ['des conjonctions'] could be read ['se lisait'].

'This revealer of the Midnight has never before ['jamais alo*rs*'] indicated such a conjuncture [*conjoncture*], for this is the one unique hour [*heure*] . . . I was the hour that has to make me pure' (Johnson, *Dissemination*, p. 264).

'Son or' is followed soon afterwards by 'vacante sonorité'. Thus the possessive pronoun *son* is transformed into the noun *son* (sound): the sound *or* ('le *son* or'); and the noun *son* is transformed into the possessive pronoun: his gold, 'son *or*'. And this homophony, the text says, 'could be read' as 'le hasard infini des conjonctions': of the conjunctions, the *or*s and the *conjonctures*.

Perhaps it is clear now why Derrida is entitled to speak of the 'double marking' of this poetically used sign (*or*). 'Le "son or" ', he says, 're-marks the signifier *or* (the phonic signifier: of the conjunction or of the noun, which latter is also the signifier of the substance or of the metallic signifier, etc.), but it also re-marks music. Which is to be expected since music, for Mallarmé, is almost always golden (*d'or*), while *or* is reduced by this play to the vacant sonority – with its chance decor – of a signifier (*signifiant*). Thus: "Sur les crédences, au salon vide; nul ptyx, / Aboli bibelot d'inanité sonore, / (Car le Maître est allé puiser des pleurs au Styx / Avec ce seul objet dont le Néant s'honore). / Mais proche la croisée au nord vacante, un or / Agonise selon peut-être le décor / Des licornes"; or *Mimique* again: ". . . un orchestre ne faisant avec son or, des frôlements de pensée et de soir, qu'en détailler la signification à l'égal d'une ode tue . . ." ' (Derrida, *La dissémination*, p. 296; Johnson, *Dissemination*, p. 264).

In such linguistic constructs *or* becomes the turning-point and point of change of a semantically oriented exegesis. The sign releases its (lexical, contextually determined) meaning, but now it 'folds' itself, bends itself back upon its unlosable capability of – through manipulation of the signifier – meaning anything else but what is prescribed by this one articulation in this one context. Picasso dreamed of making a matchbox which while being wholly

a bat would nevertheless at the same time remain wholly a matchbox (see also Sartre, *Situations II*, p. 66). And Chlebnikov devised
the image of a 'wing-beating grasshopper' (Krylyškúja . . . kuz-
néčik) which, 'filling the basket of its belly with many grasses and
beliefs' at the same time, by means of a series of poetic devices like
paronomasias, metonymies, equivalences of content and genuine
or fictitious etymological derivations reveals itself to be the (Tro-
jan) horse (*konjók*: little (hay) horse), in whose hollow interior (*kúzov*)
intruders plotting conspiracies (*kuznéc, kózni, kovát', kujú, kovárny*: all
signs spherically bound together semantically by the connotation
of 'cunningly devising plans of attack') secretly lurk – more or less
in the same way as the signifier *uškúj* (pirate ship) is anagrammati-
cally enclosed in the other – *krýlyško* (little wing) (see also Roman
Jakobson, 'Unbewusste sprachliche Gestaltung in der Dichtung',
in *Lili*, I, 1–2 (1971), pp. 101–2).

These are effects which one might call topological in order to
distinguish them from the semantic work of the language: modern
poetry is full of them. They are based on manipulation of the
material of expression, whose articulated parts are newly differentiated and/or newly combined: 'This surplus mark, this margin of
meaning, is not one valence among others in the series, even
though it is *inserted* in there, too. It has to be inserted there to the
extent that it does not exist outside the text and has no transcendental privilege; this is why it is always *represented* by a metaphor
and a metonymy (page, plume, pleat). But while belonging in the
series of valences, it always occupies the position of a supplementary valence ["position de valence supplémentaire"], or rather, it
marks the structurally necessary position of a supplementary inscription ["inscription supplémentaire"] that could always be added to or subtracted from the series. We will try to show that this
position of the supplementary mark is in all rigor neither a metaphor nor a metonymy even though it is always represented by one
trope too many or too few' (Derrida, *La dissémination*, p. 283
(Johnson, *Dissemination*, p. 251); see also pp. 288 and 309). One
could describe it as a pure possibility of constituting meaning, with
the reservation that, as is shown by the totally asemantic creations
of the Dadaists, it by no means always necessarily realises this
possibility. It is inaccessible to hermeneutics (if hermeneutic means

unlocking meaning), in the same way as music, which also suggests possibilities of meaning without fixing them in articulated language: for music is 'almost always "d'or" '; it is, as Lévi-Strauss says, 'language minus meaning'.

One may go further and say that the actual aesthetic element in a literary text is 'writing minus language'; and then 'writing' does not merely refer (as it has up to now) to the reason why a text cannot be *completely* interpreted, but the reason why in principle it *cannot* be interpreted, given that what affects us aesthetically in it is the object not of decoding nor of reading but of a perception of taste. In this context Novalis spoke of a 'general art theory and art' the object of which would no longer be a '*specific* object' but '*making the N with the N organ*' (*Schriften*, vol. III, p. 257; see also p. 283). Here we are approaching the margins of the subject of textual interpretation and will do well to admit to ourselves that those engaged in the study of literature are faced with problems beyond the understanding of meaning, problems which in their assiduous orientation towards the contents of literature they all too often fail to acknowledge. (Linked to this is the fact that the texts chosen by literary hermeneutists to illustrate their methods overwhelmingly come from pre-modern or in the broad sense realistic narrative literature, as though modern literature were not first and foremost a protest against the categories of narrative coherence, semantic availability and decipherability.)

Criteria of textual coherence

But the 'aesthetic experience', with its resistance to the assigning of meaning by the interpreter, was not the only aspect to which our opening definition of a text failed to do justice. The characteristic of cohesion (*cohaesio, cohaerentia*), which, alongside written form and the poetic element, is an essential part of the meaning of 'text', still needs to be addressed. This is more problematical for the student of literature, who also has to think of certain non-coherent and non-meaningful creations of modern literature (and does so far too little in the sentences he uses as examples), than it is, say, for the textual *linguistician*, who never ceases to invoke the *weaving together* of texts. Mephisto would probably urge him to reflect on what he

says to the student who is all too eager to put his trust in scholarship:

> 'The web of thought, I'd have you know,
> Is like a weaver's masterpiece:
> The restless shuttles never cease,
> The yarn invisibly runs to and fro,
> A single treadle governs many a thread,
> And at a stroke a thousand strands are wed.
> . . .
> This method scholars praise, and keenly clutch;
> As weavers, though, they don't amount to much'
>   (Goethe, *Faust* I, lines 1922–35, trans. Philip Wayne
>   (London, 1949))

– at least not in the case of modern examples of texts whose 'levels
of indeterminacy' often act powerfully against the imperative of
the 'good continuation' (see also Ingarden, *Vom Erkennen des literarischen Kunstwerks* (Tübingen, 1968), pp. 264ff.; Iser, *Der Akt des Lesens*,
p. 114f.).

The characteristic of the coherence of the fabric should not be
confused with that of the order or structured nature of a text,
which can also be shown to exist in the creations of surrealism or of
concrete poetry. One of the pioneers of so-called textual linguistics, R. Harweg (*Pronomina und Textkonstitution* (Munich, 1969)) gives
three criteria for the definition of *coherence*: (1) the unidirectional
arrangement of the elements (after one another, not in place of one
another); (2) the principle of a chain of pronouns, or of syntagmatic
substitution; (3) the definability of the boundaries of the text (the
criterion of delimitation, partly identical with (2) – the 'emic
criterion' – partly 'etic' in nature (book titles, headings, pauses,
greeting formulae, etc.))

Unidirectionality means the syntagmatic sequencing of the sentences of which a text is made up. Since textual linguistics, following the lead of linguistic structuralism, which was first applied to
the study of myths and then to that of literature, adopted the
working hypothesis that one could describe the structures of
language larger than the sentence in an analogous way to the
so-called 'small units' within the sentence and thus set up a kind
of textual grammar, it also had to engage in a banal attempt
to apply the characteristic of articulatory linearity (cf. Jäger,

'Linearität und Zeichensynthesis', in *Fugen* (Olten and Freiburg i.Br., 1980), pp. 187–212) to the ordering of the 'large units' too. However, whereas in the realm of linguistics the sequence of the signifiers is fairly strictly determined by the laws of morpho(no)logy, syntax and the irreversibility of the sequence, texts constructed according to poetic criteria may well not conform to analogous laws of chain-like sequences applied to units larger than the sentence. The intended sequence of the units 'in a line' is – for instance in some texts by Mallarmé, Heissenbüttel or Sollers – often quite impossible to reconstruct (there are numerous ways into the lyrical construct) or else wholly irrelevant. To the extent that the experimental texts even evade linguistic articulation they become like orchestral scores, of which Lévi-Strauss says that in them the law of unidimensional arrangement has long been contravened, given that reading them diachronically, page by page and from left to right, misses the synchronic dimension of the musical text which needs in addition to be read 'along the other axis, from top to bottom': otherwise one does not discover its *harmony* (C. Lévi-Strauss, *Mythologica* (Frankfurt am Main, 1971), vol. i, pp. 35ff.). Transferred to the poetic sphere: anyone who only follows the continuous flow of one thing succeeding another in a text will miss the nodal points of the meaning, the recurrence of its themes, the dense patterning of its symbols, the harmony of its sequences of sounds in different places – what A. J. Greimas (*Essais de sémiotique poétique* (Paris, 1971), p. 19) calls its 'isotopias' – but also the shifts of meaning which something already read undergoes as a result of everything that is read later, in short that whole criss-cross pattern of hermeneutic connections that make a unidirectionally reproduced text polyfunctional and allow it to be combined with an infinite number of co-texts.

Similar reservations are called for in relation to the *criterion of the 'concatenation through pronouns'*. This criterion tries to reinforce the cohesion of the text by systematically showing syntactically and semantically correct joins between consecutive sentences or units of utterance. This demonstration is supposed to be effected above all by means of the criterion of the 'identity of reference' between the sentences, that is to say on the basis of 'co-references' identified by grammatical means (or 'anaphora', 'recursions', 'connections',

etc.). A coherent link ('recursion') is present when several successive sentences refer to the same subject or state of affairs in a
recognisable logical development of discourse. Expressions which
effect such 'recursions' are referred to by Harweg as *Pro-Formen*
(pro-forms), by which he means not only pronouns in the narrow
sense but all expressions which refer to the same state of affairs.
This may happen *explicitly* or *implicitly*. In the case of explicit
recursions the identity of reference is directly recognisable; in the
case of implicit references it has to be revealed by means of certain
semantic features which are common to the various expressions.
An explicit recursion is present in the passage from Canetti quoted
by G. Kurz ('Textlinguistik – Texthermeneutik', *Muttersprache* 88
(1978), p. 268): 'The well-read man. B. did not care for things that
required an effort. *He does not like* to work. *He does not like* to study. *He*
is curious, and so *he* sometimes reads a *book*. But *it* must be very
simply written . . .'

Here the co-reference can be discovered in the text itself. It can,
as in the next example, be explicit but also be discovered via the
system of meaning (lexicon): '*He* went over to the desk and
scrutinised the *mail* lying *there*, without taking off his travelling
clothes. *He* was disappointed when there was no *telegram* from his
sister *among it*, although *he* was not expecting one. A mountain of
letters of condolence lay *there*, mixed with *communications* of a
scientific nature' (Musil, quoted by Kurz, *ibid.*, p. 288).

A co-reference would be explicit if, for instance, in two consecutive sentences it equated the *father* and *the old man*, or applied the
guest-house, the *room* and the *windows* to one and the same establish-
ment.

If one follows the logic of this textual-grammatical model to the
extent of accepting the precept that a 'non-text' is a sequence of
sentences in which the sentences are parts of various different texts
(Harweg, *Pronomina und Textkonstitution*, p. 386), then even the
opening of a story as conventional as Kafka's *Jäger Gracchus* cannot
be allowed to count as a text: 'Two boys were sitting on the wall of
a quay playing dice. A man was reading a newspaper on the steps
of a monument in the shade of the hero brandishing his sabre. A
girl at the well was filling her tub with water. A fruit-seller was lying
next to his wares, looking out across the lake. In the depths of a

tavern one could see, through the empty door and window open-
ings, two men drinking wine', etc.

For in these parataxes there are clearly neither explicit nor
implicit 'pro-forms' which on the basis of grammar alone would
vouch for a connection between these sentences. In order to guess
at their unity of meaning it is necessary to make a tentative
interpretation which goes beyond the text, somewhat along these
lines: 'What offered itself to the view of an anonymous observer at
time t on the quayside at Riva' or 'Memories of a holiday on Lake
Garda'; what is needed, in other words, is a readiness to respond
productively, similar to what Novalis hoped to find in a reader
who enjoys 'stories without connection': 'poems like *dreams* . . .
merely euphonious and full of beautiful words – but also lacking
any meaning and connection . . . like a collection of fragments of
the most disparate things' (*Schriften*, vol. III, p. 572). Only such texts
are – according to modern poetic theory – poetic in the true sense,
'for nothing is more contrary to the spirit [of poetry] than . . .
enforced coherence' (*ibid.*, p. 438). 'In a genuine fairy-tale everything must . . . be unconnected' (*ibid.*, p. 280).

Of course this does not apply only to the fairy-tale: even in our
everyday utterances coherence is rarely semantically and syntactically evident. We assume that our interlocutor has either background knowledge or divinatory powers of imagination which will
enable him to establish the context. Novalis recommends the
'production of mutilated fragments' as 'proof that the basis of all
effective opinions and ideas of the everyday world consists of
fragments' (*Schriften*, vol. II, p. 593). Poetry, which reflects life, will
take account of this reality; there is therefore 'in true poems no
unity but the *unity of the soul [Gemüt]*' (Novalis, *Schriften*, vol. III, p.
683). This means that the unity of a text (especially a poetic one) is
a function not of its grammar but of the mental agility of the
reader, whose 'divinatory' creative powers, brought into play as he
interprets, make up for the lack of a unity in the text itself.

Only by taking this approach is it possible to perceive the unity
of linguistic constructs which, like for instance Heissenbüttel's
so-called *Texts*, dispense with all co-references: 'everywhere: always and everywhere: ever and ever: morning noon and night
even in the office: one this this is a: whatsortofa: how at the if on or

in that is to say as what more different from: and that which if
nothing but this and so on: fixing fixed: in a position I one lead in
exactly into the one: chanical chanised crifice: meta far: domicile
micivil civil: a cel me gripping to me grasping to me keel' (*Das
Textbuch* (Neuwied and Berlin, 1970), p. 201).

If one also wanted to take into account the *pragmatic* circumstances under which readings create meaning, by means of a grammar
of the receptive attitudes and reading situations that may be
expected, which is what S. J. Schmidt has in mind in his pragmatically broadened *Texttheorie*, then this again would only be possible
at the cost of some rigorous exclusions: only what can generally be
expected, only what is bound by convention and can be derived
from a 'Taxonomy of Illocutionary Acts' (Searle, in K. Gunderson
(ed.), *Minnesota Studies in the Philosophy of Science* 7 (1975)), only what
can be understood with the same meaning in recurrent situations,
can be codified; the individual, that is to say the innovative
intentions of the subject of the text or of the concretisation slip
through the net of this model.

There could never be a universal schema of operation that had
thought in advance of all possible constellations and situations.
'Logic', writes Kafka, 'is unshakeable, but it cannot withstand a
man who wants to live' (*Die Romane* (Frankfurt am Main, 1965), pp.
444, 470). The fallacy in applying the linguistic grammatical model
– even a pragmatically revised version of it – to texts lies in the fact
that the criteria for coherence are never created by the text itself
but always by interpretative 'divination' by the reader which can
never be reduced to a mechanical system.

'Mes vers ont le sens qu'on leur prête', wrote Valéry. G. Kurz
draws the conclusion: 'Textuality or coherence is thus not a
linguistic but a hermeneutic fact, i.e. a phenomenon that is understood individually . . . There are no generally valid rules from
which it would always be possible to deduce the textuality of a
particular text' ('Textlinguistik – Texthermeneutik', p. 268; see
also 'Hermeneutische Aspekte', p. 276). And this is valid not only
from the perspective of reception theory ('the text develops its
meaning only when it is interpreted') but also in the light of
considerations of the aesthetics of production, to which Schleiermacher refers when, arguing against Wolf, he points out that the

'coherence of the ideas' ('Zusammenhang der Gedanken') has not been recognised when the text has been 'meticulously' reconstructed grammatically and historically but only when 'an author's individual manner of combining [elements], which if it had been different would, in the same historical position and the same form of presentation, have yielded a different result' has been divined (*HuK*, pp. 317ff.). Moreover, as we have seen, *written* texts, because of their situational abstractness, i.e. their virtualisation of the reference, of what is intended by their utterance, of the direct address to a recipient and of the context of communication, cannot be made subject to the maxims for establishing coherence which are applicable to everyday discourse: in every case the creation of coherence becomes an interpretative initiative on the part of the reader. This could never – despite the completedness of the text in its material form – be completed, because there is no law that limits, either in content or in quantity, the wealth of relationships that can be established in all directions between the individual elements of the text (cp. Derrida, *La dissémination*, pp. 229–30).

   Linked with this is the fact that the *criterion for the delimitation of texts* never works with certainty; for every text, given that it is articulated in the continuum of a linguistic universe, contains references to other texts with which it forms part of a chain and to which it makes its own contribution (*intertextuality*). 'Whether in the order of spoken or written discourse', Derrida says, 'no element can act as a sign without referring to another which in its turn is not simply present [i.e. present without reference to anything else]. This chaining together means that every "element" . . . is constituted on the basis of ["à partir de"] the trace of the other elements of the chain or system, which are written into it. This chaining together, this fabric, is the *text*, which is only produced by the transformation of another text. Nothing, whether in the elements or in the system, is ever or anywhere simply present or absent. There are only, and this is a generally valid principle, differences and traces of traces' (*Positions* (Paris, 1972), pp. 37–8).

TEXTUAL ANALYSIS AND TEXTUAL HERMENEUTICS

Three characteristics of the text-as-a-work

Even if the information that textual linguistics gives us about the criteria for the coherence of a text is hardly satisfying, we will not deny that even in the 'poly-functional' or 'disseminal' linguistic formations of the avant-garde there is some sort of order or structure. Even when semantic interpretation fails us we do not cease to apprehend these linguistic formations as expressions of creative and ordering activity: as *works*.

Unfortunately the meaning of this term ('work') is hardly less controversial than that of 'text'. Andreas Sandor suggested that we should speak of a text only when we mean the 'material form of expression' – S. J. Schmidt speaks of the *Textformular* – and of a work when we mean the totality of its individual transpositions into speech, interpretation or performance. According to his idea, the written text would be interpreted in 'work manifestations' of which '*the* work' would constitute the ideal unity (A. Sandor, 'Text und Werk', *DVjs* 53 (1979), pp. 478–511). Iser had already written, 'The work is the being-constituted of the text in the consciousness of the reader' (*Der Akt des Lesens*, p. 39); he too uses 'text', though not consistently, in the sense of 'objective and material, non-concretised structure of expression, *Textformular*'.

Now, leaving aside the fact that the etymologies of both *work* and *text* take us back to the meaning of 'something woven', and also the fact that in modern aesthetics (e.g. that of Adorno) the term 'work' functions as a criterion for the delimitation of pre-modern artistic creations, the meanings prescribed by Iser and Sandor cannot be shown to be part of our normal linguistic usage. It therefore seems sensible to keep to the tried and tested philological definition given by Schleiermacher. In his lectures on hermeneutics he distinguished three characteristics present in the concept of the work (Schleiermacher, *HuK*, e.g. pp. 167–70), for which he also uses the word '*Tat-sache*' (fact, or deed-thing). By it he means, quite literally, a meaningful *thing* which owes its existence to the *deed* of an individual creating meaning. As a '*Tatsache*', the work is 'structured' (it was, incidentally, he who introduced the concept of being structured into the terminology of our subject, a fact already emphasised by J. Wach (*Das Verstehen*, vol. 1, p. 133f.)).

Secondly, 'the work' belongs to a particular 'genre' (of discourse), a conventionalised 'pattern of style (usage)' – Schleiermacher also speaks of a 'type which is established in the language' or of the 'power of an already firmly established form' (*HuK*, pp. 132, 169, 321f.); it is for instance a systematic scholarly work, a letter, an article in a handbook or a lyric poem. The genre should not be overlooked: only by identifying it can one discover where the author is following a convention and where he is going beyond it. Thus in Thomas Mann's *Doktor Faustus* what was long thought to be the individual choice of a particular style by the chronicler Zeitblom was in fact an imitation of a traditional genre of hagiographic legend. Nevertheless, every work – this is the third characteristic – of course contains more or less marked traces of *individual composition*, it has an unmistakable *style* which it shares with no other work and which accordingly evades the rules of codification. Style is that aspect of a work which is irreducibly non-general.

Of these three characteristics of the work – structure, belonging to a genre, and style – we can obviously only make style, the individual use of discourse, fit in with our opening attempt at a definition of the text. For only style – whether spoken or written – is a characteristic of *discourse*, and we have up to this point defined texts as written discourses. To be *structured* and to belong to a *genre*, on the other hand, are characteristics which the concept of the text-as-work shares with Humboldt's concept of *language-as-ergon* (at least if one does not see language only as a formal system of rules but also as an objectivised expression of a societal interpretation of the world).

Basic principles of a structural textual analysis

This conclusion could also have been reached via a consideration of the related meanings of the expressions 'structure' and 'text'. For a work, being structured means two things: the substances of expression of the individual signs must firstly be clearly distinguished from all others of their kind on their own level of constitution; and secondly they must, within a hierarchy of levels of constitution, occupy a very definite position in relation to the semantic whole. This would at the same time be a rather liberal etymological interpretation of the Latin word *structura*. It is well known that the so-called structuralists analysed the system of language on the basis of this model. Already according to Schleiermacher the point of the concept of structure was that the 'linguistic values', as he calls them – that is, the meanings of the signs which are differentiated and interwoven within a system – cannot be seen as subsequent additions to the work of the articulation of the expression. The meaningfulness (of the sign) is rather the work of classification and segmentation (of the expression) itself. Thus it does not precede the sign in such a way that the expression then merely names it. On the contrary, the meaningfulness of the signs only comes into being at all at the point of intersection of the sliding layers of expression (*signifiant*) and meaning (*signifié*), which in one and the same movement are synthesised with one another and thereby defined, differentiated and identified as what they are.

This is – in rough outline – the basic insight of structuralism in linguistics. Before we examine the degree to which it may be carried over to the domain of texts, it is worth noting the semantic closeness of this understanding of the concept of *structure* to the concept of *text*. The commonly used *metaphor of being woven* in itself points to this. In texts, Husserl says (in § 124 of the *Ideen*), the 'layers' of the expressions and of the meanings are 'woven' together. If the layer of the expression were 'founded' in itself one could pull it away to reveal the equally independent layer of meaning-creating acts beneath it. But this is precisely not how it is. For the 'top layer' for its part is set into the 'lower layer', and one cannot separate the inserted element and the series without the whole fabric disintegrating. 'This compels us to correct the geological metaphor of layers by substituting the imagery of text in its literal sense (i.e. relating to the weaver's craft)' (Derrida, *Marges de la philosophie* (Paris, 1972), p. 191). Fabrics are texts (*texta sunt*). They relate the discursive (the meaning) to the non-discursive (the expression); the linguistic layer becomes 'intertwined' with the pre-linguistic layer according to a regulated system of the nature of a text.

From this parallel between *structure* and *text* it is immediately obvious that although texts are written discourses (and thus according to Saussure's distinction between *langue* – system of language – and *parole* – use of language – belong to the level of *parole*), they can be described in a way analogous to the methods of the linguists, since texts are not only actions (Ta*thandlungen*)[2] but also works (Ta*tsachen*). This was, as is well known, the starting-point for the method of *structuralist textual analysis* which grew up out of the philological practice of 'grammatical interpretation' chiefly under the influence of Saussure, the Russian formalists and the structural mythology of Claude Lévi-Strauss, and which in our day has been carried further and differentiated above all by Emile Benveniste, A. Julien Greimas, Roland Barthes and Julia Kristeva. This theory starts out by postulating that the structural methods which in phonology and in lexical semantics were tested out on units of language smaller than those of the sentence (phonemes, morphemes, syntagmas) must be extended to discourse – to chains of so-called 'large units', i.e. sentences and utterances interpreted as having intention (R. Barthes, 'Introduction à l'analyse structurale des récits', p. 3), so in textual linguistics this postulate is only making a re-appearance.

To be composed systematically is, therefore, not a privilege reserved for language; it characterises ensembles of meaning on a higher level and also the discourse of an epoch, of a myth, of an ideology, of a genre, of a single piece of writing, if their 'linguistic elements' too, as distinct complexes of meaning, are systematically linked by the unity of a viewpoint (of what 'the author had in mind'), given separate identities from each other according to the law of definition by opposition (Fichte, *Nachgelassene Schriften*, ed. H. Jacob (Berlin, 1937), vol. II, p. 355) and hierarchically graded on various levels of constitution.

This at any rate is the view of the '*structure* of a piece of writing' (Schleiermacher, *HuK*, pp. 139, 230) which Schleiermacher's 'grammatical interpretation' explained and tested publicly and probably for the first time in the history of hermeneutics. In

---

[2] Frank uses Fichte's term for the nature of the 'I', which literally means 'deed-action' (Editor's note).

relation to the process of the structuring of the text two levels of organisation need to be distinguished: the vertical relationships which the linguistic or textual-linguistic orders form with one another (the phonetic, phonological, morphological, syntactical, contextual, pragmatic, isotopic and other orders – Benveniste speaks of *integrative* relationships); and the horizontal relationships which the elements of a homogeneous order have with one another, i.e. the rules which on a single level of constitution determine their *distribution* (e.g. the arrangement of the words in the clause, of the clauses in the sentence, of the sentences in the text, of the text in the 'total linguistic area' of its epoch and in intertextuality, etc.: here the various steps in the hermeneutic spiral, as presented by Schleiermacher in his lecture to the Academy in 1828, become visible (*HuK*, pp. 329ff.; M. Frank, *Das Individuelle-Allgemeine*, pp. 305ff.)). This twofold organisation within every piece of writing, expounded by Benveniste (*Problèmes de linguistique générale* (Paris, 1966), pp. 122ff.) and applied to texts by Greimas (see also Greimas, *Sémantique structurale* (Paris, 1966); Ricœur, *La métaphore vive* (Paris, 1975), pp. 88ff.) was what Schleiermacher was already thinking of when he distinguished between the type of relationships that *co-ordinate* the units of meaning (*Elemente*) from the type that *subordinates* them in relation to the totality of the meaning of a piece of writing (*HuK*, p. 139).

As was first noted by P. Szondi (*Einführung in die literarische Hermeneutik*, p. 174), what Schleiermacher called *grammatical interpretation* anticipated in essentials the working hypothesis of the structuring of a text which in our day – and certainly with a more advanced apparatus available to the student of language – has been developed and to some extent put into practice above all by A. J. Greimas and R. Barthes (for more detail see M. Frank, *Das Individuelle-Allgemeine*, pp. 262ff.). Its advantage is that while not making the work of understanding the meaning redundant (the working out of the structural semantics or syntax of a text is always the result of interpretative conjectures or projections), it does keep it within the bounds of what can be intersubjectively monitored. After all, this aspect of interpretation is called 'grammatical' precisely because it regards each separate 'linguistic value' as an element of a 'system' (Schleiermacher, *HuK*, p. 139f.) within which it has been allotted its meaning 'by opposition, out of a common whole' (*ibid.*, p. 144). As an element in a synchronic structure each meaning is delimited in a particular way by its immediate surroundings and ultimately by the totality of the text. (Schleiermacher distinguishes between relationships of opposition – 'qualitative oppositions' and 'transitions', i.e. 'quantitative differences' (*ibid.*, pp. 144ff.).) This cannot be changed either by a different explanation of the meaning by the author or by an individual prejudice on the part of the interpreter. Once the structure of a text has been identified, the so-called 'main ideas' in a text (the textual analogues to the 'linguistic values' in a grammar) can no longer simply be regarded as products of an extra-structural invention by the interpreting subject. Schleiermacher is therefore able to state bluntly that – at least in the case of a logically composed piece of writing – the reconstruction of the tissue of signs presents 'no particular difficulty' with regard to the method to be used (*ibid.*, p. 139).

Two examples of classical textual analysis

Before embarking on textual analysis on the basis of these premises, however, it is necessary to consider a number of additional points. First there is the point that the choice of the term 'text' in the programme of textual analysis is merely an act of economy: it saves one from having to indicate more precisely the kind of text of which one is concretely thinking. A grammar of *the* text would doubtless produce only such generalities that it would be of no benefit to the practice of interpretation. At best poetics might profit by it. Thus T. Todorov seeks to discover the universals of poetry, of which the individual poetic work is a manifestation ('Poetik', in F. Wahl (ed.), *Einführung in den Strukturalismus* (Frankfurt am Main, 1973), pp. 108 and 111). All sciences, he says, are directed towards the the general: there could not be a science of bodies, but at most a physics, a chemistry, a geometry. By the same token, there could be no science of Kafka's novel, *The Trial*, but only one of its 'literaricity': in other words poetics (*ibid.*, p. 110).

Roland Barthes does not go so far. In one of his most influential essays, 'Introduction à l'analyse structurale des récits' (pp. 1–27), he attempts to give the laws governing the formation not of literature as a whole but of one genre, of the story. The kind of text is of course also something conventional: it has its rules and its universals, which it must be possible to formulate as such. This prior decision as to method is characteristic of the classical conception of structuralist textual analysis: it proves its usefulness, in the first instance, not in the field of the interpretation of individual works but in what is traditionally called genre poetics.

Barthes begins by making the point that like any semiological system the story too can be seen as a network of distributional and integrative relationships (in the sense indicated above) between elementary units of content. He calls these units of content *functions*, because they are semantically charged not in their existence in and for themselves but only in their relationship with all the others. These elementary functional units can be subdivided, depending on whether they appear among elements of the same level or different levels of text, into distributional functions (*functions* in the narrower sense) or 'functions' of an integrative nature (so-called *indices*). Functions are more likely to be found in the syntagmatic domain (on the horizontal level) and indices on the level of paradigmatic relationships between narrative units. The place of metonymy is on the first, that of metaphor on the second.

This sounds somewhat abstract, but it is easy to give examples. Let us take any story with a recurring symbol, for instance a stain which – let us say – points to some kind of involvement in guilt. According to Barthes' classification this would be a typical *index*, for it does not link narrative units in the horizontal plane but is stuck through the body of the story rather like a skewer: it is a leitmotif that goes 'straight through' and 'integrates' what appear to be quite divergent narrative sequences. For example, someone opens a door, and one would expect this to open a way through into a room. But the character catches sight of a rust-coloured stain on the door, which makes his hair stand on end and freezes the blood in his veins. The unit of opening the door, on the other hand, would be a narrative function, for this function is syntagmatically linked as in a chain with the view into a room which the horrified character who has just seen the stain now enters. This entering, or the sequence of sentences which deals with it, would be the next function. Everything which is arranged in a neighbour-ly way between successive pieces of narrative has the character of a narrative *function*.

Incidentally, Barthes' distinction between functions and indices corresponds very closely to the two fundamental rules upon which Schleiermacher bases grammatical integration. Schleiermacher distinguishes two possible ways of defining the unit of meanings in texts. On the one hand, he says, meanings are determined by the fact that they belong to a particular national language, and within this they are further defined by being differentiated from certain closely related meanings: *horse, nag, jade, chestnut, mare,* etc. would be an example of such a paradigmatic series. On the other hand, however, meanings are also defined horizontally by their 'sur-roundings', or, as we would now say, by their context: thus for instance only the syntagmatic context makes it clear whether *Fuchs* in German refers to a chestnut-coloured horse or to an animal of the dog family, the fox (see also Schleiermacher, *HuK*, pp. 101ff.).

Barthes further subdivides the functions into those whose pres-ence is essential to the development of the plot and the linking of the actions within it – these he calls *fonctions cardinales* or *noyaux* (similar to Schleiermacher's 'main ideas') – and those which act more or less as fillers, as catalysts which help in the bridging of gaps between one part of the plot and another (these he calls *catalytic functions*, corresponding roughly to the 'secondary ideas' of which Schleiermacher speaks). The *cardinal* functions create *internal* (logi-cal) relationships, the *catalytic* functions bring about external, more or less incidental relationships. Let us straight away look at another illustration from the story of Bluebeard. The knight Bluebeard, who is immediately marked as a sinister and extraordinary figure by his blue beard, marries seven women in succession and slaugh-ters them all because they all fail to resist their curiosity to enter the forbidden slaughter-chamber using a key given to them specifically to stimulate this desire. The seventh wife is (in Tieck's version) called Agnes, and when after much deliberation she finally unlocks the door of the chamber, this sequence of action ('unlocking') is obviously cardinal. By contrast, the fact that she presses down the door handle is unimportant or more *complétif* (catalytic).

Barthes makes a further, analogous subdivision of the *indices* too:

there are narrative units as *indices* in the strict sense, and as *pieces of information*. He also calls the indices 'parameters'; they run like a thread through the whole story and give hints towards a correct judgement of a character (for instance the blue-beardedness of the knight Bluebeard and his frivolous game with human curiosity), or indications of certain states of feeling, moods, attitudes. The sombre tone of the whole Bluebeard story would be a typical index, as is the characters' preoccupation with the future, for curiosity is after all only a particular way in which the characters realise their openness towards the future. By *pieces of information*, on the other hand, Barthes means hints which merely help to establish time, place and external circumstances. In Tieck's version of *Bluebeard* there is a certain Simon, Agnes' brother, who constantly broods on time and the future, and this seems to be a narrative index. By contrast, Agnes' remark – made immediately before her dramatic decision – 'How beautifully the sun has risen!' – appears merely to convey information as to the time. Now it is important to note that Barthes – again just like Schleiermacher – emphasises that these functions may at any time interchange with one another: in the course of the story the catalytic may turn out to be essential, and what appears essential to be unimportant. Similarly, an apparently incidental piece of information may prove to be decisive for the further course of the action. Once again, two examples. Earlier, we stated that it is important that Agnes fails to resist her curiosity and enters the forbidden chamber. That she uses a key to do so seems merely to form a bridge in the action and thus to be catalytic. Now the opposite proves to be the case, for from this moment onwards the key has a bloodstain which cannot be cleaned off, i.e. its function is enhanced to that of a cardinal characteristic and even to that of an index, in that the stain becomes (as the key itself already was) a sexual symbol, whose 'disseminal' occurrence at several points in the story fulfils a meaning-integrating function (that of a leitmotif). And the other example: Agnes' remark on the day on which she herself is to be slaughtered, 'How beautifully the sun has risen!', which seemed merely to give information about the time, proves to be indicative, for the reader of the text knows that the sunrise points to and heralds Agnes' imminent rescue, since her brother Simon's perpetual brooding on the future has finally communicated itself to the other brother, Anton, so that he too begins to be anxious about his sister and undertakes a nocturnal ride to Bluebeard's castle; the brothers arrive just at 'sunrise', and the reader now guesses or knows that when Agnes says that the sun has risen her brothers will appear before long.

The further course of this analysis of the narrative can be more briefly summarised; it already shows signs of a tendency to dogmatism in the method of textual structuring.

Barthes had designated the smallest elements in the story as functions. The next higher level of integration would be that at which they are linked together. In analogy with linguistics, Barthes speaks of a *syntax of narrative functions*. But he imitates the methods of linguistics to the extent of taking this talk of a syntax really seriously, i.e. he looks for an 'a-temporal matrix' of the rules of syntagmatic linking. It is important to realise what this means: what is to be examined, we are explicitly told, is not the actual sequence of individual sentences but only the syntax of their links with one another. This was already observable in Lévi-Strauss's analysis of the Oedipus myth (in a famous text from his *Structural Anthropology*): Lévi-Strauss sets out four columns, each for a different theme, and examines how the individual items of content in the columns relate to each other (*Anthropologie structurale* (Paris, 1958 and 1974), p. 236). And these relationships are dealt with purely logically: a is to b as c is to d. It makes no difference how, in the actual Oedipus story, the sentences follow one another, motivate each other stylistically and develop out of one another. By this methodical decision the transitoriness of the course of the narrative is as it were turned to stone. It is inappropriate to speak of *sequences* any more at all, for all sequences are incorporated into a stemmatic scheme, a structural tree-diagram of the kind found in the dependence grammar of, say, Tesnières.

Schleiermacher, incidentally, considers that such an approach is possible only in the case of 'systematic scientific' studies ('Here', he says, 'an idea is the direct form of the whole, and every individual element is an integrating part of it' (*HuK*, p. 138)). When, however, a lyrical, dramatic or narrative poem is to be interpreted, then it is necessary from time to time to examine how the cardinal characteristics are influenced by genre-specific 'means of portrayal' and by apparently secondary ideas – precisely the kind of effects that are excluded from study by an approach which focuses only on the syntactical aspect. Schleiermacher suggests that it follows from this that 'here hermeneutic interpretation crosses over to the psychological side' (*ibid.*, p. 142).

The danger is not that structural analysis might be forcibly taken over by the logic of incorporating elements of a work into structural tree-diagrams ('it should be noted that this is a hierarchy which remains within the level of functions' – Schleiermacher too treated the syntactical units, as far as possible, as functional schemata in changing contexts and on different levels of integration). What does give cause for concern is that for the sake of this method all consideration of the concrete links in the narrative, the style of the story-telling, etc., is suppressed. Barthes does indeed subscribe to the dream of 'écriture without style' (*S/Z* (Paris, 1970), p. 11).

This is a methodological decision which at the higher levels of integration leads to even more forced consequences. Style points to a subject who handles language in an individual way. Barthes, of course, has no use for this kind of thing. Still less is one permitted to speak of 'actions', unless it is clearly stated that *actions* are to be understood as meaning autonomous narrative sequences, with no reference whatever to acting subjects. Any one of these subjects can be treated as a grammatical subject; and this is what is done. Just as the linguists speak of two-place or three-place verbs, without having to go back to an individual using the verb, so Roland Barthes says that generally speaking every sequence implies two *actants*. For example, to one partner the unit of action 'to cheat someone' is deliberate deception, to the other it is a 'rip-off' (*fraude/duperie*). An exhaustive grammatical inventory of actions would need to list all conceivable configurations and interactions between *actants* and make them subject to a series of rules. (Todorov names two: *derivations*, when it is a matter of clarifying relationships other than the established ones, and *actions*, when it is a matter of describing variations on these which change according to the context.)

Such operations require decision-making procedures which can only be accomplished by anticipating the very highest level of the story, namely the semantic-syntactical undertaking as a whole, which is 'narration'. Just as the actants were so to speak derived from the syntax of the sequences of action (as the grammatical subjects between which these sequences mediate), so it is with the interaction of the author and the reader (the pair who are the sender and the recipient of the literary message). When for instance the author says, 'I ask you, dear reader, to take especial note of this', the apostrophe itself is only a sign in the semiotic system of the narrative: it is in no way a reference to empirical persons. Barthes makes some noteworthy suggestions as to how one can identify the narrative stance of the author within the text itself. Ultimately, of course, the effect of all this is to purge the narrative of pragmatic viewpoints. Every sentence which refers to a situation, an intention or a subject can be reformulated – this is Barthes' basic idea – in such a way that it becomes a descriptive utterance: in this way the text is hermeneutically neutralised; and the same is true of the way in which, in a final curve of the spiral, Barthes tries to include also the historical and socio-economic dimension of the text, which in its turn is reduced to a reference from one system of signs to another of different extension (*intertextualité*).

Reading Barthes' 'Introduction à l'analyse structurale des récits', one has the impression that after a brief and fruitful contact with the text itself, the textual analysis takes off so steeply into the realm of fundamental principles that the gain in scientific rigour is bought at the cost of an enormous loss in the understanding of meaning. And indeed French literary studies soon either abandoned the path of almost slavish adherence to the taxonomic model of the text – analogous to the taxonomic model of linguistic structure – or considerably relaxed that adherence. The experience of May 1968 probably marks the break between the structuralist and the so-called post-structuralist approaches to textual analysis (R. Brütting, *'Texte' und 'Ecriture'*). In revolutionary times people are more interested in changing orders than in establishing or defending them. The structural textual analysis of the early 1960s could only ensure that it remained scientific by either revealing the literaricity of the texts themselves in the light of its rules or trying to do this at least in relation to a single type of text (e.g. the story). Since then there has been more interest in the structure and the construction of *individual elements*; and here again Roland Barthes was one of the first of those who at once aligned themselves with the new tendency.

The signpost in his intellectual biography and a milestone in the development of structural textual analysis is his major interpretation of Balzac, which bears the title *S/Z*. Barthes devoted a two-year seminar (1968 and 1969) at the Ecole Pratique des Hautes Etudes to Balzac's story *Sarrasine* (1830), and then published the results (*S/Z* [Paris, 1970)).

What makes *S/Z* attractive as a methodology of textual interpretation is the same thing that separates this attempt from an orthodox structuralist tradition. (Derrida has mockingly referred to that tradition as 'ultra-structuralism' (*L'écriture et la différence* (Paris, 1967), p. 29).) For in this book Barthes breaks not only with genre poetics but with the prejudices of taxonomism in general, according to which the elemental units of meaning in a text can be derived solely from a self-contained and 'atemporal' narrative code.

This is of course also a rejection of the scientist methodologism according to which the analysis of a text has to be conducted by means of supra-subjective 'discovery procedures' and may not tolerate insoluble ambiguities. The notion that the text is a fabric of units of meaning which is forced into a particular order by a 'transcendental' cardinal meaning is rejected in *S/Z* as 'metaphysical'. The 'transcendental meaning', if there were one, would organise all other signs according to its plan, rather as a magnet arranges the iron filings over a sheet of paper or as a genome distributes certain genetic information in the code of a living organism – or, as the adjective 'transcendental' reminds us, as in Kantian philosophy the pure self-consciousness imposes its order upon the mass of the material. This view has in the meantime become unacceptable to Barthes, because it fails to fulfil the demand, made in the Bataille quotation which serves the book as a motto, that the text be recognised as a construct of multiple meaning. *S/Z* attempts to fulfil this demand by regarding the text as the intersection of codes which cross over and communicate with one another in a multiplicity of ways. Their essentially open action is not supposed to be determined by any rule that is not part of the game. Each individual seme – that is to say, each smallest unit of meaning – can and should become the germ of an endless plurality of meaning-effects, each one of which as it were produces its own set of connotatively created side-branches. .

To clarify this: it is immediately obvious that this is a wholly uneconomic way of proceeding. If it is axiomatic that a scientific procedure should reduce the diversity of the phenomena of nature to the smallest possible number of fundamental laws, and if litera-ture *as a scientific discipline* is supposed to reduce the diversity and quantity of possible meanings to the smallest possible number of structures carrying meaning, then it must be said that post-struc-turalist textual analysis attempts as it were to multiply the meaning of the text. It lets it 'explode', it supports the ambiguity of the text by revealing it (the ambiguity) as such. Of course this does not mean that it pours additional obscurity into the text; but it means that it uncovers the textual (poetic, rhetorical 'technical') pro-cedures which are at work in its obscurities and which one would suppress if by the interpretation one were to reduce the story as one reduces a sum to its bottom line. For what makes poetic works different from puzzles, charades or sums is that the interpretation does not replace and as it were resolve the poetry, as is the case with the rule of three.

Instead of making the elemental semic units subject to a specific centre of meaning which is to be presented as the outcome, S/Z aims to disperse them 'in the form of a star' (S/Z, p. 20); instead of making them less scattered it aims to make them many times more so. What does this mean in practice? Barthes demands that Bal-zac's text be dissected into all its units of action. He also calls these units of action units of reading ('lexias'). This injunction is to be taken quite literally. One is meant as it were to take a pencil and to write numbers in brackets consecutively in the printed text at the beginning of each individual block of action and of meaning; a lexia corresponds very closely to what Barthes earlier called a function. In the story, which is a good thirty pages long, Barthes finds 561 lexias. And the form that his book adopts is to list the lexias by number, quoting each one in full and then commenting on it.

This commentary is in no way arbitrary; there is no licence for a subjective stream of all the possible associations which might happen to come into the reader's mind. 'The interpretation is not open to *every* meaning . . . it is significant and can be missed'; thus there is 'an authentic interpretation' (Lacan, *Les quatre concepts fondamentaux de la psychoanalyse* (Paris, 1973), p. 225f.; *Écrits* (Paris, 1966), p. 353). The control to which Barthes subjects himself is that he looks at each lexia according to a series of 'codes'. Is this not a contradiction of the rejection of the linguistic system model? Not necessarily: Barthes still operates with the structuralist category of codes, of the system and of the 'systematic marking' (*S/Z*, p. 17), but he multiplies the codes and no longer works with just one. Each code is a systematic perspective under which every narrative sequence can be explored. 'Under the hermeneutic code, we list the various (formal) terms by which an enigma can be distinguished, suggested, formulated, held in suspense, and finally disclosed' (p. 26; English translation by Richard Miller (New York, 1974), p. 19). The allocation of a lexia to this perspective is briefly indicated in the commentary by an abbreviation such as HER (hermeneutic code) at the end of a particular lexia; this appears for instance after the title, because it raises a question and suggests an enigma and its solution: who or what is Sarrasine?

Barthes calls the second code the 'semic (or semantic)' one, the code which controls the order of the meanings: what is said and what semantic framework it fits into. It is characteristic that Barthes, as in his 'Introduction', forbids the attribution of semes to particular persons or subjects: they are to be noted only thematically, in the infinitive form. 'We allow them', he says, 'the instability, the dispersion, characteristic of motes of dust, flickers of meaning' (*S/Z*, p. 26; Miller, English translation, p. 19). (However, this restriction does not prevent Barthes from occasionally referring to this code as the 'personal code'.) This is still more true of the elements of the third, so-called 'symbolic code'. It comes into play for the first time in the second lexia, 'I was sunk in one of those deep reveries', etc., which opens up a symbolic field that points forward to all kinds of mysterious occurrences like male–femaleness, castration, coldness–warmth, stone and flesh, etc.

Fourthly there is the 'prohairetic code': *prohairesis* means the resolve, the decision by means of which I put a state of indecision behind me by deciding between two or more possibilities (and thus also the priority which I give to a thing or an action). In Barthes the term quite simply means the 'action code' or the plot structure of the story – for instance the pieces of information which I gather together under a name, the behaviours which I observe in the characters and which cause me to fear, anticipate, overlook or respond with horror to certain things, and so on.

Finally (fifthly) there is the 'cultural or reference code' (abbreviation: REF), which concerns the 'quotations from the treasury of knowledge and wisdom', e.g. when mention is made of a painting of Adonis by a particular painter or of Pygmalion or the circles of cardinals in Rome – whenever, in short, the text itself makes it apparent that it is an 'intertext', that it is intertwined with societal and cultural 'co-texts' to which it alludes and by which it constantly allows itself to be invaded, e.g. by the code of the Parisian bourgeoisie with its hunger for money, its restrained aggressiveness and vitality, its taboos, etc. If – to conclude by paying him due tribute – Barthes' revision of classical structuralism may be welcomed as the forging of a link with a hermeneutics of the understanding of meaning, one still cannot overlook the fact that Barthes does not in the last resort break with the code model of understanding. True, he corrects its most glaring defects; but even a multiply codified message continues to be decipherable by a system. The 'plural text' is 'multiple', but it is not open to interpretation. This ties in with Barthes' dismissal of reading as a process of uncontrollable discovery and assigning of meaning: the role of the hermeneutic subject is taken over by the text itself. 'In operational terms, the meanings I find are established not by "me" or by others, but by their *systematic* mark: there is no other *proof* of a reading . . . than its functioning' (*S/Z*, p. 17; Miller, English translation, p. 11). The heuristics of this finding remains as unexamined as in the concept of an objective interpretation in the manner of E. D. Hirsch. There too the claim to objectivity was confined to the examination of already completed interpretations; *how* an interpretation is motivated, how it is carried out, and whether there are rules by which it orientates itself are matters left, in both cases, in obscurity as questions on which the exponents of this science choose to remain silent (cf. R. Palmer, *Hermeneutics* (Evanston, 1969), pp. 62–3).

The limitations of the code model of textual analysis and the task of understanding style

The problem of textual analysis seemed to have been solved by the structuralism of the 1960s. But does it really provide an answer to what we understand by the concretisation of a work of literature? Had we not urged the interpreter of literary texts to investigate the flow of the meaning in the story and thus to go beyond what the structuralists, following the practice of information theory, call 'decoding'? Those and only those systems of signs can be decoded which permanently assign *one* quite specific interpretation to each expression. One has mastered the particular system when one can in accordance with its rules make the step from its expressions to their meanings, i.e. recognise them *as* signs. Now, the example of writing tells us that in the course of the story (of the communication between text and reader) the assigning of particular expressions to their meanings (can) escape from a binding prescription and so call upon the reader to contribute to the creation of meaning. This is, as Schleiermacher assures us, the point where hermeneutic interpretation changes, the point where the 'hermeneutic operation reaches across to the psychological side' (*HuK*, p. 142). Thus one can – and the grammatical or the structural interpretation essentially does – treat the text 'on the one hand' as a world-less, situationally abstract and author-less formation (see Ricœur, 'Qu'est-ce qu'un texte', p. 188f.; Starobinski, *L'œil vivant II*, pp. 21ff.; Lotmann, *Die Struktur des künstlerischen Textes* (Frankfurt am Main, 1973), p. 115). Then one explains the internal relationships within the text, i.e. its structure. One goes over to the 'other side' of interpretation as soon as one restores the link, broken by the written form, between the text and living communication; then one is no longer analysing it, one is *interpreting* it: textual analysis becomes textual hermeneutics. Now, our experience of dealing with literature has taught us that two different readings do not leave the original meanings unscathed. The meaning slides about beneath the expression ('un glissement incessant du signifié sous le signifiant s'impose donc' (Lacan, *Ecrits*, p. 502)) and, as Humboldt says, finds even and especially 'in writing, no permanent resting-place' (*Gesammelte Schriften*, ed. A. Leitzmann (Darmstadt, 1968), vol. v, p. 388; see also vol. vii, pp. 63, 45).

In order to take due account of this experience it is necessary to depart from the code model of structuralist textual analysis. As soon as structuralism makes the leap from its tried and tested method of textual analysis to a global thesis about the nature of texts, it fails to recognise the richness of the concept of the work, to which after all, besides the decodable elements of structure and of genre, *style* also belongs. Style is a characteristic not of language but of discourse. It not only brings about, in each instance, an individual choice and arrangement of the available lexical material; it also shifts the hitherto valid boundaries of linguistic normality. This is why it has to be defined as the non-conventional element in the text that cannot be shown to derive from anything else; and it will be difficult, if not impossible, to subject it to scientific analysis of the grammatico-structural type which dreams of a 'writing without style' (Barthes, *S/Z*, p. 11). What Schleiermacher calls the 'other side' of textual interpretation calls for productivity on the part of the subject; this is why he also calls it 'psychological' or 'technical' (i.e. artistic, inventive) interpretation. Its *'whole aim'*, he says, *'may be defined as a complete understanding of style'* (Schleiermacher, *HuK*, pp. 168ff.), where 'style' is to be understood as meaning 'an author's individual way of combining' words, not as the combining of the words according to a syntactical rule or a *genus dicendi* (*ibid.*, p. 171, section 5): two perspectives which Leo Spitzer (*Stilstudien*, 2 vols. (Munich, 1928; 2nd edn, Darmstadt, 1961)) had distinguished under the headings of *Sprachstil* and *Stilsprache* (see also Starobinski, *L'œil vivant II*, p. 36f.). The sentence or the discourse or way of speaking or expression as examples of the application of universal regularities are 'objects of grammatical interpretation' and relate only to 'the language as a general concept', namely as the apparatus for the production of all 'necessary forms for subject, predicate or syntax' (Schleiermacher, *HuK*, p. 171). These, however, Schleiermacher continues, 'are not positive means of explaining' the individual choice and linking together of words, 'but only negative ones, because what is

contrary to them . . . [cannot] be understood at all' (*ibid.*, p. 171f.).
Thus syntax, semantics and (in so far as it is itself bound by rules)
pragmatics do constitute the necessary preconditions for the use
of language; but this is not to recognise any of these instances as
the cause which brings about the individual combination through
which the 'energeia' of the subject of the text manifests itself in its
'individual quality' which could never be produced under the
compulsion of rules and which can therefore also never be wholly
schematised (*ibid.*, p. 173). 'We see that the person of an author
combines, in relation to the "average" language of a given state of
culture, with a system of (syntactical, lexicological, etc.) deviations
and differences – a deviation that finds its ultimate expression in
the *excess which dispenses with all rules* in certain extreme works'
(Starobinski, *L'œil vivant II*, pp. 24–5). The individual quality of a
style cannot therefore 'be constructed a priori'. Indeed, 'one cannot sum up an individuality grammatically in a term . . . There
can be no concept of a style' (Schleiermacher, *HuK*, p. 172). All
models which – like the structuralist ones of, say, M. Riffaterre
(*Strukturale Stilistik* (Munich, 1973)) – would like to subject style as a
rule-led or multiply codified process to a generative apparatus are
doomed to failure. And this is not because style introduces an
extra-verbal quality, or is contrary to any existing rule (Schleiermacher actually says that rules 'are a precondition' for it), but
simply because it is only the style that inserts the signs of the
relevant text-system into the particular meaning in the light of
which they reveal their chromatics. Retrospectively – above all
when (for instance by way of critical interpretation) the culture
wins back the stylistic excess for ordinary language (Starobinski,
L'œil vivant II, p. 25) – one can perhaps also characterise in general
terms the technique of *this* style and then *know*; until then, it is
necessary to 'divine' it.

Ultimately only the general is known or recognised; and the
style of a text could be the object of knowledge only to the extent
that it is not a single thing but reproduces – say – the discourse of
its epoch, of its class, its stratum, its profession, etc. (a so-called
stratum of style: simple style, developed style, elevated style, poetic
style, etc.) or merely that of a particular type of *use* of language
which has become established among a number of participants in

the language (a so-called stylistic *type*: situational style, functional style, the style of certain sorts of text, etc.) (cp. W. Sanders, *Linguistische Stiltheorie*, (Göttingen, 1973), pp. 93ff.). In all of these examples style is not something individual but something shared in common by a number of speakers. And only by removing the individual facts can a scientific description be confident of its generalisability. That is provided for by the rule which has made it possible for the multiple and changeable elements of the (textual) material to be gathered together as *one* characteristic and so to be expressed by a concept. This condition might be called *the criterion of being repeatable in the same form and with the same meaning*. This criterion dominates the field of all the disciplines orientated towards the concept of the sign (the so-called 'semiological' disciplines), including the methods of structural textual analysis.

By contrast, what is individual, e.g. style, is, in the literal meaning of that word, indivisible and thus immediate (the Anglo-Saxons say 'unshareable', combining both meanings). Not in the sense of the classical model of the atom, meaning the non-fissionability of an infinitesimally small substance, which has relationships 'only' with itself (since Leibniz's infinitesimal calculus science has in principle had no problem with such quantities); but in the sense of that which exists without an inner double and without relationships, which has therefore literally nothing the same as it and which *thus fails to fulfil the criterion of being repeatable with the same meaning*. To write down an individual utterance and to re-produce (that is, re-create) it in the act of reading then means not (and this is the decisive point) *to articulate the same linguistic chain again and with the same meaning* but *to undertake a different articulation of the same linguistic chain*. For, says August Boeckh (one of the great, forgotten methodologists of our subject from the first half of the last century), 'one can never produce the same thing again' (*Enzyklopädie und Methodologie der philologischen Wissenschaften*, ed. E. Bratuschek (Darmstadt, 1966), p. 126). The same view is put forward by R. Musil when he calls 'that which is individual something absolutely unique [*einmalig*, literally "occurring only once"]', something which 'cannot be fixed . . . [something] anarchic', which 'permits of no repetition'. If one talks about it, one does so 'in the knowledge that no word can be said twice without changing its meaning' (Musil,

Gesammelte Werke in 9 Bänden, ed. A. Frisé (Reinbek, 1978), vol. VIII, pp. 1404 and 1151; vol. IV, p. 1212).

Humboldt had shown the reason for this: in every linguistic communication situation – even in the special case of communicating with oneself and communicating via texts – two ways of thinking about something collide, and only the conventional part of each matches the other, while '*the more individual* [part] *juts out*' (*Gesammelte Schriften,* vol. V, p. 418). That the two coincide completely 'at one indivisible point' is not possible, for every communication conveyed by signs or by text delivers a historically unstable union of the general with an individual *view* of the general, which could not also be general. The attempt at communication could attain objectivity only on condition that one could control its meaning from an Archimedean point outside language; but we are involved in what happens in language, and this also applies when we are interpreting texts. 'Every day and every speaker', says Sartre, 'changes the meanings *for everyone*, indeed the others turn them around in my mouth' (*Crd,* p. 180). This is why every articulation is not only re-productive (i.e. repeating – bringing back again – a rigid convention), but inventive in a way that cannot be systematically controlled. The individual style always challenges the synthesis of signs which orders writing and meaning, it always shifts the boundaries of normality that have hitherto been valid. This is why a decision as to the 'true meaning' of a written utterance has in principle only the character of a supposition.

Every interpretation therefore remains *in the last resort* hypothetical. Sartre speaks of a 'hypothesis of understanding' ('une hypothèse compréhensive, notre compréhension conjecturale') which has to be set up so that what has not been made clear by the convention of discourse and of words, in other words the radically 'new' element in an utterance, can nevertheless be understood. Of course 'the truth of this restoration cannot be proved, its probability cannot be measured' (Sartre, *L'idiot de la famille,* vol. I, p. 56). But here there is no choice: either the interpreter tries also to give some account of the imponderables of the individual style – and then his hypothesis may well be mistaken – or he refrains from doing so and confines himself to reconstructing the purely literal meaning (a task which, sufficiently strictly regarded, is indistinguishable from the first alternative, since determining the literal meaning of the words must always happen communicatively, which requires the formation of hypotheses and a reciprocity of recognition (Sartre, *L'idiot de la famille*, vol. 1, pp. 159ff.)). It is this irreducibly hypothetical character of understanding which distinguishes textual interpretation from the methodical and deductive procedures of scientism. The reason why one cannot simply derive the meaning of an utterance in the form of a text from the grammar and the dictionary is because whatever has meaning is not caused but is motivated. Those actions are *motivated* which can be both triggered and understood only through the mediation of a (Peircian) interpretant. The suggestion of a cause (of the motive or impetus) which is supposed to 'explain' the action retrospectively and show what preconditions gave rise to it only repeats on a reflective level the interpretation which the action itself – prior to any reflection – had given of its own situation in anticipation of a particular future for that situation (M. Frank, *Das Individuelle-Allgemeine*, pp. 322ff.; *Das Sagbare und das Unsagbare*, pp. 239ff). The grammar which a speaker or an author internalises in order to be a competent participant in the contemporary conventions of linguistic actions never acts with the certainty of a machine which repays the input of particular expressions with the output of meanings firmly assigned to them. For every meaning in a language has first to prove itself in the situation and for the situation to which the author – *acting* linguistically – applies it. To this extent the language *motivates* him (he cannot simply say what he wants to), but it does not condition his linguistic usage (he can always say more than, and something different from, what is provided for by the rules codified up to this time in the grammar and the dictionary). This ties in with the fact that language attains its ultimate meaningfulness only in the act of utterance and that in this externalisation it distances itself necessarily and in an uncontrollable way from the syntheses of expression and meaning which average linguistic usage up to this time had preserved as the norm in discourse. In order not to miss this (possible) innovation in meaning, the interpreter must go beyond the deductive system of a linguistic-pragmatic code by forming suppositions and hypotheses; and precisely this overstepping of such limits leads, if it is successful, to *understanding*. The understand-

ing of a text is, as Schleiermacher already emphasised, inexhaustible (for the process of communication constantly absorbs new
meaning, i.e. it also shifts the concretisation projects undertaken
up to that point by the community of recipients (*HuK*, pp. 8of., 94,
196)). 'A thousand possibilities will always remain open even if one
understands something in this phrase that makes sense' (Derrida,
'Limited Inc. abc', *Glyph* 2 (1977), p. 201; French version, *Glyph* 2
(Supplement, Baltimore, 1977), p. 35). And 'so long as even one
such possibility has not been wholly rejected one surely cannot
speak of a necessary insight' (Schleiermacher, *HuK*, p. 317). Derrida mocks the scientistic option chosen by the supporters of
'objective interpretation', using the metaphor of the 'wolves of the
type "indecidability"' which break into the sheepfold of codifieds
and prevent the shepherd of generative textual grammar from
counting his sheep and determining where the borders lie between
text and concretisation ('Limited Inc.', p. 216).

For a theory of textual interpretation, what is significant about
Derrida's criticism of hermeneutic objectivism and of the model of
generative grammar is that he does not carry his argument *against*
the minimal consensus on the nature of a communication system
but on the contrary derives the argument from it. In this respect he
also corrects the scientistic option of classical structuralism itself.
This minimal consensus is based on the insight that semiotic
systems intersubjectively lend meaning to their elements by articu-
lating the available graphic or phonic material of expression in the
same way, i.e. they make very definite cuts into the hitherto
unarticulated and meaningless matter of signifiers, always in the
same places, and through these the individual blocks are split apart
from each other and precisely as a result of this are endowed with
profile, outline, individuality, in short with 'differential characteristics'. Only after the work of distinguishing and forming intervals
between the 'full and positive terms' has been completed can the
'distinctness' of the signs (as syntheses of intelligible meanings and
material bearers of signs) be achieved (Saussure, *Cours de linguistique
générale*, ed. T. de Mauro (Paris, 1972), pp. 155ff.). For the differences between the terms of an already constituted language Saussure
used the term 'oppositions' (*ibid.*, pp. 166–8). The concept of the
constituted language (and, analogously, of the completed written

text) implies a state of completeness and unchangeability in the system. It is, after all, no mere accident that the model that forms the basis for structural linguistic and textual theory is the crystal lattice, in which, if the temperature is low enough, all the molecules are fixed motionless in their places, both distinct from all the others and linked to them. Now, unlike the world of the elements, the historical-cultural world cannot be cooled down to absolute zero; language thrives only with a certain warmth which permits a flow – the exchanging and rearrangement of the signs. Texts, says Derrida, are always transformations of other and earlier texts, just as signs are always re-articulations of other signs used previously. For the idea of differentiality also means that no sign is directly and atemporally present to itself, as is assumed in the 'opposition' model. After all, the idea of differentiality says that if a sign only acquires its particular meaning – what Hirsch calls its 'determinacy of meaning' – in that way, then obviously it does not refer primarily to *itself*. It has no original identity, and acquires identity only by making a detour via all other signs (*différer* in French means to defer as well as to differ from) before returning upon itself. It may thus be said that it is separated from *itself* by nothing less than the universe of all other signs – and, if one is arguing at the level of the text, by the universe of all other texts. If one accepts this and is also clear about the fact that this path leads through infinity, then one has broken with the scientistic notion that there is an original and timeless presentness or familiarity of at least *one* meaning at and with itself; so much so that on all paths that I tread by means of signs I am always certain of finding my way back to it. Such a meaning extracted from the play of structure would be the *principle* of structure – Derrida calls it the 'transcendental signified'. But the unity of this Archimedean point is always already lost; none of the many paths which I take through the web of connections in the text in order to discover its wealth of oppositions/meanings and its total meaning reliably leads back to the starting-point. For this value is a function of the infinitely open series of all its opposita. The paradigm of re-flection (of the speculative return to the starting-point) cannot withstand the experience of the no longer limited economy of semantic oppositions (cp. Derrida, *La dissémination*, pp. 422ff.; 'Limited Inc.', p. 183ff.).

This does not mean that as a result anarchy must break out in the system of signs (and in textual interpretation). For Saussure's recognition that the 'differentiation of a specific *value* for a term *x*' takes place 'through the formation of associative series of "oppositions"' can be strictly formulated as a universal law. This states that the value of a term *x* is dependent on its being in a relationship of fundamental negation to any number of terms *a*, *b*, *c*, etc., 'with the "non" . . . being understood in the sense of "different from"' (C. Stetter, 'Peirce und Saussure', *Kodikas/Code* 2 (1979), p. 135). However, this rule leaves it wholly open which oppositions and how many of them I write into the associative series, 'because there are neither logical nor empirical grounds to assume the opposite, but on the contrary one can prove the possibility of producing infinite quantities of expressions' (*ibid.*). It follows from this that the addition of a new differentiation (which shifts the meaning of the oppositions constituted so far) – and this kind of thing occurs in every moderately profound textual interpretation, as well as in every productive conversation – that the addition, then, of a new oppositive term to the series of the others is not calculable (in advance) (*ibid.*, p. 136), and so the meaning of an expression cannot be decided from outside the conversation in which it crops up.

As soon as one introduces the idea of processuality – and thus the idea of time – into the system of the text, its edges become blurred – much to the discomfort of the scholar, who can now no longer assume that the semantic economy is complete and closed, and therefore can no longer guarantee the recursivity of the linguistic types and that they are used each time with identical meaning.

In order not merely to state in the abstract that the meaning is constantly sliding about beneath the writing but to show this as an event taking place within the literary text itself, I will return to the example of Kafka's story *Der Jäger Gracchus*. Like the Flying Dutchman, like the Wild Huntsman and Coleridge's Ancient Mariner, Gracchus too is punished for the crime, born of curiosity about the world and of presumption, of overstepping a boundary (in both the geographical and the religious sense). It costs him his heavenly home and forces him, dead but alive, to sail for all eternity on earthly waters and to reflect on the undesirability of his hunt and of his error (Kafka, *Sämtliche Erzählungen*, ed. P. Raabe (Frankfurt am Main, 1970), pp. 258ff.). What is special about the story is of course that in it the aimlessly drifting ship begins its wanderings upon the waves of poetic discourse itself. The very fact that it is called a 'bark' may be seen as an allusion to the metaphorical tradition of the 'ingenii barca', of poetry as navigation and as a transgression. Moreover, Kafka does not omit to attribute to the course of the bark the characteristics associated with the artist (already presented in the story *Odradek*) of fickleness and undefined meaning, in which there is also a reminiscence of the curse of Cain: 'a fugitive and a vagabond shalt thou be' ('now high, now low, now right, now left, always moving. The hunter has turned into a butterfly'). But the *Barke* (bark) is also shown by its phonetic similarity to *Bahre* (bier) to be a symbol of the writer: already in Coleridge's *Rime of the Ancient Mariner*, which Kafka knew, the Mariner's final penance for the criminal act of killing the sacred animal is an insatiable urge to communicate, which transports him, neither truly alive nor dead, into the imaginative realm of poetry: 'I pass like night from land to land; / I have strange power of speech' (see also Frank, *Die unendliche Fahrt*). It is the same with Kafka's writer. He is, as an entry in Kafka's diary says, 'dead in his lifetime and the real survivor' (*Tagebücher 1910 bis 1923*, ed. Max Brod (Frankfurt am Main, 1973), p. 340). Finally Kafka makes the hunter as it were leap out of the text and introduce himself as his author: 'No-one', he says, 'will read what I am writing here.' So the 'misfortune' of not reaching that paradisaical place in which man is really at home would then be a reference to the process of writing itself, which elsewhere too Kafka characterised as a transgression, as the questionable overstepping of a threshold (*ibid.*, p. 347), and indeed as a 'hunt', that is, as the 'storming of the [ultimate earthly] boundary' (*ibid.*, p. 345). The unending nature of the wandering becomes a warning image to itself in the instability of the literary production of meaning – as a Fall from the simplicity of meaning, which now shines out only in the 'stillness' of a child's 'knowledge' (see also Kurz, *Traum-Schrecken*).

Modern French literary theory expresses this by speaking of the infinite text, of the 'texte général'. While Odysseus finds the way (back) to his Ithaca, for those who overstep the boundaries like the

hunter Gracchus there is no home any more. Similarly there is no
longer a home-meaning which would be the starting-point for the
fabric of meanings in a modern text and to which – through
interpretation – it would be brought back. Derrida spoke of the
removal of the boundaries of the textual economy, which deprives
every sign of its identity and 'sweeps [it] uncontrollably into the
whirlpool of writing' ('Le retrait de la métaphore', *Poésie* 7 (1978), p.
105). In the infinite text the meaning has no anchor – that is, no
definitive, no certain interpretation – indeed, it shows, as Derrida
says, 'an irreducible and *creative* multiplicity. The supplementation
and the turbulence of a certain lack ["le supplément et la turbulence d'un certain manque"] break up the boundary of the text
and preclude an exhaustive and final formalisation of it or at any
rate a completed taxonomy of its themes, its meaning, its intention' (Derrida, *Positions*, p. 62; see also 82).

The inadequacy of a pragmatics of the understanding of style

It will perhaps be objected that recent linguistic and literary studies
have moved away from the orientation towards the code model
and insistence on the non-ambiguity of the utterance. For some
years so-called *pragmatism* in linguistics has been teaching us not
only to pay attention to the grammatical correctness and the
meaning of sentences but to concern ourselves with the intention
with which they are used (see also S. J. Schmidt, *Texttheorie*; K.
Stierle, *Text als Handlung* (München, 1975)). One and the same
sentence-content (e.g. 'I will refute what you say') may be interpreted as a threat, as irony, as a promise, as a boast, as a programme, even (under certain circumstances) as flirtation. Now one
might suppose that style too (as the *manner* in which language is
used) is the expression of an intentional action and can be scientifically examined with the same precision as Austin's and Searle's
so-called 'illocutionary acts' or 'speech acts'.

This extension of the textual model to apply to linguistic acts
and also to style is very questionable. To the pragmatist, 'to
understand an intention' never means 'to understand an individual', but means to be familiar with a convention according to
which the individual encodes his intentions. Conventions by their

very nature follow rules and are thus, as Searle says (*R*, p. 207), capable of being repeated with the same meaning. (To return to Derrida's image, there are no wolves of undecidability here: the pragmatic shepherd has them all under control.)

On this premise, then, the style of a text would be nothing other than an application of a universally (or at least regionally) valid rule or – as Abrahams and Braunmüller put it – 'a function of pragmatic variables' ('Stil, Metapher und Pragmatik', *Lingua* 28 (1971), pp. 1–47). The pragmatic conception of style which for instance R. Ohmann has in mind ('Instrumental Style', in B. B. Kachru and H. W. F. Stahlke (eds.) *Current Trends in Stylistics* (Edmonton, 1972)) is inspired by Austen's and Searle's theory of speech acts which was supposed to pay as much attention to the fact that speaking is an action as to the 'network of circumstances and social conventions' (Sanders, *Linguistische Stiltheorie*, p. 123). Of course this also means that the area of what Saussure called the 'acte de la parole', which, as an area of individual choices and innovations, was contrasted with that of linguistic sociality ('la langue'), is only subject to a kind of pragmatic grammar, namely the system of the rules of context and of action. One can easily admit the existence of such rules without thereby having to reject Saussure's insight that *in the last resort* it is always only the *individual* act of speech – and not the intersubjective norm, which is a motivating but never a compelling factor – that decides the pragmatic meaning of the utterance (without this decision also binding the *understanding* of the utterance): 'In the *langue*', writes Saussure, 'there are thus always two sides which correspond to one another. The *langue* is $\frac{\text{social}}{\text{individual}}$

... If one leaves aside one of the two aspects, this can only be for the purpose of abstraction. There is the social and the individual langue. Forms and grammars exist only socially. But the changes originate with an individual' (*Cours de linguistique générale*, ed. R. Engler (Wiesbaden, 1968), vol. I, p. 28). However, the concept of a 'pragmatic stylistics' goes so far as to define the single stylistic choice merely as the manner in which the author realises the linguistic action (or the intersubjective convention written into it):

'By actualising these choices the writer chooses his own rule, his public and a kind of relationship to the reality of society' (Ohmann, 'Instrumental Style', p. 131). A deviation from or transformation of the rule is not provided for, because then it could no longer be decoded as a special case under the rule. This scientistic premise shows the limitations of the pragmatic conception of style. Every case is a particular instance of the general. But one must not confuse the individual with the particular. The particular can always be identified as an element in an order made up of elements similar to itself, whereas the individual, in its uniqueness, has to be discovered by *guessing*. But to guess does not mean merely to make visible the already inherent or intended meaning of a thing; for, as Peirce recognised, there is no meaning which is inherent in the sign by virtue of a rule, but only fallible conclusions drawn from previously established interpretations (see also S. Weber, 'Das linke Zeichen', in *Fugen*, p. 61). Accordingly, there can be no grammar of style, and thus no grammar of the text, although some exponents of the flourishing science of textual linguistics, influenced by structuralism (especially by Barthes and Todorov), claim that there can. (Both Barthes himself and Todorov originally held this view but have since corrected it. And in the *Dictionnaire encyclopédique des sciences du langage*, ed. Todorov and Ducrot (Paris, 1972), pp. 375–82, Todorov rejected the thesis that a text can be subjugated to a system as 'untenable and obsolete'.) By its unrepeatability, i.e. untransferability, the 'individual addition (*Beisatz*)' (as Boeckh calls it (*Enzyklopädie und Methodologie*, p. 83)) breaks apart the synthesis of the type of the speech act formed in accordance with convention, in which an intention and a proposition exist side by side. And it is only because this is so that 'habent sua fata libelli', i.e. books have their destinies in terms of meaning and participate in processes of linguistic change and of shifts of meaning, processes in which pragmatics or textual linguistics has no interest and for which, indeed, it can offer no explanation. This distinguishes it from literary studies, which set out from the experience 'that every [poetic] work of art offers not only a direct experience but one which is actually never wholly repeatable, not fixable, individual, even anarchic', which constantly extends the limit 'of everything that has been said previously'. Each experience exists in an unstable unity with the term with the help of which it was made; but 'each new experience goes beyond the formula of those previously gained . . . What we call our intellectual being is continuously engaged in this process of expansion and contraction. In this process art has the task of indissolubly reshaping and renewing the picture of the world and of behaviour in it, by [providing] experiences which explode the formula of [previous] experience' (Musil, *Gesammelte Werke in 9 Bänden*, vol. VIII, pp. 1151–2).

Essential features of a model of 'technical interpretation'

If textual *pragmatics* also fails to give a satisfactory answer to the question of what it means to understand a literary text, then one must look around in other areas of the formation of theory. There are, it is true, a large number of contemporary models of interpretation; but, with one exception, these have no adequate criterion for the description of a stylistic utterance. And only when such a description has been arrived at – this was already stressed by Schleiermacher – is the business of textual interpretation, the *technical interpretation*, complete (*HuK*, p. 168, see also pp. 170ff.).

The one exception is Sartre with his *Questions de méthode* and its 'application to a man and an *œuvre*', *L'idiot de la famille*, a book whose impressive stature matches its ambitious aims. This masterpiece, incidentally, provides the most powerful testimony to the continuing relevance of what Schleiermacher had called 'technical interpretation: the complete understanding of style'.

A human being, says Sartre, (and this applies also to Sartre's concept of the text) is a 'singular universal' (*L'idiot de la famille*, vol. I, p. 7; see also Starobinski, *L'œil vivant II*, p. 56), an *individual instance of the general* (Sartre, *L'idiot de la famille*, vol. III, p. 432). He is *general* in that, by the way in which he links together the words and sentences he reveals not only the drama of an individual socialisation but through it the totality of the rules of his epoch in all linguistic strata – what can be covered in a patiently carried out structural analysis (for instance along the lines advocated by Barthes). But beyond that the text is *individual* in so far as it internalises, applies, interprets and so transcends this totality of rules, that is pre-given and divided into the layers of its semiological varieties, in a way peculiar to *itself* alone. If the individual is dependent with regard to his *stock* of available signs but free in the use that he makes of them, then (not the meaning, but) the worldliness and the style of our texts always constitutes itself only in the interplay between 'structural causality' (L. Althusser and E. Balibar, *Das Kapitel lesen* (Reinbek, 1972), vol. II, pp. 250–1ff.) and 'individual projection of meaning' (Sartre). After all, no element in a symbolic order (e.g. a linguistic order or that of a literary genre) is master of its own application-in-a-situation, and this is because the order – the social code – does not appear itself and as such at the level of the *use* of symbols. For the universals of a grammar, no matter how liberally defined, that which is *not* the general, in other words the individual and his style, represents an uncrossable boundary. If one calls the order of codified signs and types of utterance the 'sayable', then style would be the 'unsayable' (*l'indisable*, as Flaubert calls it (Sartre, *Situations* IX (Paris, 1972), p. 111f.)); namely the potential meanings not, or not yet, expressed by the linguistic system as it is, which the creativity of the speaking/writing individual is able to articulate in it. Sartre speaks of a 'hermeneutics of keeping silent' (*L'idiot de la famille*, vol. III, p. 29); only it marks the true achievement of textual interpretation, which is not reached at all by the reconstruction of the lexical, syntactical and pragmatic codes. Of course *silence* is only a heuristic and transient element in textual interpretation: 'In the temporary detour via non-communication one arrives at an expression and a communication which are consequently all the more intense, and thus at an activation of the powers of language' (Starobinski, *L'œil vivant* II, p. 56).

This being so, the work of the interpreter will consist of discovering in every structural element of the text the 'individual addition (*Beisatz*)' and conversely of identifying in the author's individual style the traces of the superseded symbolic order (Sartre, *Crd*, pp. 85–6ff.; see also Frank, *Das Individuelle-Allgemeine*, pp. 293ff., *Das Sagbare und das Unsagbare*, pp. 256ff.). Schleiermacher called this the objective–subjective, historical *and* divinatory method of interpretation (*HuK*, p. 93f.), 'divination' meaning the attempt to guess the act of the author's original finding of meaning prior to the use of the linguistic convention (*ibid.*, pp. 169ff.).

No one gives the interpreter a guarantee that he will in fact correctly identify the individual style of the author (or, to put it more cautiously, of the text's subject), or indeed that he will bridge the time-gap which separates his world from the world of his text. Jürgen Kreft has shown very well how problematic even the maxim is that the interpreter must put himself in the place of the 'original reader', for instance by acquiring all the knowledge which he can assume in a contemporary of his text as a participant in a social system (*Grundprobleme der Literaturdidaktik* (Heidelberg, 1977), pp. 133ff.). The 'ideal reader' is a scientific fiction which ignores the fact that the 'objective mind' of an epoch comes into play unevenly, indeed heterogeneously, in an infinitely complex communicative field and appears fragmented into as many facets as there are individuals who appropriate it or vary it each in his own way. Who, for instance, is the 'intended or primary addressee' of Sophocles' drama *Oedipus Rex*? Is it the audiences who watched Sophocles' tragedies? Hardly, for they were the addressees of the tragedies of Sophocles' predecessor, Aeschylus, the performances of whose dramas those of Sophocles were intended to follow without further preparation. 'If Sophocles, who like the other dramatists was a creative theologian, gives a new interpretation of human existence, then this means that his dramatic texts have to create an adequate reader for themselves' (*ibid.*, p. 140). And *we* can be this 'adequate reader' just as well as (or indeed, in Schleier-macher's sense, 'better' than) the Athenian public of the fifth century BC. Identifying with the spirit of the times of the author is an effort which must not be confused with that of 'divination'. Even if the interpreter has studied the structure of an epoch as meticulously and made it his own as thoroughly as for instance Sartre did with the structure of Flaubert's period, he has still not gained an understanding of Gustave Flaubert's individual way of writing: he knows (or has an inkling of) the general, but the individual remains closed to him. In order to guess at the 'individual', a 'differential interpretation' is required (see also Schleier-macher, *HuK*, p. 92, §. 16,2; Sartre, *Crd*, p. 88; Starobinski, *L'œil vivant II*, pp. 24f., 51, 53, 63). This aims to make visible the distance between two contemporary 'sections' or 'layers' of historical 'objectivity': what L. Spitzer (in his *Stilstudien*) called the 'stylistic divergence'. In a division of labour, *regressive analysis* concerns itself with the relatively universal element in the text, while *progressive synthesis* 'divines' whether and in what way the text has gone beyond its predetermined structure. 'It is really', Sartre explains, 'the difference between the *shared features (communs)* and the idea or the concrete attitude of the person being studied, their enrichment [i.e. the enrichment of the shared features], their type of concretisation, their variations, etc., which *above all else* give us a clearer insight into our object. This difference constitutes their individuality and uniqueness' (*Crd*, p. 88). When this has been found – by means of 'comparison' and 'differentiation' – then the textual datum that has been extracted in this way can, by means of 'conjectures' and 'hypotheses of understanding' (*L'idiot de la famille*, vol. I, p. 56), be made transparent in its singularity for the purpose of the whole project (*Entwurf*) and be examined to find out in what way it has altered, preserved or reorganised a particular layer of the social code (in the gradation of its levels of constitution) compared with the state of affairs at the outset ('progressive synthesis').

All these approaches and methods may in a particular case spring from an overriding interest either in structure – to the extent that it is the structure that forms a basis for the project and to the extent that every project must realise itself in a (new) state of the structure – or in individuality – because the individual internalises the structure in an individual way and distinguishes himself from the general – and so one encounters again the multiplicity of perspectives outlined in Schleiermacher's 'positive formula' of hermeneutics (quoted above) (see also M. Frank, *Das Individuelle-Allgemeine*, p. 289ff.).

In Sartre too hermeneutics has two levels, one above the other: on the first is the relationship between the circumstances of the epoch and the totality of the author's life (biography), on the second the relationship of his 'seminal decision' ('projet fondamental, intuition embryonnaire') (Sartre, *L'idiot de la famille*, vol. II, p. 1490) to the totality of his individual projects (documents, records of his life, works, etc.). In both cases the interpretative emphasis is on the break, the difference, by which the individual goes beyond what is given, i.e. on his *style*. Just as the style, as the author's individual way of combining elements, points back directly to a particular world-view ('conception du monde') and indirectly to a life-story (Schleiermacher, *HuK*, p. 168; Sartre, *Crd*, p. 90), so the life-story for its part points to broader social structures of the epoch, from which it must in turn be distinguished by interpretative differentiation, so that behind the generality of the stage of development of the intellectual and material productive forces or meaning-creating energies, and also of the forms of interaction in society and family specific to the epoch, the unique drama of a childhood and ultimately of a whole life can become visible: 'We must *divine at one and the same time* social structures . . . and a *unique* drama of childhood' (Sartre, *Crd*, p. 91). Motivated by questions which the work asks of life, regressive analysis seeks, while continually extending the horizon of its questioning, to reveal the *situation* in which the universal and the individual engage with each other. Regressive analysis will advance step by step through the biography to the social–historical and ultimately to the universal-historical context, making use in the process of psychoanalysis, sociology and the different branches of historical studies (to name only these).

Between the individual utterances and the general circumstances to which they refer – though the two do not always completely correspond to one another: the work may say nothing about its motivations, or over-determine them, but it will in every case interpret them somehow – there arises in this way a kind of 'to-ing and fro-ing' which extends through several levels hierarchically placed one above another and finally 'makes it possible to assess, approximately', the object of study, the human being and his goals, 'in their whole historical depth' (Sartre, *Crd*, p. 92).

Sartre instructs the interpreter of the text to compare his work with one's attitude towards the injunctions of an ethic: no-one forces the textual interpreter 'to guess the individual element'. Nor can this element be theoretically objectivised by demonstration. It is imposed as a task upon the will to understand, rather than simply given to it. Through its style the work asks questions of life and of the times, i.e. it calls them into question. It is precisely by doing this that it appeals to the future and as it were asks the interpreter to take up these questions once again, to appropriate them in a different form. Sometimes it uses its beauty in order the better to achieve this end; poetic works are after all, to quote an expression used (though with a different purpose) by Novalis, 'aesthetic imperatives' (*Schriften*, vol. III, p. 413). They call upon the reader or interpreter to contribute creatively, by reminding him, as though of a task, of his ability to step beyond constituted structures of meaning, in other words of the fact of freedom. It is not the piece of writing but *we* who are responsible for the meaning. The appeal to understanding also contains another lesson which points beyond the field of the academic study of literature, namely the need to stand up for the rights of the individual in their irreplaceability and distinctiveness. Of course it is more convenient to overlook the 'individual addition' (Boeckh) and to stick to what is brought to light by the scientifically testable methods of textual analysis: 'a writing without style' (Barthes, *S/Z*, p. 11). Measured by the ideal of method in the exact sciences, the idea of the irreducibility of the individual to the structure appears unimportant or sentimental; the world can continue to exist quite well without it.

But – as Sartre reminded us (*Situations II*, p. 316) – it can even more easily continue to exist without human beings.

CHAPTER 3

The 'true subject' and its double: Jacques Lacan's hermeneutics

To speak of Jacques Lacan's hermeneutics, as I propose to do in this chapter, must seem questionable right from the outset. Are those 'objections in principle to the phenomenological, hermeneutic and dialectical project of thematism',[1] the narrowing down of textual analysis to the semantic aspect of the interpretation of meaning, not also raised in Lacan's writings? Anyone who is familiar with them knows that the term 'hermeneutics' is used only seldom and with reservations, although there can be no doubt that Lacan's *Seminaire sur la Lettre volée* follows a 'parcours admirable'[2] (admirable trajectory) of classical textual interpretation. Yet the caution about terminology is not surprising. For one thing, the philosophical hermeneutics which developed in Germany in the nineteenth century and acquired a new dimension through existentialist ontology has, all in all, met with only a limited response among French intellectuals. Significant exceptions, like Groethuysen (who, however, must rather be said to have imported Dilthey's approach to the humanities to Paris) or Sartre, who incidentally is also cautious in his use of the term, despite being the author of the most significant work of modern hermeneutics, confirm the general impression. Following this, the triumphal progress of so-called structuralism began to undermine an epistemological premise so fundamental that it was thought that hermeneutics must stand or fall by it, which I shall be speaking

This lecture, which I gave at the Berlin Lacan Symposium in April 1978, was first published in the first special issue of the psychoanalytical journal *Der Wunderblock* (Berlin, 1978), pp. 12–37.

[1] Jacques Derrida, 'La double séance' II, in *La dissémination* (Paris, 1972), p. 281.
[2] Derrida, *Positions* (Paris, 1972), p. 118.

about later on. I am referring to the idea that consciousness has access in principle to the meaning of its life-utterances, even if these may at first be disguised and – as Merleau-Ponty put it – need to be recovered by means of 'archaeological' reconstruction work.[3]

It is immediately obvious that on this conception Romanticism and Cartesianism are in complete agreement. The discovery of an 'unconscious' or 'real activity of the mind' (Schelling), the thesis of the 'primacy of the will in self-consciousness' (Schopenhauer), the discovery of the 'drive-nature' and of the 'dark side' of the life of the soul did not in principle make it necessary to abandon the classical reflection model. For if the self is defined, as it is for instance by Kierkegaard, as 'a relationship that . . . by relating to itself, relates to another',[4] then that fully takes account of that minimal but effective distancing and concealment by means of which the self escapes from its authority and distances itself from its own consciousness. *Reflection* is after all a relationship between two moments, whose self-conscious identity never emerges otherwise than from the depths of a split. Every presence is the presence of something to something or to somebody: thus it always presupposes an absence, by means of which it (temporarily) escapes from itself and destines itself for indirectness. A life-utterance has access to itself, certainly; not directly, however, but by deriving its meaning from the signs and reflexes through which its self-consciousness is, objectively as it were, mediated. I think that this is the formula – if one were required – which, stopping just short of excessive simplification, could be used to characterise the psychoanalytical hermeneutics of Habermas/Lorenzer and that of Paul Ricœur: both approaches are based on a kind of Cartesianism which, though corrected by the achievements of historical and sociological consciousness and of the Romantic 'unconscious', nevertheless retains the paradigm of reflection and dreams of once again, by means of an archaeological exertion, subjecting layers of meaning that have been covered over or of desymbolised discourse to the control of the autonomous self.

[3] Preface to A. Hesnard, *L'Œuvre de Freud* . . . (Paris, 1960), p. 9.
[4] Søren Kierkegaard, *Sickness unto Death*, trans. and ed. Walter Lowrie (Princeton, 1968), first section, A.

Freud's saying, which has so strongly appealed to twentieth-century writers, that the self is 'not master in its own house',[5] is also quoted, it is true, by the exponents of existentialist, i.e. Heidegger-inspired, hermeneutics in order to reject the illusion of an 'infinite consciousness'. What is meant is, firstly, that, as Gadamer says, every self-understanding contains within itself in a way that is not controllable 'more being than consciousness',[6] and therefore in the movement of reflection does not by any means get to the bottom of itself or become transparent. (Lacan is saying the same thing when he writes, 'the place which [on a given occasion] I occupy as the subject of the signifier [is not] . . . concentric' with that which I occupy as the subject of the signified.)[7] Secondly, the narcissism of self-presence is humiliated by the discovery that the structure of consciousness is ecstatic. The *Cogito* experiences its meaning not through world-less self-contemplation but as a reflection which shines back from the things and signs of the world, to which it has totally externalised itself. 'Being', dark and not yet written upon, becomes 'world' by being passed through and as it were written upon or, as Heidegger says, 'cleared' (*gelichtet*), by the projects and purposes, by the symbolising and designating activities of subjects, so that henceforth, as a structure of the type of a general 'context of involvements', it provides the background for every individual attempt at self-understanding. The 'I' finds itself inserted into a world already imbued with meanings, which it must first inter-nalise before it can acquire an understanding of itself. 'I find myself in a world which is already significant and which reflects back to me meanings which I did not put there',[8] in a world, then, which has the structure of a language, of a 'symbolic order'. One could say that the speaking self – introduced into the symbolic order – is separated from itself by nothing less than the whole world. And to this extent the reflexivity of this movement indeed bears little similarity to the closed circuit of Hegelian consciousness, which at the end of its process 'reach[es] a point at which it lays aside its appearance of being encumbered with what is alien to it, which is

---

[5] Hans-Georg Gadamer, *Wahrheit und Methode*, 2nd edn (Tübingen, 1965), pp. 260, 264.
[6] Gadamer, *Kleine Schriften* (Tübingen, 1967 and 1972), vol. I, p. 127.
[7] Jacques Lacan, *Ecrits* (Paris, 1966), pp. 516f.
[8] Jean-Paul Sartre, *L'être et le néant* (Paris, 1943), p. 592.

only for it and is as an other, or where appearance becomes the same as essence'.[9]

The reflection of consciousness made over to its world and mediated by the order of signs unites the poles of the historical– social world and of the subject in a dialectical 'effective unity' (*Wirkungseinheit*),[10] without the consciousness which understands meaning ever succeeding in freeing itself from the prescribed linguistic world-view which Gadamer, following Hegel, calls 'substance'.[11] While the consciousness immersed in the linguistic universe has the status of an experience which has direct knowledge of itself, it is forced to derive the theme of its self-understanding from the meaning which the interpreted thing throws back as a reflection on to the interpreting consciousness. In understanding something, instead of being able to place itself before itself, especially objectively, its self-consciousness comes to it wholly from that which is other to it, without its having the possibility of bringing its message methodically under control or being able by itself to anticipate it prognostically.

The reason why I place such emphasis on this characteristic of existentialist–ontological hermeneutics is that, at least at first sight, it shows undeniable similarities to Lacan's psychoanalytical approach. This has been shown in detail by Hermann Lang.[12]

I will briefly recall the parallel. Lacan starts out from the analytical experience that there is no continuous transition from the being-for-itself of a meaning to its linguistic articulation. To release the silent need (*besoin*) from the relationship with itself alone (to generalise it into a meaning which exists for others) requires that it be externalised to the 'ordre symbolique'. The ontogenetically premature birth (*prématurité*) compels the 'sujet *infans*'[13] to convey its vital needs symbolically – via other people (and first of all via the mother). But precisely at the point of intersection of the co-ordinates of the still pre-symbolic intentionality of the speech-

[9] G.W.F. Hegel, *Phänomenologie des Geistes*, ed. J. Hoffmeister, 6th edn (Hamburg, 1952), p. 75.
[10] Gadamer, *Wahrheit und Methode*, p. 267.
[11] *Ibid.*, p. 286.
[12] Hermann Lang, *Die Sprache und das Unbewußte. Jacques Lacans Grundlegung der Psychoanalyse* (Frankfurt am Main, 1973).
[13] *Ecrits*, p. 497.

less wish[14] and of the demand that has become a symbol, an unexpected distortion takes place.

The act which the subject hoped merely to use as a transparent means of achieving its desire no longer beams back the familiar features of its pre-linguistic self from the signifier (to which it had entrusted itself), but instead the strange face of an order of the Other. The mere fact of having to speak distorts the pre-linguistic – or, as Lacan says, the 'imaginary' – intention in the medium of the 'demand' conveyed by the symbol and causes its message, spoken by itself, to come back to it in the alien form of a message spoken to it from the place of the Other.[15] This movement of inversion therefore makes the person who speaks become the place through which 'It' speaks, turning their action into a passion.[16] The meaning's supposedly prior possession of itself has to cede its authority – its position as the originator – to the activity of the signifier, which prescribes the effects 'by means of which the signifiable undergoes its marking and by undergoing it becomes the signified [où le signifiable apparaît comme subissant sa marque, en devenant par cette passion le signifié]'.[17]

Grammar itself, by using the passive form, *signifié*, hints at the fact that the symbolically conveyed meaning must in principle be understood as an effect, and moreover a subsequent effect ('effet après coup, rétroaction'),[18] of the chain of signifiers, and that its stability always exists only inside the limits within which their 'constant sliding' has just stopped, and that it can thus be revoked by a new 'attachment' of the meaning to the chain.[19]

Of course one will not expect the vital need to acquiesce in this alienation and distortion: it nominates desire (*désir*) as its successor (*rejeton*). In the realm of the symbolic order itself, desire represents the intention of the need, but at the same time it deepens the 'split'[20] undergone by the subject in the 'original alienation', a split which sets up a barrier between its intelligible and its empirical side. For this reason Lacan – like Sartre – calls desire a 'useless

---

[14] The fact that the wish lacks language does not prevent it from having the form of a *propositional attitude*.

[15] *Ecrits*, p. 41; p. 439. [16] *Ibid.*, p. 688. [17] *Ibid.* [18] See also *ibid.*, p. 838f.

[19] *Ibid.*, p. 502.

[20] *Ibid.*, p. 689.

passion'.[21] At this point I have to underemphasise the psychoanalytical implications in order to focus on the closeness, and the
distance, between Lacan's approach and existentialist hermeneutics. Instead of asking how well or how badly the apparatus
of linguistic theory interprets the scene of the mother–child relationship and its reciprocal desires, I must concern myself with
showing the logic of the model as such. Here we find that Lacan
presents the feeling of lack and of failure inherent in every desire
as a necessary effect of what he calls the dialectic of the 'entry of
the signifier into psychism [l'intrusion du signifiant dans le
psychisme]':[22] the speechless and as it were not yet written-on
subject could not possibly entrust itself to the symbolic order
without *ipso facto* being broken into pieces by its sections, articulations, distinctions and breaks. For language itself – the condition
for any communication – stands on the ground of an ineradicable
lack; it pays for its functioning with the expulsion of a full signifier
which from now on appears as a sliding emptiness between the
other signifiers and keeps alive the memory of its absence.[23] It is
the signifier of the subject, which has been 'crossed out by its first
intention [en barrant le sujet par première intention]',[24] split
(*séparé*) and forced into the distanced form of being of 'exsistence'.[25]

The terminological allusion to the existential ontologists' concept of existence is, I think, unmistakable. And with the concealed
quotation Lacan is also bringing comparable implications into his
own theory:[26] for Sartre too, to name only him, the subject
externalises its substance – ecstatically – to the being to which as a
result of this transformation it applies all the determinations via
which it understands itself: the subject is – in relation to being –
something relatively non-existent[27] which as it were deducts itself
from the wealth of being, in order, by the emptiness of its negations, to 'clear' (*lichten*) the context of involvements of a world, of a
linguistic order. Without doubt it is not the ground of its being, but
only of its non-being – of the negations which it inflicts on being.

---

[21] *Ibid.*, p. 812.   [22] *Ibid.*, p. 555.   [23] *Ibid.*, p. 806f.   [24] *Ibid.*, p. 848.
[25] *Ibid.*, p. 11.
[26] That 'connotations, if not concepts of post-war existentialism' crop up in Lacan's work is
obvious. Derrida did not 'discover' this. (See also Derrida, 'Le facteur de la vérité', in
Poétique. Revue de théorie et d'analyse littéraires 21 (1975), p. 124.
[27] A 'néant' (μὴ ὄν) – as opposed to a 'rien' (οὐκ ὄν).

It is no different in Lacan, who takes up a familiar comparison which Sartre had used in *L'être et le néant* (and elsewhere): 'The effect of language', says Lacan, 'is the cause brought into the subject. By means of this effect it is not the cause of itself (*causa sui*), it carries within it the worm of the cause, which splits it. [L'effet de langage, c'est la cause introduite dans le sujet. Par cet effet il n'est pas cause de lui-même, il porte en lui le ver de la cause qui le refend].'[28]

Even the ontological status of this *sujet-néant* (subject-nothingness) is defined similarly by Lacan and by Sartre. True, in and for itself the intention of the subject at the imaginary stage is nothing (*rien*), lacking substance and definiteness, similar to that 'amorphous fog' to which Saussure – following Herder and Humboldt – compared the state of the intention prior to the 'semiological synthesis'. But this nothing is as it were carried by being (*est été* – 'is been', as Sartre says) and is thus preserved from disintegrating into absolute *non*-being. Lacan expresses himself quite similarly: the subject, he says, is a *manque-à-être*,[29] a 'lack which is to be been', i.e. a lack which has to be taken up by the symbolic order ('qui est à soutenir', in the sense in which a Christian 'has to take up' the Cross, or in which Heidegger and his French translator Corbin said of Dasein that it is not but 'has to be its being' [a à être son être]). 'Now', Lacan continues, 'this nothing (has) existence, (namely) on the basis of this insertion of it in its function (within the symbolic order) which was brought about at this moment by the appeal issued in the Other to the second signifier [Mais ce rien se soutient de son avènement, maintenant produit par l'appel fait dans l'Autre au deuxième signifiant]'.[30]

This enigmatic formulation, which Lacan repeats rather than explains in a few key passages of *Ecrits*, requires detailed analysis, for it touches the nerve of the argument by which Lacan attempts to substantiate his equation of language and the unconscious and thereby at the same time to shed light on the function of subjectivity and of understanding.

---

[28] *Ecrits*, p. 835.
[29] To translate this into German as *Seinsverfehlen* does not seem to me to make sense: it overlooks the ontological problem which Lacan addresses here.
[30] *Ecrits*, p. 835.

For if one supports the thesis that the subject is originally 'decentred'[31] and, as the 'signified', undergoes – in a process over which it has itself no control – the marking of the 'signifier' as the absolute cause,[32] then one is taking on the obligation of showing the constitution of that potential infinity of meaning (which transcendental hermeneutics sees as being produced by the subject) in the subjectless mechanism of signification as such. The theory which questions the precedence of the philosophy of consciousness must be able to offer an explanation at least equally good for the genesis of meaning: it must not fail to do justice to the phenomenon itself.

For this purpose Lacan undertakes an idiosyncratically accented rereading of Saussure's theory of language, according to which the linguistic system consists of a synchronically self-regulating combinatorial system of distinct elementary values, each of which is defined by being clearly distinguished from all the others.[33] Saussure, though not the first to do so, had, of course, shown most appropriately that semiosis, the movement of the creation of signs, cannot be seen as a relationship of depiction or representation between the meaning which looks at the thing and its graphic or phonic expression. No inner bond mediates between the non-sensuous and the sensuous aspect of the sign. On the other hand meaning needs expression, in order to present itself to itself, not only because it would otherwise remain invisible or inaudible but because as a purely intelligible entity it would have no contour and profile by which it could distinguish itself from other meaning. The basic requirement of a sign is its 'identity', and that means its distinctness from other signs. But it cannot acquire this directly from the relationship-only-with-itself; for a meaning cannot be expressed by itself, any more than one could imagine a price that was not embodied either in a number or in a quantity or a coin. So it is not that there is first a meaning which then, by a simple reduplication, makes itself present again in the chain of signs: instead the 'semiotic synthesis' which attaches the meaning to a signifier which is differentially profiled against others allows the meaning to appear for the first time as that meaning in the

---

[31] *Ibid.*, p. 621.   [32] *Ibid.*, p. 688.   [33] *Ibid.*, p. 414.

determinate unity and within the boundaries of its schema. Fichte spoke of the 'law of reflection of all our cognition – namely, that nothing is *known* as what it is without our also thinking what it is *not*'.[34] This law makes no exception of the thought 'I'.

Without doubt this condition is even more radical, in two ways, than the concession that existential hermeneutics is prepared to make to the priority of language over the subject; and structuralism has, in my view rightly, insisted on this. For one thing, it is not enough to describe hermeneutic reflection as the mediation of the subject through a pre-existing linguistic world-view: for this relationship can be understood, as Gadamer quite explicitly does, as a *speculative structure*, i.e. as a play of essentially similar elements which are 'mirrored in one another': in the process of the consciousness of effective history one mind always speaks to another mind, or to put it more pointedly, the context of meaning of a tradition speaks *to itself* in the form of an understanding which is open to this tradition. In this way the hermeneutics of effective history, both in Gadamer and in Ricœur, is able to make the connection with the paradigm of reflection for which the alienation of consciousness from itself can only be a stage on the route of its constant return into itself.[35] Secondly, existentialist hermeneutics has failed to take account of an alterity of quite another order. For within the order of a linguistic world-view every element, even before it is able to grasp itself as what it means, carries within itself the trace of all other elements of the structure of signifiers, i.e. it acquires its identity-as-meaning precisely not from its specular relationship to itself but from its total externalisation to what is other than it. 'An interval', says Derrida, 'must split it off from what it is not, so that it can be itself'.[36] Thus the meaning which is to be understood is based not on a continuum consisting wholly of meaning like itself but on something which is itself not meaningful, namely the constitutive gap which, as a negation which can never be (in a

---

[34] Johann Gottlieb Fichte, 'Wissenschaftslehre nova methodo', in *Nachgelassene Schriften*, vol. II, ed. Hans Jacob (Berlin, 1937), p. 368.

[35] This of course poses a contradiction to the second structural requirement of the notion of 'I' – its *direct* acquaintance with itself prior to any reflection. I have discussed this problem fully in *Das Individuelle-Allgemeine. Textstrukturierung und -interpretation nach Schleiermacher* (Frankfurt am Main, 1977), pp. 96ff.

[36] Derrida, *Marges de la philosophie* (Paris, 1972), p. 13.

Hegelian sense) overcome to form a unity, separates every 'positive term' from itself and only thereby determines it. The immediate transparency of the meaning is thus already clouded at its origin; and if one wanted to designate meaning as the conscious or the sayable, then one would indeed have to call its origin the unconscious or silence, as Lacan does.[37]

Only now, I think, can one judge the full significance of Lacan's formulation, quoted above, to the effect that the nothing of the subject realises itself by existing as an 'appeal issued in the Other to the second signifier'. Without this lack 'all others would represent nothing. For nothing is represented unless it be for someone or something [tous les autres ne représenteraient rien. Puisque rien n'est représenté que pour quelqu'un ou pour quelque chose]'.[38]

Here the reflexive 'for' of the representation does not – and this is probably the most conspicuous offence committed against classical hermeneutics by Lacan's idiosyncratic definition – refer to a transcendental subject. Instead the subject itself is revealed as the reflexive gap, the interval of a regulated play of reference between (at least) two signifiers which stand out positively, in their presence and determinacy, against the empty background into whose depths the subject flees and as it were makes itself nothing. Does this mean – as some have tried to interpret Lacan – that strictly speaking there is no subject? Not at all: it survives as the order of the symbols, which without the effect of the 'subjective gap' would after all remain mere insignificant letters, as meaningless as stones and just as dumb. Since, as Lacan says, 'in the symbolic order the empty spaces are just as significant as the full terms [dans l'ordre symbolique, les vides sont aussi signifiants que les pleins]'[39] it may be said that it is precisely the deferral, the pausing, the constitutive growing silent of significance which present (represent) the subject, given that the subject is nothing but the 'Being beyond all communication . . . Nothingness'.[40] Lacan does not hesitate to call it the 'ground of constitution' of all significance.[41] So he acknowledges a semiologically irreducible function of the subject – and he

---

[37] *Ecrits*, p. 819.　　[38] *Ibid.*　　[39] *Ibid.*, p. 392.
[40] Sartre, *L'idiot de la famille*, vol. III (Paris, 1972), p. 377.
[41] See also for example Lacan, *Le séminaire*, XI, *Les quatre concepts fondamentaux de la psychoanalyse*, 1964 (Paris, 1973), pp. 44, 46.

does this, I think, deliberately and undeterred by the accusations that he is reverting to logo-phonocentrism – even if the name of 'subject' can no longer be taken to mean the reflexive self-certainty of the Cartesian 'cogito'.

I see in this an advantage of Lacan's theory (over, say, Derrida), which can be of benefit to hermeneutics. For this theory is able to distance itself equally successfully from two other kinds of approach: on the one hand from all the so-called structuralist attempts to overcome the concept of the subject, which suffer from the weakness that they do not show the motive for its 'decentring' explicitly in the structure of the decentred concept itself, and even in their rejection of it have no consistent theory of self-consciousness; but on the other hand Lacan also departs from the quasi-dialectical approaches (including the hermeneutics of the 'merging of horizons') which heuristically orientate the process of self-understanding towards the reflection model and so in principle run the risk of mistaking the discourse of the other for the specular echo of the dialectical discourse with oneself.

It is well known that Lacan interprets[42] Freud's famous saying from the thirty-first of the *Neue Vorlesungen* (New Lectures), 'Where It was, I should become' in a way that is as far removed as possible from the interpretation that would like to see it as a late echo of the self-reflection of subjectivity presented in Hegel's *Phänomenologie des Geistes*: as the act of liberation of an intelligence which reappraises the opaque contents and burdensome obsessions of its history and finally brings them into view as what they truly are and literally appropriates them. Assigning every piece of content which can be represented as one side of a relationship of a self-presence in the traditional sense to the sphere of influence of the imaginary *moi*, Lacan avails himself of the opportunity offered by the French language to reserve the pronoun *Je* for the function fulfilled by the subject-of-the-Other, the 'sujet véritable', which cannot be adequately represented in any reflection (since it is in a certain sense in-existent).[43] In this context the unconscious is not a merely

---

[42] *Ecrits*, p. 417.
[43] In what follows I use *ich* (I) with a small 'i' when referring to the relationship with the self (*moi*), to distinguish it from the irreflexive *Ich* (*Je*) of the unconscious, which is written with a capital letter.

hidden or virtual self-consciousness which has only been waiting
for the archaeological operation to bring it to light, but an area
from which all bridges to reflection have been broken. If one
assumes that it is an 'I' (*Ich*) distinguished in this way that It is to
become (*not*, then, the 'I' [*ich*] of self-reflection), then one has an
inkling of how strange Lacan's paraphrase of Freud's sentence will
seem to anyone who has learned to use psychoanalysis as a
demystifying tool in a teleologically and semantically conceived
hermeneutics.

For, far from situating 'It' in the reflection which it would like to
objectify and put behind itself, self-consciousness which is disguised and caught up in the nets of narcissistic ego-ity is to be
re-integrated into the founding area of that Other which cannot be
reduced to the concepts of presence, of positivity and of the
relationship to oneself and whose manner of being of 'absolute
subjectivity' Lacan indicates by using the almost mystical neologism of *s'être*,[44] letting himself be inspired (as is his way) by the
homophony of the German *es* (= it) with the initial phoneme
shared by 'subject', 'signifier' and the reflexive pronoun 'se' ('s' '
before a vowel).

Thus Lacan distinguishes two levels or potentials of subjectivity,[45] and it is precisely at this point that he departs not only from
structuralism in general but even from such a carefully considered
approach to overcoming it as Derrida's grammatology. For this
too can be accused of not deriving its criticism of the trap of
representation, which it sharp-sightedly finds established everywhere in classical metaphysics and especially in hermeneutics, and
even in Lacan's work, immanently from the structure of subjectivity, i.e. by proving that it is not possible to form an appropriate
concept of this structure using the classical apparatus. Lacan
wishes to make good this omission.

He does this by showing in the middle of the 'dual relation from
the me to the me' ('relation duelle du moi au moi')[46] – the hovering

---

[44] *Ecrits*, p. 418.
[45] The coherence of these, however, remains theoretically undetermined. This is so despite
Lacan's fondness for devising structural sketches and graphs in which all kinds of
constellations of *Je* and *moi* are considered. In this matter Ricœur is more precise.
[46] *Ecrits*, pp. 428, 454, 607f.

of the meaning between 'duel' and 'dual' is just as deliberate as is the association with the binary nature of the sign – by showing, then, in the middle of the dual relationship of selfhood, the *effect of a lack* by which the full presence of the 'I' (*ich*) in the 'image spéculaire', the mirror-image, is undermined from within, de-completed, driven out of the pre-linguistic/mythical domain of imaginary transferences and wish-led identifications and handed over to the 'ordre symbolique'. An unprejudiced reflection on the apparent self-sufficiency in which the baby seems to remain in the imaginary identification with the primary object which it inter-prets as a mirror-image, with the other (Lacan writes *autre* with a small 'a') – an identification which gives it the false impression of an integral personality not yet fragmented and differentiated by the scansions of the chain of signifiers – an unprejudiced reflection on the 'capture imaginaire' is sufficient to reveal the basic negativ-ity against the background of which the pleasure of an integral feeling of self first finds the way to its understanding. In other words, the lack (*Mangel*) first felt in the ineradicable failing (*Fehl*) of the primary object of identification (the mother) and inadequately replaced in the metaphor *Nom-du-Père* (Name-of-the-Father) cross-es, as the 'discourse of the Other' which cannot be dissolved into selfhood by any dialectical manoeuvre, the fortress of the specular fascination, forcing it to admit a fundamental 'dependence' on a *Third* which transcends it.[47]

This means that the attempt at a phantasmatic self-grounding of the 'I' (*ich*) which evades the incisions and articulations of the symbolic order fails precisely because *the wish to preserve itself from the Other's intervention in the delineation of the 'passion imaginaire' has itself already been produced by the Other*. The very vision of a *causa sui*,[48] of which reflection dreams, is already an illusory creation of the wish that has become aware of its 'radical heteronomy':[49] a construct, as Lacan can say with only apparent paradox, of the 'highest narcissism of the lost cause'.[50] The 'I' (*ich*) of self-consciousness exists essentially as something which the Other addresses and makes demands upon (ein vom Anderen in An-spruch Genom-menes), even before it has been able to resort to the dialectical ruse

---

[47] *Ibid.*, pp. 437, 812.   [48] See also *ibid.*, p. 835; p. 840.
[49] *Ibid.*, p. 524.   [50] *Ibid.*, p. 826.

of rejecting the trace of this Other in favour of that 'second-degree alterity' through which A both offers itself to the view of consciousness in the mirror-image of the reflection and at the same time withdraws itself from view.

It offers itself to its view by imparting knowledge of the Other in the 'mediating position' of the *petit autre*; at the same time it withdraws itself from it, in that it is not adequately represented within the specular duplication in which the 'I' (*ich*) always recognises the Other only as its counterpart (*sui simile: son semblable*). The over-determination of the 'I' (*ich*) by the Other which results from this inappropriateness makes itself felt as a lack which also forces the lie of its binary fascination with itself to call upon the Other to vouch for the truth in which it exists.[51]

For, arching above the 'image spéculaire', there is already the point of that pyramid (Λ), in an ink invisible to the wish, which completes the measured straight line of the dialogue which the 'I' (*ich*) has with the other (*autre*) of itself (−), to form the 'symbolic triangle',[52] that is, in quite general terms, the signifier of a constitutive lack in the midst of the Other and its discourse (S[A̶] → S̶) – *of a lack* which makes the Other 'inconsistent' [53] and *which drives self-consciousness to admit its essential dependence on a 'Third'* which no dialectics could prove to be the motive force of the happening of the self-mediation as such.[54]

Lacan's curt condemnation of consciousness as a weapon used by the insincere strategy of reflexive self-grounding now becomes understandable. The 'one homogeneous function' that he grants to consciousness consists of the 'imaginary capture of the me [*moi*] by its specular reflection' and of its inherent function of misrecognition.[55] Is it then wrong to conclude that 'ubi cogito, ibi sum'? Not at all – so long as one is aware that this conclusion 'limits the I [*ich*] to existing in its being only to the extent that it thinks itself [me limite à n'être là dans mon être que dans la mesure où je pense que je suis dans ma pensée]'.[56] Schelling, in his Munich and Berlin lectures, had already made this point as a reservation in relation to Descartes: the 'cogito sum' does not reach being (*Sein*) itself – irreflexive being – but being *which* is 'only for me' and *because* it is

[51] See also *ibid.*, p. 524.   [52] *Ibid.*, p. 524.   [53] *Ibid.*, p. 819f.
[54] *Ibid.*, pp. 607ff.   [55] *Ibid.*, p. 832.   [56] See also *ibid.*, p. 516.

only in relation to me (i.e. 'essential being [*Wesen*]'). 'Indeed, true thinking must even be objectively independent of that subject that reflects upon it; in other words it will think all the more truly, the less the subject interferes with it.'[57]

Recognising *oneself* and *misrecognising* oneself are thus, quite independently of the play on words provided by the homophony in French of *me connaître* and *méconnaître*,[58] names of one concept. In order for it to be seen clearly one must analyse the ambiguity of the concept of the subject which makes it susceptible to equivocations. Just as there is an 'Other beyond the other',[59] so there is a 'subject in the subject, transcending the subject',[60] a 'sujet véritable' (*Je*) in and at the same time beyond the 'sujet narcissique' (*moi*). Their relationship does not obey the law of representation (for there is no original and repeatable presence of the 'I' (*Ich*) which could be made present again – re-presented – in the 'I' (*ich*): the two subjects are 'not concentric'), but is determined by an order of radical inversion. 'Reflection', as Schelling strongly emphasised, means 'mirroring' and consequently 'inversion'.[61] The being of one party in the relationship is reflected in the other as non-being and vice versa ('I think where I am not, therefore I am where I do not think').[62] Novalis called this law the 'ordo inversus'.[63] It corrects, as it were from within, the illusions of the idealistic view for which the world stands on its head. It is precisely not the equal possibility of two points of view (only inverse in relation to each other) that is put forward in its name; rather the experience of the self-negation of thinking (*cogito*) demands the location of the being of subjectivity beyond the reflexive dyad 'in a third place',[64] that of the Other, 'to which I am bound more closely than to myself, since in the utmost depth of my identity with myself it is it which is active through me

---

[57] Friedrich Wilhelm Joseph Schelling, *Sämtliche Werke* (Stuttgart, 1856–61), part I, vol. x, pp. 5ff. (English in F.W.J. Schelling, *On the History of Modern Philosophy*, trans. A. Bowie (Cambridge, 1994), p. 47–8); 11f. See also part II, vol. I, p. 301: 'Just as we ourselves had to see from the "I am" of Cartesius that it expresses after all only a being that is doubtful, admittedly not to me who pronounces it but *in itself.*'

[58] *Ecrits*, p. 808.   [59] *Ibid.*, p. 439.   [60] *Ibid.*, p. 437.

[61] Schelling, *Sämtliche Werke*, part I, vol. x, p. 234.   [62] *Ecrits*, p. 517.

[63] For a detailed discussion of this see M. Frank and G. Kurz, 'Ordo inversus. Zu einer Reflexionsfigur bei Novalis, Hölderlin, Kleist und Kafka', in *Geist und Zeichen*, Festschrift für Arthur Henkel (Heidelberg, 1977), pp. 75–97.

[64] *Ecrits*, p. 525.

[à qui je suis plus attaché qu'à moi, puisque au sein le plus assenti de mon identité à moi-même, c'est lui qui m'agite]'.[65]

This expression very clearly marks the crossroads at which a speculative dialectic must part from a 'dialectic of desire', although the latter quite frequently flirts with concepts borrowed from the former. Certainly Hegel too sees the ground against which contradiction is smashed to pieces as a Third in relation to the moments of reflection which exclude but at the same time demand each other.

But the programme of his logic of essence (*Wesen*) promises to derive this third element from its own organisation of reflection, in other words immanently. This is why Lacan accuses him of having, by his successful criticism of the narrowness of self-consciousness, which imagines that it possesses the general immediately in the law of its own heart, achieved only an apparent victory over narcissism. Just as the 'raging of crazy self-conceit' [66] is intent on blaming its own invertedness on the generality of the Other outside itself, so too the Hegelian system avoids tautology, which it denounces, only at the cost of grounding the 'tauto-ontics of the beautiful soul' all the more firmly in the completed mediation of the original invertedness with the order of the self.[67]

It is also appropriate, however, to have similar reservations about a philosophical hermeneutics which abandons the ideal of absolute self-mediation on the part of the historical subject without at the same time refraining from orientating itself towards the methodological model of a dialectic of self-understanding in being Other – i.e. towards a teleology of meaning. Gadamer's reversal of the path of Hegel's dialectics remains, as we have seen, committed to dialectics.

This objection ought to be considered, because precisely Gadamer and Lacan (Hermann Lang's study lays strong emphasis on this) appear to be in agreement when it comes to obtaining a hearing for the true claim of the discourse of the Other against the self-appointed authority of individual empathy on the one hand and its reduction to reified standards of decoding on the other. Behind the intuitionistic and the scientistic approaches they both

---

[65] *Ibid.*, p. 524.　　[66] Hegel, *Phänomenologie des Geistes*, p. 271.　　[67] *Ecrits*, p. 415.

detect defence and/or transference mechanisms in the service of reflection, which attempt to dissolve the 'Other Discourse' in the sulphuric acid bath of imaginary identifications of the self and of objects. While placing the pure *relation* between interpreter and interpretand above these elements,[68] and thus truly acting as a corrective to extreme subjectivism, Gadamer's dialectic nevertheless does no more than come up against the limits of dialectical speculation from the inside. For the relationship between the communicating horizons to be justifiably described as a process analogous to living experience, it must be possible for it to be internalised by the interpreting subject. But to introduce a centre of internalisation means, however unintentionally, to bring into play the structure of self-relationship. And instantly the humility, undeniably intended, of dedication to the happening of tradition shrinks to a mere intention: all understanding ultimately remains – in an involuntarily limiting sense – specular self-understanding[69] (not necessarily on the part of the individual, but certainly on the part of the happening of language thought of as the subject). Thus with Gadamer too, under the headings of 'language as the speculative centre' and the 'merging of horizons', the cunning of dialectical self-consciousness triumphs over its humiliation as self-conceit.

In this way one becomes convinced that the agreement between the 'merging of horizons' and what Lacan calls 'parole pleine'[70] exists only as an intention.[71] For anyone who thinks of subjectivity as I-ness (*moüté*) – and neither Hegel nor Gadamer escapes this consequence – precisely the fact of the completed merging of two 'I'-horizons becomes a trap set by narcissism, a trap which invites one to repress the otherness of the 'grand Autre' by means of the 'autre spéculaire' of reflection (it is no accident that Gadamer, while analysing his method, hits upon the 'speculative structure of

---

[68] Gadamer, 'Zur Problematik des Selbstverständnisses. Ein hermeneutischer Beitrag zur Frage der "Entmythologisierung"', in *Einsichten*, Festschrift für G. Krüger (Frankfurt am Main, 1962), p. 77.

[69] Gadamer, *Wahrheit und Methode*, p. 246.   [70] *Ecrits*, pp. 247ff.

[71] Of course Derrida ('Le facteur de la vérité', pp. 128ff., 142f.) sees precisely the chain *parole, plénitude, propriété, authenticité, vérité qua* 'adéquation de la parole pleine à elle-même' (p. 129) as the main evidence for his thesis that in the last resort Lacan adheres to traditional 'phonologocentrism'.

language': it is a reflection of the self in the Other, 'a doubling which is nevertheless only the existence of one').[72] But beyond the *certainty* which it has of itself the conversation which carries the consensus is revealed in its *truth* as a metaphor (and thus as a disguise) for a discourse which can be neither specularised nor anticipated by prior understanding, a discourse which is spoken in another arena than that of communication and which is protected by the irremediable absence of a subject-originator from in any way solidifying to become a representer of truth.

In order to realise the ambiguity of the discourse spoken *ad hominem* (to which hermeneutics and the linguistics of communication confine themselves), so as to perceive behind the staging of the manifest discourse the action which is performed in the '*other arena*', we must, Lacan says, first and foremost 'be imbued with the radical difference of the Other, to which (our) discourse is to be addressed, and of this second other, namely of the one (we) see before (us) and by whom and through whom the first speaks to (us) in the discourse which it conducts here before (us). For only in this way shall (we) be able to be (those) to (whom) the discourse is addressed [pénétré de la différence radicale de l'Autre auquel sa parole doit s'adresser, et de ce second autre qui est celui qu'il voit et dont et par qui le premier lui parle dans le discours qu'il poursuit devant lui. Car c'est ainsi qu'il saura être celui à qui ce discours s'adresse].'[73] It is precisely the visibility of the Other and the audibility of its discourse, but also the discursive logic, abstracted from the discourse as its *rule* of formation, which it obeys,[74] in short the presence of the Other and the agreement between its discourse and the discursive order of communication as such and in general that enable dialogue to become the entry-point for *misrecognition*, i.e. for the inverted order of reflection, whose metaphysical legacy hermeneutic discourse also feeds on.

A simple linguistic analysis does indeed reveal that talk of the happening of tradition as a setting itself to work of truth thinks of the textualisation of being as re-presentation (the use of the reflexive pronoun in such contexts is never accidental). If the 'grand Autre' were radically imagined as that *Néant* which by its removal

---

[72] Gadamer, *Wahrheit und Methode*, pp. 432ff., 441.   [73] *Ecrits*, p. 430.   [74] *Ibid.*

allows the empty trace of an unstable parasemic context to be glimpsed between the 'termes pleins' of the battery of signifiers ('it is that which is not which determines that which is'),[75] it would not be possible to treat this trace as the material reflection of a signified. The logic of the order of signs does not reflect something represented: it replaces or rather stands in for its absence. There is simply no other pole of the dyad of reflection (unless one were to speak – questionably – of something that is not as being represented by something that is).

The subject of the Other has 'no mirror-image, in other words no alterity'[76] at all. Therefore the discourse of the Other could never testify to its own truth (dire 'le vrai sur le vrai' – say 'what is true about what is true'):[77] for it would then need not only to exist but at the same time to see the yardstick of its truth before it and thus to be able to be at the same time in the truth and outside it. But the truth of the unconscious (if one can use this metaphysical title at all here) has no specular double, and one cannot look over the shoulder of its discourse from a meta-language situated at an Archimedean point: 'One does not see oneself as one is'.[78]

This invisibility of the *'true self'* – is it not connected with its radical *uniqueness*? The individual is that which is by its nature unrepeatable and uncommunicable (and it is 'only' with it, Lacan says in the foreword to the German translation of his *Writings*, that analysis is concerned).[79] Nevertheless, the true subject is not a beyond of communication: it is by withdrawing itself from the linguistic happening that it invests the material signifiers with the meaning that is exchanged. The same is true of the rules of formation of discourses, the grammar of texts, the structure of symbolic connections, in fact of all intersubjective and codified orders. Only something radically individual (unique and impossible to reduplicate) could successfully withstand the paraphrase which would seek to subject the various utterances to one common deep semantics and declare the law of identical repeatability to be the law of their being. It is the law of *truth* which always makes the claim to divisibility/communicability and can demonstrate its validity only by the fact that its propositions are capable of

---

[75] Sartre, *L'être et le néant*, p. 130.   [76] *Écrits.*, p. 818.   [77] *Ibid.*, p. 867.   [78] *Ibid.*
[79] Lacan, *Schriften*, 2 vols. (Olten and Freiburg, 1973 and 1975), vol. II, p. 12.

generalisation. The universal structure does indeed depend, irre-
versibly, on the 'particular'[80] and the individual:[81] 'What the structure of the chain of signifiers reveals', says Lacan, 'is the possibility
that I can use it, precisely to the extent that the language is common to me and others, i.e. that this language exists (as a codified
system), to designate by it *everything other* than what it says [Ce que
cette structure de la chaîne signifiante découvre, c'est la possibilité
que j'ai, justement dans la mesure où sa langue m'est commune
avec d'autre sujets, c'est-à-dire où cette langue existe, de m'en
servir pour signifier *toute autre chose* que ce qu'elle dit].'[82] In other
words, the intersubjective generalness of the structure contains no
definitive prescription for the semantic effects of discourse (as
Peirce has shown). 'What belongs to the same structure [has] not
necessarily the same meaning.'[83] We know how Lacan mocks the
exponents of information theory who take the language of bees as a
model for the process of understanding – 'with the most confused
results'.[84] The obsession with lack of ambiguity and rule-led deciphering which is typical not only of methodical hermeneutics and
analytical philosophy but also of the analysis of discourse as in-
itiated by Foucault, bears all the marks of a repression of what is
perhaps 'a little too self-evident' and so can expect to meet with
ridicule from Lacan. After all, he shows in details (though without
making explicit references) that these procedures (which, incidentally, Derrida mentions in one breath: Ricœur, Searle, Foucault[85])
hold up a model of discourse oriented towards reflection: it is precisely the relativity of the discourse to the 'acceptance of the principle of a rule of debate which does not proceed without an explicit
or implicit agreement about what is called its basis' – precisely this
dependence on a 'corpus of rules' which is always historically codified – Foucault's 'archive', Searle's 'universals of linguistic use', etc.
– that keeps discursive reason in the thrall of the narcissism of

---

[80] *Ecrits*, p. 14.
[81] For this reason, as Derrida has rightly objected, one should really not speak of a 'truth' (=
generalisability) of the 'I' ('Le facteur de la vérité'). For Lacan, however, 'science' and
'truth' are not names of a concept. (See also 'La science et la vérité', *Ecrits*, pp. 855–77:
'There is no science of man, because man does not exist, but only his subject' (*ibid.*, p.
859).) There is a 'division of the subject between truth and knowledge' (*ibid.*, p. 864).
[82] *Ecrits*, p. 505.   [83] *Ibid.*, p. 14.   [84] *Ibid.*, p. 18(f.) (see also p. 297).
[85] Self-quotation by Derrida in 'Limited Inc. abc', *Glyph* 2 (1977).

specularisable and 'almost always anticipated prior agreements about what is at stake (presque toujours . . . un accord anticipé sur son enjeu)' in the debate which it wants to conduct.[86]

What is it that ultimately foils the efforts of the Prefect of Police in Poe's detective story *The Purloined Letter*? Was the search perhaps poorly planned, were the logistics at fault, or the organisation? Lacan lays great emphasis on the fact that it was undertaken 'as a theoretically incontestable exhaustive search of the area' in which the letter must be, and that the police action displays all the characteristics of a correct execution of the imperative of a rational criminalistic plan.[87] The mistake does not lie in the area of logistics and of the deductive conclusions. What prevents success is the structure, the plan itself, because it believes it can discover a radically *singular thing* (matérialité du signifiant . . . *singulière*)[88] in the domain of an order of the *general*:[89] equipped, naturally, with legal hypotheses and corresponding anticipations and of course using a methodical approach. Here of course a *category mistake* with far-reaching consequences is at work; and the oracular commonplace that Dupin takes a malicious pleasure in writing in the 'faithful replica' of the letter on the card-rack is very appropriate to it: 'Un dessein si funeste,/ S'il n'est pas digne d'Atrée, est digne de Thyeste.' Lacan, incidentally, quotes the first words as 'un destin',

---

[86] *Ecrits*, pp. 430–1.   [87] *Ibid.*, p. 23.   [88] *Ibid.*, p. 24.
[89] 'But if we have first of all insisted on the the materiality of the signifier, this materiality is *singular* in many ways, the first of which is that it does not allow any division . . . This is because the signifier is a unity because of its uniqueness, being by its nature a symbol only of an absence' (*Ecrits*, p. 24). Derrida sees in this phrase a movement of 'idealisation of the signifier', which understands it as the 'intangibility of an identity of its own displacing itself without alteration' ('Le facteur de la vérité', p. 126): Derrida confuses individuality and subjectivity, conceiving of the former according to the model of the 'interrupted identity', i.e. the relationship of the self to itself; but it makes no sense to think of the 'individual' (*das Einzelne*) as an instance of truth, of reflection, of identically repeatable presence, as Hegel's furious outbursts against 'the individual' (*das Individuelle*) show. (On this point there are conflicting assertions in Derrida's text: on the one hand he says that Lacan 'disqualifies the insertion of the privileged signifier into a register, its repeatability' ('Le facteur de la vérité', p. 130) – after all, 'it implies an irreplaceability, it excludes all deceptive images of a double' (p. 127); on the other hand precisely its singularity is supposed to 'guarantee [it] a repeatable identity' (p. 132), as though the individual (*das Individuelle*) had a 'registered', iterable and communicable 'meaning'.) Lacan is consistent here: could he otherwise call the individual (*das Einzelne*) a *symbol of absence*? As a privation (something robbed of true being, something which *is* not) it has always been excluded from the metaphysical order of *truth*: it is the invisible limit of that order and, as becomes apparent, a challenge to it.

Poe has 'dessin' and the the German translators write 'dessein',
which is undoubtedly philologically correct. However, the ambiguity is welcome, as Lacan's paraphrase shows:[90] what seemed to
be a baneful 'plan' changes for the owner of the signifier in question
to a 'destiny' which has him dancing on a string and ties together
his desires. It is the destiny of *reflection*, whose methodical acuity is
ruined by the uniqueness of the Other. (This does not mean, by the
way, that interpretation is arbitrary: 'Interpretation is not open to
all meanings.' It isolates, as Freud says, a *core of non-meaning*, without
wishing wholly to free it from ambiguity. All the same, 'interpretation is significative and can be wrong',[91] and consequently there is
'an authentic interpretation'.)[92]

If I have presented the corrective qualities of Lacan's criticism of
reflection in an exaggerated way, I am – as I must confess in
conclusion – not convinced that his theory of the subject has an
adequate foundation. What remains unclear above all is the core of
the matter, the interaction of *Je* and *moi* which – despite their
'excentricity' and 'heterogeneity' – must somehow be connected, in
order – and everything depends on this – to be valid in relation to
different aspects of a *single* 'I'-structure. Also it does not by any
means follow from the 'supremacy of the signifier in the subject'[93]
that it would be possible to explain phenomena such as meaning
and consciousness – however much they may 'slide' or 'flow' – *solely*
on the basis of the relationship between signifiers. (This objection
may of course be directed even more strongly against Lacan's critic,
Derrida.) Leaving aside the fact that so-called 'neutral monism' –
the theory of consciousness of some Anglo-Saxon pragmaticists –
already failed because of a similar problem,[94] there lies concealed
behind Lacan's apparently idiosyncratic phrase about the 'signifier
that represents the subject for another signifier'[95] a loose quotation
from Marx, 'One use value represents the exchange for another use
value.'[96] In this *quid pro quo* too the subject is 'subverted' and now
appears only as a value-reflex of the commodity-signifier: but

[90] *Ecrits*, p. 40.   [91] Lacan, *Le séminaire*, xi, pp. 225f.   [92] *Ecrits*, p. 353.
[93] See also *ibid.*, p. 20.
[94] See also Dieter Henrich, 'Selbstbewußtsein', in *Hermeneutik und Dialektik* i (Tübingen,
     1970), pp. 257f., 262f.
[95] *Ecrits*, p. 819.
[96] Karl Marx, Friedrich Engels, *Werke* (Berlin, 1956), vol. xxiii, pp. 67, 70f.

behind the conclusion that it is non-existent, or even merely that it is deferred, there lurks the trap of commodity fetishism, which Sartre rediscovered, rightly, I think, in the structuralist 'chosisme du signifiant' ('thing-ism of the signifier').[97] The symbolic order is after all the codification of a living world-view: should the *great Other* – as a super-individual who, acting as the highest instance, expropriates the practices of the speakers – take responsibility for its constant change? I am noting these reservations, which I have dealt with more fully elsewhere,[98] merely in passing, in order to avoid giving the impression that I think that 'on points' Lacan defeats existentialist hermeneutics on the one hand and the structuralism of the theory of discourse on the other.

It is my view, however, that overall there is justification for speaking of Lacan's hermeneutics. Derrida practically does so, albeit with a nasty look: 'What is going on there is hermeneutic deciphering, despite appearances or the denial.'[99] If Lacan is nevertheless rather wary of that designation, this is probably chiefly because the hermeneuticians – especially his disloyal pupil Ricœur[100] – use it for a programme that makes too many concessions to the dialectic of specular self-mediation on the one hand and to the model of codes and decoding on the other (as well as Ricœur, L. Goldmann also shows how little these approaches are mutually exclusive). 'Traditions', too, which play such a prominent role in Gadamer, are of course symbolic *orders*, as truly as they are languages; and it makes little difference that Gadamer – unlike the structuralists and system theorists who have revised his work – dislikes using the concept of a 'rule' because of its closeness to that of a method.

---

[97] Sartre, *L'idiot de la famille*, vol. III, p. 100. Of course this is not the only reference. Sartre has also repeatedly justified the comparison with commodity fetishism.

[98] Manfred Frank, *Das Individuelle-Allgemeine*, pp. 87ff.

[99] Derrida, 'Le facteur de la vérité', p. 113.

[100] But how could one be a 'disciple' of Lacan without becoming an apostate? In any case Derrida suggests, though not explicitly, that Lacan's psychoanalysis differs only in inessential points from the analytical hermeneutics of Ricœur – which has many advantages in terms of concepts and textual theory. For Lacan too, he suggests, the signifier is only the detour which the subject has to take in order to return to its original act of existence: a circular movement which is certainly indisputable in the case of the seminar on *The Purloined Letter*. (*The Purloined Letter*: the letter delivered by a circuitous route.) See also 'Le facteur de la vérité', p. 111.

If Lacan keeps his distance from hermeneutics in this sense, he does come close – this claim sounds a little forced, I know – to Romantic hermeneutics, in which the concept of the individual and thus of the radical non-harmonisability of the Other were central. Not every use of the category of subject has narcissistic interests: this prejudice persists only on the basis of inadequate differentiations, which have not always been avoided even in existentialist hermeneutics or so-called post-structuralism. The intensive preoccupation with the problems of individuality, for instance in the hermeneutics of Schleiermacher and Humboldt, has ensured that no-one could believe that the individuality of the Other could be merged with the horizon of one's own. And this is not because it would not fit into the framework of the context of a tradition, the rules of grammar or the principles of formation of a so-called discourse, but simply *because sharing in these general structures does not of itself make it an* individual.

The individual, which could not be represented by a sys-tematised knowledge – at best a 'proper name' could do this[101] – is, unlike the particular, not a 'case' which can be subsumed under a 'rule'. It slips, just like Lacan's 'sujet-néant', through all the meshes of the structure, for it is *what has no counterpart.* How could one possibly extract it from the general by means of 'comparison', i.e. separating it out by distinguishing and comparing? Schleiermacher demonstrated the vicious circle in which anyone who tries to extract a singular meaning from a totality of general meanings becomes embroiled: if the meaning has not previously, in an original 'divina-tion', been instituted and fixed within its limits as that unique meaning, it could not become accessible to any structural analysis (Schleiermacher says to any 'comparative method').[102]

Have we – at the very end of this chapter – strayed right away from Lacan? I do not think so. What is the sudden inspiration (Derrida skirts round it like the devil avoiding the pentagram) by which Dupin in *The Purloined Letter* thwarts the plans of the Prefect of Police and the minister? We have read it aright: it is the *'thorough* identification' with the mind of his opponent, the divinatory 'ad-

---

[101] *Ecrits*, p. 868.
[102] F.D.E. Schleiermacher, *Hermeneutik und Kritik. Mit einem Anhang sprachphilosophischer Texte Schleiermachers*, ed. Manfred Frank (Frankfurt am Main, 1977), p. 169f.

measurement of the intellect with which (he) is engaged'. What led the Prefect into his 'perpetual error' was not the lack but the hypertrophy of 'highly ingenious resources'. 'A certain set of highly ingenious resources are, with the Prefect, a sort of Procrustean bed, to which he forcibly adapts his designs. But he perpetually errs by being too deep or too shallow for the matter in hand.'[103] He should not have leapt over subjectivity – neither his own nor that of the Other – but only have taken care to reach the 'true' subjectivity, the 'sujet véritable' and not the 'moi imaginaire et duelle' and its rule-obsessed shadow-boxing. The 'truth as an effect of the unconscious' is not to be prejudged by any kind of 'classificatory order': that would be a reduction in which the *true subject* and its *thought* (in the sense in which Freud speaks of dream *thoughts*) would fall by the wayside ('C'est pourtant là une réduction qui y néglige le sujet – And yet that is a reduction which neglects the subject').[104]

If, as Derrida stresses, Lacan leaves no doubt that Dupin's successful approach represents as an ideal type that of the analyst, it is worth looking at it very closely. 'The identification . . . of the reasoner's intellect with that of his opponent depends . . . upon the accuracy with which the opponent's intellect is admeasured.' And this is done not by over-hasty 'empathy' in the sense that one's own idea is as it were pulled over that of the Other. On the contrary, 'The Prefect and his cohort fail so frequently . . . [because] they consider only their *own* ideas of ingenuity; and, in searching for any thing hidden, advert only to the modes in which *they* would have hidden it' (i.e. the letter).[105] The identification succeeds precisely through an extreme measure of distrust of one's own intellectual horizon and the phantasmagoria of the 'I' (*moi*), in other words through an extreme effort at putting oneself aside.

Let us understand this correctly: in order to find an idea in its uniqueness, one must not apply the anonymous principles of formation of an 'archive' (like that of Foucault) – a sort of hermeneutics of observances – nor follow the imperatives of a strategy valid *in all comparable cases*; one must invent as an addition to the signifier in question its own thoroughly open meaning (its

[103] *The Complete Tales and Poems of Edgar Allan Poe*, with an introduction by Hervey Allen (New York, 1938), pp. 215f.
[104] *Ecrits*, p. 871.   [105] *The Complete Tales and Poems of Edgar Allan Poe*, p. 216.

'interpretant', as Peirce calls it), if one wants to make it speak. Signifiers just do not speak of their own accord. And 'thoughts' are happenings which never come about *without* an underlying structure, but that does not mean that they are brought about *by* the structure (the *necessary cause* is not in itself the *causa per quam* of a meaning). This, I think, is the intended meaning of the admonition contained in the motto placed at the head of Lacan's *Séminaire*: it is 'luck' and 'fate' which make the find possible; it does not look as if it can be forced by means of a method . . .

Let us listen to Lacan himself:

'I want . . . to show that what belongs to the same structure does not necessarily have the same meaning. For this reason, too, there is only analysis of the particular: an identical structure by no means arises from a unified meaning, especially not when it affects discourse.

'There is no general meaning of the hysterical, and what the identification focuses on in this or that case is (merely) the structure and not the meaning.'

Is this really something different from what Schleiermacher says? Lacan continues:

'The fact that the analysts, or let us say those who . . . regard themselves as such . . . whether they follow me or not, have not yet grasped that what goes into the matrix of discourse is not meaning but signs, gives an exact idea of what is meant by the passion for ignorance.'[106]

And:

'The meaning of meaning in *my* practice can be grasped [se saisit] from the fact that it . . . flows – as from a barrel, and not in the sense of running away.

'By flowing (as from a barrel) a discourse acquires its meaning, that is to say, by the fact that its effects would be impossible to calculate.

'The point of meaning, one feels it, is the riddle.'[107]

I believe that today's theory of discourse and hermeneutics should be reminded of this, in the name of Lacan – and of Romantic hermeneutics.

---

[106] Lacan, *Schriften*, vol. II, p. 12f.
[107] *Ibid.*, p. 7.

CHAPTER 4

The entropy of language: reflections on the Searle–Derrida debate

'Das ächte Dividuum ist auch das ächte Individuum' (The
truly divided is also the true individual)
                    Novalis, *Das allgemeine Brouillon*, no. 952

Many are the theories of truth. Yet whether one defines truth as
bringing thinking into line with reality, or as a 'thought' (*Gedanke*)
through which what is the case can be asserted; as the disclosed-
ness of being, or as harmony between the beliefs of subjects who
communicate with one another – in the classical view truth still
remains a matter of strict universality. This differentiates it from –
to use Frege's terminology – the *Vorstellung* (representation), which
is always bound to one and only one carrier and, despite its
certainty, can be neither shared nor communicated. An essential
quality of truth is that it is valid not only for me or you but for *all*
individuals who take hold of that particular thought, and also for
all cases covered by it. The actual propositions which have been
declared to be true or false at different stages in the history of
mankind have evidently not remained the same. However, this
does not in principle alter the fact that at the time when these
propositions were being asserted as truths, universal (if hypothetical) validity was always claimed for them. Another characteristic
seems to me important: a single statement that is 'obviously true'
is, precisely for that reason, no longer individual but a formulation
of a general fact. It appeals to a wider logical syntax[1] which defines

I wish to thank Rudi Keller for critically reading through the manuscript of this chapter.
The present version takes account of many of his objections.

[1] I use this term not in the sense in which it is used by Rudolf Carnap and others, but to
mean a structure of relations between the terms of a scientific system.

its place and raises it to the status of a function affecting all other true statements. Functions are elements of a system and consequently not individuals.

Now there is no reason to suppose a priori that an ordered arrangement of ideas is more basic than a juxtaposition of concepts together or side by side in no particular order. If, just for fun, one were to draw an analogical conclusion from the Second Principle of Thermodynamics – known as the Law of Entropy – it would rather suggest that there is a greater probability of disorder than of order, and that closed systems are most strongly inclined, unless hindered by a supply of energy, to bring about their own disintegration. Philosophy should therefore, to quote a humorous piece of advice from Whitehead, 'evolve a general concept which allows room for both [order and disorder]'.[2]

Now, to create an order of thoughts means first and foremost to eliminate individual representations in favour of a standardised knowledge which a community of researchers unanimously regards as having universal validity. And this exclusion of the individual is not suspect: it is intrinsic to the concept of the calculation or the law which governs scientific work. Unlike intuitions, which according to the classical understanding relate directly to individual things, cognitions are indirect: they too relate to things, but only 'by means of a characteristic that is common to several [and in the case of *pure* concepts, all] things' (Kant, *Critique of Pure Reason*, A 320/B 377). Representations which have been defined by the consciousness of their unity and thus raised to the level of a cognition are by that very fact put together according to a rule. The rule prescribes how the intuition is to be guided in order that it shall relate the many possible aspects of something that exists to a concept by means of which it can at the same time be defined as a complex of elements of an order. Now there are no set criteria for such a unification and order; and 'by reason of the essential individuality of the many things, there are conflicts' between different attempts at synthesis: the orders that are produced are and remain relative to the choice of perspective and ultimately of the world-view which guides the

---

[2] Alfred North Whitehead, 'Understanding', in *Modes of Thought* (Cambridge, 1938), p. 70.

search for insight and under which the manifold has been synthesised. In this way the order of the whole and the chaos of the
individual aspects – or, let us say, system and entropy – are not
scientific rivals but aspects of a twofold movement which is that
of the scientific process itself.[3]

One could imagine that if Whitehead were able here and now to
express his opinion on such an 'improbable' (*LI*, g)[4] debate as the
one carried on in the periodical *Glyph* between John R. Searle and
Jacques Derrida, he would characterise this debate as a 'confrontation' between options that are by no means incompatible. One
of the protagonists is an analytical philosopher striving by means
of a class of pragmasemantic universals to bring under control the
multiplicity of speech acts that occur; the other disputes the possibility of such an order – if it sees itself as definitive and thus 'true' –
on the basis that there is no criterion for two uses of one and the
same linguistic type having identical meaning or even just playing
the same 'illocutionary role'. I hasten to add that this characterisation is entirely my own and is terribly simplified; but as it is not my
last word but as it were my first word on this controversy, it may be
permissible and even welcome as a signpost in the jungle of
arguments and objections.

THE BACKGROUND TO THE DEBATE

This is how it all came about: in August 1971, at the *Congrès
international des sociétés de philosophie de langue française* (in Montreal) –
the theme was 'Communication' – Derrida had presented a text
of some length entitled *Signature événement contexte*. In the two final
chapters he had discussed Austin's analysis of performatives,
which he characterises as 'patient, open, aporetical, in constant
transformation, often more fruitful in the acknowledgement of
its impasses than in its positions' (*Sec*, p. 383; English, *Glyph* 1,

---

[3] *Ibid.*
[4] In what follows, I use the abbreviation *LI* to refer to the text of Derrida's reply to Searle's
intervention, 'Limited Inc. a b c'. I am using a proof copy of the French original, which
subsequently appeared in print in an English translation (and also as a 'supplement' in
French) in *Glyph* 2 (1977). To enable my quotations to be checked, I give, after the
abbreviation, not a page number but the letter which Derrida uses (in alphabetical order)
as a heading for each unit in his argument.

p. 187).[5] In particular he had discussed possible motives for Austin's exclusion of so-called 'infelicities', i.e. unsuccessful speech acts, from the corpus of *standard* or *normal performatives*.

For the moment I will confine myself to this aspect. In order to maintain control over the proliferation of infelicities, Austin is obliged, in Derrida's view, to operate with the concept of an exhaustively definable context ('total context'). This premise in its turn requires – implicitly or explicitly – the concept of an intentional consciousness which is wholly transparent to itself. It suggests a 'conscious presence of the intention of the speaking subject in the totality of his speech act' (*Sec*, p. 383; English, *Glyph* 1, p. 187): furthermore, this presence of the intention in its utterances must be complete and adequate, i.e. there must remain 'no residue, either in the definition of the requisite conventions, or in the grammatical form, or in the semantic determination of the words employed; no irreducible polysemy, that is, no "dissemination" escaping the horizon of the unity of meaning' (*Sec*, p. 384; English, *Glyph* 1, pp. 187–8). On the other hand there *are* these infelicities, and Austin cannot avoid admitting that they constitute not only a 'constant' but actually a 'necessary and internal possibility' of the use of language. From this Derrida draws the conclusion that the meaning-effects of discourse can never be conventionally 'mastered' (*maîtrisé*) and controlled with Cartesian certainty, that there is no pre-stabilised harmony between the animating intention and its expression, and that every 'iteration' of a speech act calls into question the identity of the type and thus the norm of *standard discourse*. Austin's downgrading and devaluation in principle of indirect speech, 'metaphorical' (*uneigentlich*) or 'parasitical speech' is therefore, Derrida says, at best strategically understandable but not justified.

What Derrida is concerned about may perhaps be summed up as follows: 'If a misunderstanding (for example of Austin's theses) is possible, if a *mis-* in general ("mistake", "misunderstanding", "misinterpretation", "misstatement" . . .) is possible, what does that imply concerning the structure of speech acts in general?' (*LI*, g).

Searle replied in 1977 in the first issue of *Glyph*, selectively and

[5] Under this abbreviation I quote from 'Signature événement contexte,' in *Marges de la philosophie* (Paris, 1972), pp. 365–93; English version by Samuel Weber and Jeffrey Mehlmann, 'Signature Event Context', *Glyph* 1 (1977), pp. 172–97.

focusing 'on those [points] that seem to me to [be] the most important and especially on those where I disagree with his conclusions' (*R*, p. 198).[6] As an analytically trained thinker, he admits to not finding Derrida's style of argument especially clear, and in particular he levels at him the accusation that 'Derrida's Austin is quite unrecognizable. He bears almost no relation to the original'; 'thus the confrontation never quite takes place' (*R*, pp. 204, 198). At one point he briefly considers a more 'sympathetic reading of Derrida's text' (*ibid.*, p. 207), but this kindly impulse cannot dispel his general impression: 'Derrida has a distressing penchant for saying things that are obviously false' (*ibid.*, p. 203).

Searle's two-part reply contains a series of discussions, of criticisms of Derrida's arguments and of attempts to reformulate certain positions of speech act theory more rigorously, where possible creating new definitions. Where Searle merely rejects Derrida's conclusions or complains about his divergent use of analytical scholarly terminology, I feel that on the whole what Searle indicates at the opening as a possibility is indeed the case, 'that I may have misinterpreted him as profoundly as I believe he has misinterpreted Austin' (*ibid.*, p. 198). However, what proves to be fruitful and significant for the further course of 'this improbable confrontation' (*LI*, g), which only now develops into a real debate between Searle and Derrida, is Searle's somewhat discursive attempt to specify what he understands by 'meaning' and 'intention'. His discussion of the role of the 'parasitical' and of 'infelicities' is closely linked with that attempt.

Derrida's latest response (of which I am using a hand-corrected proof copy in French) quotes Searle's 'Reply' almost in its entirety. Instead of first having to give some account of the course of the debate, therefore, I can turn to it straight away.

Derrida – I have quoted this twice already – calls the debate 'improbable'. And the very precondition without which it would not only 'not quite' take place, but not take place at all, is improbable: namely that there is a kind of minimal agreement between the two protagonists about the nature of a system of 'types' which bring about communication.

---

[6] Under the abbreviation *R* I quote in my text passages from John R. Searle, 'Reiterating the Differences: A Reply to Derrida', *Glyph* 1 (1977), pp. 198–208.

THE MINIMAL CONSENSUS: CONVENTIONALITY AND ITERABILITY

It is – in the view of Searle and Derrida – a necessary condition of semiotic systems that all the participants in a particular linguistic group identify the meaning-bearing elements as the same by means of identical materials of expression. Any number of 'tokens' in spoken or written discourse can be traced back to a finite number of 'types', of which they are the concrete realisation. In other words, every participant in the language must traverse the materials of expression that are in circulation in order to get at the same meanings, and link them together according to uniform rules.

Ever since Humboldt, if not before, this structural requirement of every symbolic interaction has appeared trivial. Trivialities, however, always have the advantage of being acknowledged as 'obviously true' – even when it is a matter of starting up a dialogue between a continental European and an Anglo-Saxon thinker. (The English Channel, which separates the British Isles from the European mainland, has in philosophical works of the last twenty years acquired a considerable value as a metaphor for the irreconcilability of two styles of thinking; though this view is emphatically denied by Derrida (*LI*, g): he takes up his own position outside this epistemological rejection.)

Let us remember, then, that there is a 'minimal agreement' here (*LI*, r). Searle himself stresses this several times, thereby making it clear that he does not regard it as trivial. 'Without iterability', he says, 'there is no language at all' (*R*, p. 206). 'Iterability . . . is a necessary condition of the particular forms of intentionality that are characteristic of speech acts' (*ibid.*, pp. 207–8). 'As Derrida is aware, any linguistic element, written or spoken, indeed any rule-governed element in any system of representation at all must be repeatable, otherwise the rules would have no scope of application. To say this is just to say that the logician's type/token distinction must apply generally to all the rule-governed elements of language in order that the rules can be applied to new occurrences of the phenomena specified by the rules. Without this feature of iterability there could not be the possibility of producing an infinite number of sentences with a finite list of elements; and this, as philosophers since Frege have recognized, is one of the crucial features of any language' (*ibid.*, p. 199). And finally, 'any conventional act involves the notion of the repetition of the same' (*ibid.*, p. 207).

Thus Searle. In order to see where his conclusions differ from those drawn by Derrida, I will first attempt to show the metaphysical implications which are contained in his definitions. In Searle's view the iterability of conventional symbols is, firstly, a basic requirement of functioning communication. Secondly, by virtue of the recursivity of linguistic rules it includes an ability to communicate 'an infinite number of different contents' (*ibid.*, p. 208), and thirdly it is the necessary repetition of something identical, since otherwise the completeness of the system could not be guaranteed. By taking into account all conceivable contexts, the proliferation of which is again controlled and limited by a finite number of types of possible linguistic use, every speech act by any competent participant in the language can be identified as a realisation of this and only of this quite specific meaning-intention, because all have the same access to the universals of linguistic use. Already at this point one can observe that there is no fundamental difference between the system of pragmatic conventions and the traditional grammatical model. The latter had focused only on the codification of descriptive utterances and was able to ignore the intentional 'animation' of these statements in specific contexts of action. Statements are linguistic units; their elements are called expressions. Austin and Searle, on the other hand, devote themselves to the analysis of utterances, i.e. of situated sentences, as the pragmatic–semantic units of discourse. If they introduce the aspect of intentionality into the spectrum of linguistic philosophy, this is not in order to jeopardise the structuralist or generative-grammar concept of the 'linguistic system'. Searle speaks, in terms that cannot be misunderstood, of a 'taxonomy of illocutionary acts'.[7] One could say, with some simplification, that the encoding and decoding of the utterances follow the same model of operation as the input and output of utterances.

---

[7] The title of an article in *Minnesota Studies in the Philosophy of Science* 6 (1975).

The *use* of language can thus still in principle be 'mastered' by everyone who shares in the convention concerned; and it is certain that not only the identity of the message but also that of the intention in the act of communication – through which the signs exchanged are duplicated as those of the sender and those of the receiver – is preserved. For this reason – and this would be the fourth implication of Searle's theses – the category of 'intention' could never act as a disturber of the peace or trouble-maker in the system of meanings. True, an explicit right is conceded to it (and this is, as Derrida admits, an undeniable advance on the classical grammatical model); but the intention, as Searle significantly says, is always realised in the sentences themselves; 'there need be no *gulf* at all between the illocutionary intention and its expression. The sentences are, so to speak, fungible intentions' (*R*, p. 202). Leaving aside for the moment the scope of possibility which Searle himself leaves open by his negation of an apodictic utterance ('need be no . . .'), one could paraphrase his view as follows: intentions are themselves functions in a homogeneous pragmasemantic system, the generalness and completeness of which ensure that repeated use does not render them unrecognisable. When intentions are recognised they are deciphered as that which has been encoded and are not communicable in any other way. For – as Wittgenstein says – 'only in a language can one mean something by something' (*Philosophische Untersuchungen*, note to §§35–8). Intentions could thus never be strictly private: they merge with the universal types of meaning: 'one forms one's intentions (or meanings) in the process of forming the sentences' (*R*, p. 202). 'Intentions *or* meanings', Searle writes, and I understand this to mean 'intentio *sive* significatio'. The uttered sentences therefore become one with the intentions which situate them to form fixed schemata, i.e. invariant prototypes of the use of language, each of which survives the act of communication unchanged and shows the same face to all speakers/hearers. It is an analytical consequence of the *determinacy of meaning* that – as E.D. Hirsch says – it represents 'an entity which is self-identical . . . always remains the same . . . is changeless'.[8] And: 'Validity [in

---

[8] E.D. Hirsch, *Validity in Interpretation* (New Haven, 1967), p. 46.

encoding or decoding] requires a norm – a meaning that is stable and determinate', and 'the author's meaning, as represented by his text, is unchanging and reproducible'.[9] Thus the iteration of understanding is a case of 'recognising again' the intention of the speaker – and this intention (despite all that we have learned from Fichte, Solger and Sartre about the negativity in principle of the self) coincides with itself just as opaque substances do.

When dealing with the epistemological premises of this model, one can observe clearly how the virtually dual nature of the sign – as the expression of the individual intention of its author *and* as an element in a system of types – is surreptitiously reduced to an identity of the two aspects. Iterability is a recognised characteristic of communication by means of signs; but the sign – as a type – survives the act of transmission by virtue of its permanence and likeness to itself (they are vouched for not by the speaker but by convention). One must see, Searle stresses, 'that an adequate study of speech acts is a study [not of *parole* but] of *langue*' (*SA*, p. 17).[10] The theoretician is in principle concerned with speech acts only as types, not as concrete and living speech events. For what makes the performance of a speech act into an utterance is not that it occurs in a historically unique context but that 'as an event' it can serve to communicate any number of different contents and that the receivers of speech acts can understand an infinite number of meanings 'simply by recognizing the intentions of the speakers in the performances of the speech acts' (*R*, p. 208). This presupposes, as we have said, that for the sake of 'recognisability' these intentions have previously been schematised according to permanent and generally binding rules – in other words that they represent protocols of convention.

The same applies to the duplication of the conventional sign into expression and intention. When Searle – very much like Hirsch – characterises the text as 'the expression [indeed as the "precise expression"] of the intentions of its author' (*R*, p. 202), one might at first think that he wishes to underline the greater authenticity which the first person singular 'normally' – 'in the standard

---

[9] *Ibid.*, pp. 126 and 216.
[10] This abbreviation refers to quotations from John R. Searle, *Speech Acts* (Cambridge, 1969).

case' – has with regard to the possibility of assessing the appropriateness of intention to what is said.

What happens when the author really means what he says? Can one say – with Husserl, who inevitably comes to mind when intentionality is under discussion – that the speaker represents his 'pre-expressive intentions' through expressions? He would in this case need a criterion for the identity of his meaning and his saying, a common measure for both – similar to Kant's schema which mediates between the generality of the category and the individuality of the concrete instance. Since, however, the expression – for the sake of its communicability – must be common to all speakers (a social fact), then a priori only an intention that shared this generality would be really appropriate to it. In that case not only the linguistic expression but the pre-linguistic intention would have to submit to the law of iterability, and Searle does assume this: 'Iterability . . . is a necessary condition of the particular forms of intentionality that are characteristic of speech acts' (*R*, p. 208). There can thus be no difference between intention and expression as to the degree of generality or privateness of what is meant. At most there could be a difference between the articulation of one and the same chain of signs before it is expressed and when it is being expressed, i.e. a difference between the silent and the audible use of signs. In short, despite the rhetorical emphasis with which Searle makes the terminological distinction between intention and expression, he still reduces them to just as strict an identity as he insisted upon for the sign (the type) and its double: if any communication that is at all 'serious' is being carried out, the intention is a 'functional' feature of the expressions which circulate on the market of public communications and which, like coins, show the same face to all concerned.

Searle here brings into play a methodological premise which is intended to dispose of two difficulties from the outset: for the sake of the possible objectivity of understanding it is assumed, first, that the author has access to the authentic meaning (*Sinn*, *vouloir-dire*) of the individual intention of his utterance (otherwise neither he nor someone else – for instance his interlocutor or interpreter – could judge with certainty whether he has really said what he meant: the problem of undecidability would already be creeping into the inwardness of the projection of meaning).[11] The second presupposition is that what the author meant is identical with what he said, i.e. with what he entrusted to the sign which is valid for all those who share the language. (Otherwise one would have to reckon with the possibility that occasionally one might understand adequately what the author said without also understanding what he really meant. There would have been a successful understanding of his utterances, but it would not have been in accordance with what the speaker himself had in mind. It is necessary to understand *him*, if understanding is really to be objective and capable of being verified.)

By these premises an apparent concession to the individuality of a speaking subject and to the individuality of his utterance is surreptitiously destroyed and retracted in favour of the necessary generalness and iterability of what has actually been said. So that no gulf opens up between the two elements, the further premise is needed that in 'standard discourse' only such utterances are passed on from mouth to mouth as 'precisely' (*R*, p. 202) 'represent' (Searle's expression!) the intentions of the subjects involved in the conversation, and that in doing this they are at the same time of the nature of 'types': 'The author says what he means' (*ibid.*, p. 201). 'Understanding the utterance consists in recognizing the illocutionary intentions of the author and these intentions may be more or less perfectly realized by the words uttered' (*ibid.*, p. 202). Of course the whole problem with this theory lies in this 'more or less'. It is very difficult to explain the meaning of this restriction on the basis of Searle's model. Curiously, he suspects that Derrida harbours the 'illusion' of the existence of illocutionary intentions before or beyond the utterances (*ibid.*, p. 202). But Searle seems unable to exclude precisely this idea from his own model. For the possibility of 'saying what one means' logically also includes the other possibility, that of not saying what one means, or of realising one's intentions 'less perfectly' in one's utterances. In short, even Searle – particularly Searle – cannot exclude the structural possibility (cannot exclude it *from his theory*) that the 'pre-expressive intention'[12] and the utterance made are not congruent with one

---

[11] One would never know for certain what the 'literal' meaning of an utterance was once it had been made.
[12] As Husserl calls it.

another – and this presupposes that intention and expression, although they come together in the utterance, are after all not simply the same. But Searle must insist on this sameness if he does not want to give up the claim that the intention can be mastered by the linguistic (and institutional) convention – and thus give up the rule-model of language and understanding.

To sum up: Searle's premises are based on the following theoretical construction. In the process of communicating with one another (whether in a verbal exchange or by the interpretation of written discourse), the aim is always 'a perception or construction of the author's verbal meaning'.[13] But the intention of the speaker, whom we shall have to imagine as an individual, must always be a complex of meaning which can also be represented by the marks of utterance provided and definitively determined by the 'convention'. Now Saussure showed – and he was not the first to do so – that a meaning can only become distinct, and this distinctness of meaning be intersubjectively 'shared', in an encounter with a carrier of expression (*signifiant, sôme*) which for its part is differentially profiled. But this makes the dichotomy of a (pre-semiotic) will to utter and a (material) expression vacuous.[14] At the very least one must take into account that at the moment of its 'representation' by the word-sign the pre-linguistic *vouloir-dire* suffers a radical change which splits its semantic–pragmatic identity, making it from now on an entity that is dual in nature.

SAMENESS AND DIFFERENCE OF LINGUISTIC TYPES

As such, the analytical postulation of a 'determinacy' of meaning of utterances finds itself on slippery ground on the basis of its own premises. And this happens to it through the very instance which is invoked to vouch for the scientific nature and objectivity of the procedure: the instance of the 'code', the linguistic and institutional 'conventionality' itself.

---

[13] Hirsch, *Validity*, p. 143.

[14] Linguistics is concerned with signs, speech-act theory with utterances (as units). In this context this difference may be ignored, since utterances too – as soon as they appear, as Searle suggests, in the framework of a 'taxonomy' – obey the criteria of a general semiology.

In what way? Derrida answers this question by setting out his reservations about the convention model of speech-act theory in several steps. First he analyses the meaning of the concept of repetition (*répétition, itération*). This is a safe starting-point, since Searle and Derrida are united in recognising it as such. Derrida too emphasises that the iterability of signs or utterances is a structural possibility of rule-governed speech and obeys the logic of a recursive model in which any number of 'token'-events do not endanger the unity of the underlying 'type' – at least not in the strictly synchronic perspective of speech-act theory. This model, according to Derrida, requires a certain distancing ('absence') of the speaker from his utterances. Only on condition of their 'relative' independence from the individual, 'actual' and historically unique meaning-intention of the speaker, after all, can the 'tokens' which he utters become repeatable elements of a supra-individual convention, in other words 'types': the individual retreats in order to make space for the generality of the system. If both conditions – the absence and the iterability – represent possibilities of logical order, then they cannot be pushed aside by *de facto* arguments, e.g. by reference to the actual uniqueness of a situated utterance or the physical presence of the speaker at the act of utterance (*LI*, n). Iter*ability* is not necessarily iteration, 'the possibility of being absent' does not necessarily mean being absent. Like the Kantian 'must be able', these conditions cannot be excluded *as* possibilities without thereby being declared to be fundamental necessities. But as soon as codified types are exchanged, it *must* be *possible* to replace their first or original articulation by a second and so to move away from the (always virtually absent) convention. '*Curiously*, this re-mark [i.e. this always possible renewed marking] constitutes *part* of the mark itself' (*LI*, n).

Searle imagines a case where the sender and the receiver of a message are the same person, for instance where someone aids his memory by making a shopping-list (*R*, p. 200). Here, as in the other case where someone passes a written note to his neighbour – during a concert, so as not to disturb others by whispering – it seems indisputable that the sender and the receiver are in the presence of each other and of their utterances and that the signs are identical with themselves after their repetition. Strictly speaking this does not in fact follow from this example: every form of being-present-at has the structure of a differentiation between 'something is with something', and 'something comes after something';[15] two elements are involved. The presence separates the self and what is the same from itself – as is shown by the grammar of the use of the pronouns and reflexives – and then after a minimal but never insignificant interval re-unites it with itself. The meaning is separated from itself, it becomes distorted: who can prove that *after* passing through the gap of iteration it consists of the same synthesis as before? 'The very shift in meaning would confirm the law here indicated: the time and place of the *other time* already at work, altering from the start the start itself, the *first time*, the *at once*' (*LI*, r, *first possibility*, 1st section). In other words, every presence temporalises itself, it couples its future moment with its past, and no-one would wish to claim that future and past are the same merely because, each time, they are now combined (even if both phases were to have the same content, which, if the problems are sufficiently rigorously examined, cannot be the case, but which in practice is not always of any consequence). 'This necessitates, obviously, a rigorous and renewed analysis of the value of presence, of presence to self or to others, of difference and of *différance*' (*LI*, n).

Not only the identity of the person who at different times in his process of communicating with himself designates himself by the reflexive pronoun or the first person singular pronoun – 'perhaps [as] *himself at another moment*' (*LI*, o), but also the identity of the sign by which he denotes himself or something else shows itself to be mediated via the gulf of a distance (the French 'différer' expresses both deferment and difference). There is a difference to be overcome, a delay to be bridged before the sign can prove its identity with itself. Of course it would not be able to perform this act of identification by a roundabout route if there were not a 'minimal remainder [*restance*]' (*LI*, o) of the sign-pod (to imitate Derrida's neologism) – a remainder which, like Saussure's *aposème*, must not be confused with a timelessly instantaneous presence of the sign (*sème*) to itself (this is why Derrida speaks of a

---

[15] 'For the problem of idealization and of iterability is already posed here, in the structure of temporalization' (*LI*, r, first possibility, 2nd paragraph).

'non-present remainder'). So *restance* does not mean *permanence*. A thing would be permanent if through its as it were unshiftable instantaneousness it remained unaffected by the flow of temporalisation. In this sense a sign could never be permanent, for the structure of iteration implies identity and especially difference (*LI*, o). The sign is identifiable in its sameness if and because it carries its double ('son autre') with it. It is marked by a difference even and especially when after passing through the gap of representation (becoming present again) it proves to be still identical. There is never a simple and seamless immediacy. This is what Derrida wishes to express when – already in *Sec* – he speaks of the 'non-present *remainder* [*restance*] of a differential mark' (*Sec*, p. 378; English, *Glyph* 1, p. 183). If one concedes that this splitting of the meaning-identity of the sign is a positive condition of any discursive utterance, one cannot deny that the prefix *re* in the noun *repetition* serves as the index of an – albeit minimal – transformation: if this were not so, this index would be superfluous in the economy of speech.[16] One could not logically recognise the shift away from its origin which the sign undergoes through its iterability as the basis of its making of meaning if one wanted at the same time to maintain that what is involved here is something external to the sign (and indeed in the 'standard' case the discourse functions even without such considerations). Incidentally, the split which the sign undergoes in iteration is only a special case of a general structural condition of semiological systems, and it is independent of whether one takes a representationist or an instrumentalistic model of language as a basis. As in earlier publications of his, Derrida pays special attention to this. An intention – seen as a mental phenomenon which passes, leaving no trace – could not of itself have a particular meaning if

---

[16] The distrust which such a statement must expect to meet with in our culture is similar to that which little Malte Laurids Brigge feels in relation to music: 'I was,' he says, distrustful of it, 'not because it lifted me out of myself more strongly than anything else, but because I had noticed that it did not put me down again in the place where it had found me' (Rilke, *Sämtliche Werke* (Frankfurt am Main, 1976), p. 824). Incidentally, Lacan too – with analytical intent and following Freud – provides the concept of *repetition* with the index of a transformation: 'Everything that is modified, modulated by repetition is only an alienation of its sense . . . [There is] that more radical difference which repetition in itself constitutes.' (*Die vier Grundbegriffe der Psychoanalyse* (Freiburg, 1978), p. 67). (*The Four Fundamental Concepts of Psychoanalysis* (Harmondsworth, 1979).)

it did not differentiate itself from the form of other meanings. In order to do this the 'amorphous fog' of the pure stream of consciousness must as it were become condensed and precipitated in articulated segments, i.e. it must attach itself to the sections of a substance of expression that can be modified in many ways. The elements of this substance differentiate the unity of the intended meaning to the extent that each element differs from all the others in a very specific way. This has an important consequence for the discussion of iterability: it is not that there is a prior meaning which then authentically makes itself present again (re-presents itself) in the chain of signs; there is not, therefore, a kind of original and non-sensuous presence which has merely been reproduced and made sensuous in the sign (what would be the common measure for mind and senses?). Instead, because – like the value of goods according to Marx – the meaning *cannot* be expressed directly through itself, it is forced to exist as a game of relationships and references between several materials of expression. Meaning's 'non-sensuousness' or 'non-presence' can thus easily be explained: it is formed in the gap between any two 'marks' which are comparatively amenable to the senses and which acquire profile and distinctness, i.e. are induced into their function as signs, before its retreat. Meaning, one might say in a very metaphorical paraphrase, is hindered in the perception of its identity until it is designated.

There is a further consequence: anything that only gains its identity by giving itself totally to that which is other than it may be said to be separated not only from everything else but also from itself (*LI*, n). Also from itself: for it only has access to itself – *as* to that particular sign – when it has first taken the detour via all other signs. Its 'self' is formed by the detour via all other identities, and every repetition of this detour *can* (does not necessarily) modify its identity. For want of adequate language I will again resort to a metaphorical paraphrase: the sign is hindered in the *direct* perception of its identity, for between it and itself stands the mass of all other signs on which its 'value' depends and which at every moment challenge its identity by processes of linguistic change (for no-one ensures that the existing structure will become 'permanent'). The relationship might also be characterised like this: the sign conveys its presence-to-itself (which to begin with does not exist) via the relationship to what is other, and that is a relationship which logically precedes its 'self' and of which one can thus say that it constitutes this its self. Saussure – who, with Hegel, is everywhere present in the background of Derrida's arguments here – had already had recourse to a similarly paradoxical formulation when he noted that it is 'the peculiar characteristic of language, as of every *system*, that it permits of no distinction between what distinguishes a thing and what constitutes it (because the "things" referred to here are signs which have no other mission than to be differentiated and distinct)'.[17] In the sign there is nothing inherently positive. Its being is pure being-distinct ('être distinct'), or – in the terminology of the *Notes item* – each seme is in itself necessarily a paraseme, a secondary sign or a sign-alongside-all-other-signs (separated from itself διὰ πάντα τὰ σέματα παρ[ὰ] αὐτοῦ).

A constitutive characteristic of the sign could not be inessential: one cannot abstract from it, one cannot trace it back to something else. The *Veränderung* (to use a word coined by Rosenkranz – the making into something other) 'works parasitically within the very inner core of the iter', not leaving its identity within its previous boundaries but repeating it (uncontrollably) (*LI*, x). In order to be resurrected *as* a renewed presence, the presence would have to be interrupted for a moment. For the duration of this moment – it is the moment of the absence 'of sender and of receiver: that is, of *determinate, actually present* senders and receivers' (*LI*, n) – the meaning is as it were precariously balanced. The intention which 'animates' the sign (or signs) is in the balance: it is deferred (*différée*) and thereby virtualised. It is uncertain whether the 'meaning' of the signs will survive as this particular 'type' or whether it will change. But whichever way the decision goes, there can be no question that the 'original' or 'literal' meaning flows continuously into its renewed presence, i.e. into its representation, or that it brings it about mechanically. Neither possibility – neither the preservation of the first use *nor* its transformation – can be seen as direct effects of the convention. In the end the

---

[17] Ferdinand de Saussure, *Cours de linguistique générale*, ed. R. Engler, vol. II, fascicule 4 (Wiesbaden, 1974), (N) 47, 3342.

iteration threatens to change the boundaries of the synthesis of signs, the unity of the 'type' concerned.[18] (The permanence of conventions – or even merely their 'relative purity' (Austin) – cannot be adequately explained by reference to the logicians' type-token distinction; after all, the conventions are in fact constantly changing, even if this change seldom or never takes the form of a radical break.) To exaggerate somewhat, one might say that the repetition of a speech act (like that of any other 'mark') is not the same use again (though perhaps in a somewhat different context – that is irrelevant to a sufficiently abstract theory), but another use of the same *marque restante*. Speech acts, like all conventional types, maintain their existence only through use. Between themselves and their repetition an *interpretation* intervenes which cannot be thought of as determined by the 'type' or as a case which necessarily results from the rule governing use. (I will return to this point.)

SAYING AND MEANING

It is, I think, quite clear now why Derrida rebuts the suggestion that he maintains that the intention is in principle absent from the 'mark' (*LI*, q). What he claims is merely that my or your actual intention, determined to the last degree by the situation in which the conversation takes place, does not provide, i.e. 'fill up' the meaning of this utterance permanently. A sign 'animated' by an intention, if it is iterable, is never in the strict sense 'meaning*ful*' (*LI*, q). The individual meaning never permeates the sign in such a way that it merges with it to form the unity of an unchangeable type. After all, it is only the fact that the linguistic types are relatively independent of the meanings attached to them on given occasions by the historically situated speakers that makes the totality of the signs a *system* of signs, i.e a *supra-individual convention*. In other words, if the fact of the meaningfulness of linguistic signs ('types') were in principle dependent on being created by an 'I' that was 'now-present' on each occasion (by a *'particular* and *actually* present sender and receiver'), that would invalidate the idea of

---

[18] 'The line delineating the margin can therefore never be determined rigorously, it is never pure and simple' (*LI*, r).

signs being meaningful in a way that is more than merely individual and related to the present – and thus invalidate the idea of the code and of iterability. Rightly, therefore, Derrida underlines the fact that he does not deny the necessity of intentionality-in-general for the constitution of signs, but only the necessity of its *actuality* – implicit in the concept of the speech *act* – i.e. its absolute attachment to the 'present moment' at which each speech act takes place (*LI*, q).

Once again: the conclusion which Derrida draws from the iterability of linguistic (and pragmatic) types is not that of the absence of intentionality. Rather he concludes that the actual 'animation' of the signs by an *individual* intention is not a fact that can be deduced from the concept of the convention. Only in this sense does he maintain that the intention can never be quite present to itself: freed, as an element in a supra-individual system, from the actuality of a 'moi-ici-maintenant' (me-here-now), it also, conversely, has no complete determining power over the individual meaning-effects of my discourse uttered here and now. The intention (seen as a characteristic of conventional types) cannot escape from the general structural law of a type-system, the law of iterability: 'the iterability which, in every case, forms the structure of the mark, which always divides or removes intention, preventing it from being fully present to itself in the actuality of its aim, or of its meaning [*vouloir-dire*]'. 'The possibility of a certain non-presence or of a certain non-actuality [of the intention] pertains to the structure of the functioning under consideration [of the mark], and pertains to it *necessarily*' (*LI*, q). The loss in plenitude which the intention suffers through the uncontrollable activity of the formation and shifting of difference is the precondition for signs being able to break with their codification[19] and open up to human language the infinite domain of history. Linguistic theory can only enter into it at the moment when it cuts through the fetters of the code and provides the concept of the iterability of types with the index of their possible change in meaning.

---

[19] It is of course also the condition for the possibility of codification: 'Once again, iterability makes possible idealisation – and thus, a certain identity in repetition that is independent of the multiplicity of factual events – while at the same time limiting the idealisation it makes possible: *broaching* and *breaching* it at once [elle l'*entame*]' (*LI*, r, a, first possibility).

This is precisely what Searle does not do. For him it is an accepted fact 'that any conventional [or, as Derrida calls it, "coded"] act involves the notion of the repetition *of the same*' (*R*, p. 207; (my italics, MF)). The strategic necessity of this supposition is immediately obvious. Searle states that he sees his theory of speech acts as being the analogue in the field of linguistics to the idealising method used in most of the natural sciences (*SA*, p. 87). In order to attain this goal he must assume that the intentions are, as it were, nailed to their expressions and that the vagueness of the available concepts is reducible: one can 'idealise' them and free them from the effects of 'chance' and from 'impurities'. In this way one arrives at unproblematic 'ideal speech situations' or 'pragmatic universals' under the auspices of which one can communicate seriously – an analytical conclusion drawn from the methodological premises and not from the nature of everyday speech. Serious, i.e. non-metaphorical or non-fictional, discourse is thus a theoretical construct. The exact sciences seek to identify in the objects in their field of study, which are finite in number, extent and duration of existence, relationships which are repeatable and which are the same for all present, past and future objects under essentially similar conditions. These are the so-called objective laws which in the domain of finite things show us relationships which, repeated infinitely many times, show no change. Speech-act theory deals in the same way with the linguistic data. It abstracts from its empirical multiplicity until it has listed a finite number of essences and rules which free it from the need to take into account concrete divergences in actual linguistic usage – in short, from any kinds of irregularities. In order to understand a speech act, Searle says (I will for the moment keep to the text of the 'Reply'), 'it is necessary to know that anyone who said it and meant it would be performing that speech act determined by the rules of the languages that give the sentence its meaning in the first place' (*R*, p. 202). In other words, the idealisation methodically excludes the 'parasitic' use – the transforming reproduction – of the type and works on the basis of a convention model which assigns to every material of expression – according to a typology of 'forms of intentionality' – one and only one quite specific meaning with which it can be used. This model *can* only work if the 'permanence' of the signs, i.e. of the codified units of meaning and expression, remains intact, if the intention completely 'fills up' the expression. In order to guarantee this Searle must systematically abstract from a possibility which incidentally he himself acknowledges to be a 'structural precondition' of any use of signs (see also *LI*, v) – the possibility of the inauthentic and meaning-altering use of language which he characterises as 'parasitic' or 'non-normal' (so it is not 'normal' for language to change in use in such a way that the convention existing up to that time no longer interprets its present meaning) and which he tries to bring back under the control of the existing norm by saying that it is 'logically deduced' from normal linguistic usage.

Now it is not clear, firstly, why a relationship of logical dependence should lessen the dignity of a thing: what logician would maintain that because B follows from A it is therefore 'inauthentic', 'abnormal' or 'parasitic'? (One might, on the contrary, point to Hegel, who declares that only what follows from a premise is its 'true essence'.) Of greater significance, however, is – secondly – what emerges from an analysis of that 'logical possibility'. For that concept also implies that the 'norm' could not simply be put in quarantine and isolated from the parasites of the abnormal (otherwise it would be an eventuality, not a logical possibility). The realisation of the parasitic quality of the inauthentic, the 'pretended' promise, for instance, does not require the theatre stage or the novel (to which Searle – in keeping with his style of organisation which tidily deals with seriously meant and merely pretended speech in two separate publications – would really like to consign them). 'It is a temptation for philosophers', says Whitehead in his lectures on *Modes of Thought* (1938) 'that they should weave a fairy-tale of the adjustment of factors; and then as an appendix introduce the notion of frustration, as a secondary aspect', and he continues, as though anticipating the need to counter the theory of infelicities: 'There is no reason to hold that confusion is less fundamental than is order.'[20] But even if one accords them equal status, even the ordered, in the process of its various applications, does not escape the law of uncontrollable repetition. The ghost of

[20] Whitehead, 'Understanding', pp. 69–70.

relative disorder – that is, of the distortion of what the speaker intended the words to mean – crops up anew, again and again, as a logical possibility of any realisation of a general speech-act type; any everyday process of communication can serve as an example showing that there is neither 'full' meaning nor 'full' understanding. Our 'real life' itself inescapably shares in the possibility of the lie, the illusion, the misunderstanding, the *parasitage*, so much so that anyone who examined 'normal language' in terms of the norm would be approaching it under a misconception. It is part of its definition that the infelicity can never be simply external to standard discourse, can never be excluded from it and consigned to the appendix of exceptions (see also *LI*, v).

Incidentally, Searle justifies that exclusion as merely a matter of the *ordo inveniendi* ('a matter of research strategy' (*R*, p. 205)). But unofficially, as it were, he interprets it – as I have said – as being founded on a 'logical and ontological order': the serious use is 'logically prior' to the non-serious, the latter 'logically depending' on the former. Thus there is a clear hierarchy here of what is essential and what is inessential, with a tendency towards a reduction of the latter to the former. 'The "standard" case of promises or of statements', says Derrida, 'would never occur as such, with its "normal" effects, were it not, from its very inception on, parasited, harboring and haunted by the possibility of being repeated in *all kinds of ways*' (*LI*, v).

One can now see quite clearly, in retrospect, the methodological purpose of Searle's equation of *meaning* and *saying*: these are the two elements of the synthesis of signs the *complete* matching of which stands as a necessary condition for the attempt to define the sign as an element in a taxonomy or as a 'case' of a universal order of intention–expression pairs. Anyone who doubts the match between the two (and attributes the achieving of the shift to 'iteration', of all things) jeopardises the scientific describability – at least in the sense in which Searle uses the term 'science' – of facts of everyday language. And the same is true of anyone who considers contexts as something other than 'protocol[s] of the code' (*Sec*, p. 376; English, *Glyph* 1, p. 180), and therefore makes not only the signs but also the surroundings in which they occur subject to general universals of context.

SYSTEM AND EVENT

With such reflections (which should not be confused with a critique of the structure and organisation of Searle's theory as such) Derrida makes a quite general attack on the fetish in the humane sciences of forming rules and laws. There would be no objection if someone – on the basis of the achievements of structuralism and analytical philosophy – set about examining traditions, social orders, forms of discourse, patterns of speech and also literary and artistic 'texts' in order to discover the structures which the mass of 'events', as cases of general regularities, makes it possible to recognise. For the orders I have mentioned are alike in that individuals can acquire a competence in them (that is trivial). After all, the concept of competence, which – since Chomsky – has sometimes taken the place of Saussure's *langue*, Hjelmslev's *schematism* or Humboldt's concept of the *system* – designates, like these, a capability, a potential – something which exists only virtually, a *mè ón* in Plato's sense. Now a pure possibility could never occur as an antecedent in a real causal chain.[21] Competence could have consequences only if a being that was capable of action and was self-conscious realised one or other of the possibilities. 'Language', says Schleiermacher, 'must individualise itself. Otherwise it can only be conceived of as a capability, but not really exist.'[22] But what happens in the act of individualisation which changes a general speech type into an event? Nothing less than a threat to the continued existence of the whole code. Its rules can in principle – as potentialities and as idealisations of real utterances – only claim validity for the period of time from the stocks of which they have been recruited by scientific abstraction. This is why all rules carry an index of the past: this is how people spoke, up to the time when

---

[21] As is suggested by some linguistic philosophers (e.g. with the idea of a 'structural causality' (Althusser)). Once again Saussure himself is unambiguous on this point: 'The synchronic law is generally valid, but it has no power to command. It exercises a power over individuals through the compulsion of collective usage, but that relates only to the speaking subjects. What we want to say is that within the linguistic system no power that prevails at any point guarantees the maintainance of regularity' (*Cours de linguistique générale* (Paris, 1964), p. 131).

[22] F.D.E.Schleiermacher, *Hermeneutik und Kritik. Mit einem Anhang sprachphilosophischer Texte Schleiermachers*, ed. Manfred Frank (henceforth cited as *HuK*) (Frankfurt am Main, 1977), pp. 363–4.

the rules were formulated – nothing follows from this for the future of linguistic usage.[23] It is a free iteration – and thus, perhaps, a transformation – of the *status quo* of the convention. Anyone who denies this must set up the power of tradition as the norm for the future: this is how people have spoken (up to now), this is how they must to continue to speak. This view is quite frequently expressed by nomologically orientated linguistic philosophers, and it offers an obvious explanation for their conservatism. Wittgenstein, for example, says: 'Philosophy may in no way touch the actual use of language, it can ultimately only describe it . . . It leaves everything as it is' (*Philosophische Untersuchungen*, §124).

Of course no one will wish to deny the fact that conventions change. But a characteristic feature of a certain strand of analytical philosophy is a terminological tendency to describe the transformation of conventions as a process in which the social and cultural heritage reproduces or transforms itself 'by itself', i.e. without any intervention by subjects capable of action and with the power of meaning. Expressions like that of the 'power of traditions', however, do not fall into the category of what Searle would call serious speech. They borrow from the rhetoric of metonymy, interpreting human acts as forces inherent in things.

But what conception must we have of the linguistic (and also the pragmatic) 'type' in order to account for both intersubjectivity – the code level – and transforming iterability – the level of concrete language use? I would remind the reader of Derrida's formulation: 'Iterability supposes a minimal remainder [*restance*] (as well as a minimum of idealization), in order that the identity of the *selfsame* be repeatable and identifiable *in*, *through* and even *in view of* its alteration' (*LI*, o). Schleiermacher called the indispensable boundaries within which a meaning must be attached to a substrate of expression in order to be still just identifiable as that particular meaning, the 'schema' of the sign in question. The 'minimal remainder' is only one side of the schema. On the other the schema is a function of the 'surroundings', which 'affect' its mean-

---

[23] The Saussure quotation given in note 21 continues: 'The synchronic law is merely the expression of an existing order and describes an existing state of affairs . . . Diachrony on the other hand presupposes active forces which bring about an effect' (*Cours de linguistique générale*, p. 131).

ing.[24] For with regard to the contexts the schema is not a concept fixed once and for all, but an intuition 'movable within certain limits' (*HuK*, p. 106) – related to Wittgenstein's language game, which is of course also defined as 'a concept with blurred edges' (*Philosophische Untersuchungen*, §71).

Derrida sees the possibility of such movement – and thus the 'corruptibility of serious or normal discourse' – as an analytical consequence of the iterability of the 'marks' (*LI*, r, *Secondly*). Even if one concedes to him that iterability is the negative condition for the 'positivity' of any conceivable linguistic 'value' – 'this condition of possibility is structurally divided or differing-deferring [*différante*]' (*ibid.*) – one has still by no means established through what instance the pure capability of repetition (iter*ability*) is set in motion: is it iterability itself and as such, or the individual who iterates the 'marks'?

I will discuss the problems posed by this theoretical ambiguity later on. Here it is enough to show that the 'minimal consensus' which exists between Searle and Derrida about the conventional preconditions of communication makes their theories, apparently so divergent, comparable on one decisive point: Derrida follows the usage of the Wittgensteinian school when he ascribes the capability of changing meaning to the code itself. This agreement exists despite the fact that Derrida sees in the code chiefly its tendency to entropy, while Searle seems to be interested in defining it as a force for order. This is of course a decisive difference, and yet it is not sufficient to characterise Searle's and Derrida's positions as wholly incompatible with one another. I now propose first to show the difference as clearly as possible and later to investigate what it is that prevents both Searle and Derrida from having recourse to the category of a meaning-creating and meaning-altering individuality.

THE UNCONTROLLABILITY OF THE MEANING-EFFECTS

First Derrida. It is noticeable that he avoids the classical term 'sign' (the 'sem' in Saussure's sense), preferring the expression 'mark'.

---

[24] Schleiermacher, *Hermeneutik*, ed. H. Kimmerle (Heidelberg, 1959), p. 47.

He himself states his reason for this: he wants to avoid the classical implications of the representationalist sign model. These consist, in his view, of the notion that the 'meaning' is given to the sign by a subjectivity that freely interprets the world (or was formerly given: the fact that *I* do not know myself to be an instituter of the schematisation of signs that is now valid does not exclude the possibility that this instituting was effected – before my time – by other subjects, and thus in no way represents a natural event). What happens is not that a subject 're-presents' his intentions in the sign, but that 'meaning' and 'significance' (*Sinn* and *Bedeutung*) appear as effects of the differential relationships between the 'marks', as a process of autonomous differentiation of the world. Certainly Derrida stresses that the differentiality of the marks can never be systematically mastered and that the flow of the meaning-relationships can never be frozen in a crystal-lattice of rigid conventions. 'Iterability', he writes, 'blurs a priori the dividing-line that passes between these opposed terms [of the serious and the unserious, the genuine and the ungenuine, the strict and the vague] . . . The line delineating the margin can therefore never be determined rigorously, it is never pure and simple' (*LI*, r, *Secondly*). Is this perhaps because there is an individuality which cannot be deduced from the concept of the free play of the marks? Not at all; the reason is that the economy of a sign system is itself without boundaries because the systematic frame of the convention shifts with each new use of types, because the ensemble of the differential marks cannot be imagined as an iron grid in which the elements are fixed in their places, like the atoms in a crystal so long as the temperature remains constant, but as an endless process of melting and hardening caused by iterability. Under such circumstances it would be impossible to assign a particular sign a priori to a particular context. Any mark can break with any context. Not because in this way it can create meaning free of a context, but because history lets no pre-stabilised harmony arise between the signs and a context which is allegedly 'original' and 'natural' (*LI*, s). The wealth of communicative situations in which possibilities of meaning not anticipated by the system come into effect cannot be deduced from the hitherto valid rules governing the linguistic use concerned in each instance; for firstly there are any number of contexts without an absolute centre of anchorage (*ibid.*), and secondly it is impossible to deal exhaustively or even adequately with the infinite number of filiations between the contexts and the (spatially and temporally limitless) universe of discourses that have been uttered (see also *Sec*, pp. 389–90). It also follows from this that an utterance could never be quite *filled* with meaning or the understanding of a speech act be wholly complete (*LI*, q).[25] Incomplete understanding and misunderstanding cannot be dismissed simply as transgressions of the rules or corruptions of the standard communications.

It is perhaps Whitehead who has shown most brilliantly the paradox that lies in the methodical demand for complete understanding. 'Full understanding' of the performance of a discourse, he says, would amount to its tautologically cancelling itself out: for within it every individual aspect of what is to be understood must, as soon as it has been gone through, be part of 'what is already clear. Thus it is merely a repetition of the known.'[26] Only tautological repetition would guarantee complete understanding, and precisely that does not allow understanding to occur at all.

By its nature understanding is a never quite controllable way of not understanding. It is worth recalling that this view was already expressed most emphatically by Humboldt and Schleiermacher – theoreticians who have often been accused of 'objectivism'. According to Humboldt, language attains 'its final determinacy only in the individual. In relation to a word, no-one thinks precisely and exactly the same as another, and the difference, however small, ripples outwards through the language like a circle in the water. All *understanding* is therefore at the same time a *non-understanding*, all agreement in thoughts and feelings is at the same time a divergence.'[27] And Schleiermacher, who in his hermeneutics gives reasons why the achievement of understanding can never be

---

[25] Wittgenstein would say that it also functions without this ideal of exactitude. On the other hand he too postulates that 'where there is meaning . . . there (must) be perfect order. So the most perfect order must be present even in the vaguest text' (*Philosophische Untersuchungen* (Frankfurt am Main, 1971), section 98).

[26] Whitehead, 'Understanding', p. 71. (See introduction by G. Boehm to H.-G. Gadamer and G. Boehm (eds.), *Die Hermeneutik und die Wissenschaften* (Frankfurt am Main, 1978), p. 27.)

[27] Wilhelm von Humboldt, *Gesammelte Schriften*, ed. A. Leitzmann et al. (Berlin, 1903–35, Neudruck 1938), vol. VII, pp. 64ff.

completed, adds that 'non-understanding will never finally dissolve' (*HuK*, p. 328).

Certainly neither Humboldt nor Schleiermacher nor Whitehead would object to the formulation that non-understanding
constitutes a structural condition of any achievement of understanding. Of course this concession need not imply that they would
be convinced by Derrida's reasoning. After all, it is possible that his
arguments are coloured by his minimal consensus with Searle. For
if one leaves aside the fact that the two of them draw incompatible
conclusions from the code model of language, it is nevertheless
striking that they both talk of linguistic acts as *codificates* (whether
they designate them as 'types' or as 'graphemes'). Why Derrida
does this I shall (as I have said) examine later. In Searle's case it
seems clear to me that he sees no other way of taking account of
the requirement of identity and the recursivity of the speech-act
types. I will turn first to the motives for Searle's choice of method.

THE LIMITS OF THE METHOD AND THE PROBLEM OF INTERPRETATION

Now, as far as his turning towards the code model is concerned,
the theoreticians who prepared the way for Searle were not so
much Austin or even Peirce but rather Morris and Chomsky. At
the time of its appearance, Morris' pragmatics claimed to give an
account of the regularities of linguistic communication. It did this
in the form of a systematic interpretation of so-called intentional
acts, i.e. acts which determine the communicative role in which
the uttered sentences make themselves known as speech acts, e.g.
as a wish, command, threat, statement, plea, etc. The epistemological framework within which this systematisation was supposed to take place is not fundamentally different from that of
classical information theory. Grice formulates this most clearly: 'I
have stated my maxims, as if the purpose of conversational talk
were a maximally effective exchange of information.'[28] In this
discipline communication processes are thought of as forms of

[28] H.P. Grice, 'Logic and Conversation', in P. Coles and J. Morgan (eds.), *Speech Acts* (vol. III
of *Syntax and Semantics*, general editor J.P. Kimball (New York Academic Press, 1975)), p.
47.

exchange of information, messages, or meanings or (in Frege's sense) thoughts, which are conveyed via a consensus, a convention, a code, etc. Once this code has been identically internalised by those holding the conversation – but who confirms this identity, if not the success of the communication itself? – everything proceeds perfectly straightforwardly. Any possible non-understanding never arises from uncertainty of a hermeneutic nature, but comes about either because of physical-physiological obstacles which hinder the exchange, or because there are signs in circulation which one of the 'interlocutors' does not or cannot decipher correctly, or because generally recognised principles of conversation have not been adhered to. Now Morris' pragmatics extends this code model, supposedly by adding precisely the missing hermeneutic–pragmatic dimension; however, it inserts this extension into the traditional model of grammar itself. If the component parts of grammar had hitherto been morphonology, syntax and semantics, it now had incorporated into it the additional area of pragmatics, as the doctrine of the relationships, universal and capable of being described in terms of laws, which the syntactically linked signs have – on the descriptive level – with the intentions of their users and the surroundings of the conversation situation by which they are more closely defined. The formulation which Morris uses is very significant: 'The representamen', he says, 'is a mere object, and its designation of other objects has its basis in the fact that *rules* for use exist which correlatively link the two series of objects' (my italics, MF). In other words the intentions too are mediated by an apparatus of rules which is inviolable for any two speakers, namely the pragmatic code, from the repertoire of which they can – wholly in accordance with the generational-grammatical model of competence – be produced and deciphered. Just as the conveying of chains of meanings presupposes the identical iterability of the signs and the invariance of the laws governing their combination, so also the conveying of speech acts presupposes their iterability without a shift in meaning. The illocutions are thus *general types* of speech acts, such as, for instance, asking, requesting, stating, or being ironical about something – they are thus universal patterns of the use of discourse which form part of the uniform and indispensable stock which all who share a

particular culture or a tradition of discourse possess. Now it is plain
to see that the epistemological framework of the underlying model
in itself excludes a priori any consideration of the understanding of
what has historically occurred only once and its unique meaning.
For something which has been, in the radical sense, uttered only
once, which moreover would vouchsafe its intention *only* in *that
particular* context in which it has been used, would not accord with
the law of identical reproducibility and thus the concept of the
linguistic type (as also used by Searle).

Of course this is not the direction in which Derrida's objection
to the theory of the speech act is aimed. If he disputes the certainty
of the code model he does so on the basis of that minimal consensus with Searle, which lies in the fact that they do not take refuge in
the concept of a (transcendental) individuality. Even though the
fetish for regularity shown by the linguistic philosophers may have
its comical aspects, Derrida would still not think of challenging the
shared epistemological premise that codification and iterability are
names of the same concept. Each new use of a sign, in his view,
modifies its meaning and challenges the notion that the code
controls its use with machine-like certainty. What is not challenged, however, is the concept of the code itself and the notion
that the meaning is always accessible only via the detour through a
convention.

Two things strike one about this line of argument. Following the
Kantian tradition, Derrida sees the codification of the signs as a
merely hypothetical guide. And he justifies this by saying that the
use (or the reading) of a sign changes that sign ('iteration . . . is at
work, constantly *altering* . . . whatever it seems to reproduce . . .
Iteration alters, something new takes place' [*LI*, i]). Thus he
identifies the distance between the sign – as an element of *parole* –
with the distance between each two uses of a *single* 'mark'. This
really seems to me to be a 'category mistake'.[29]

For the concept of competence or of the code (or of iterability)
refers, as we have said, to a system of pure virtualities; and the
elements of the *langue* only acquire actual meaningfulness through

---

[29] In his reply Searle calls it a confusion between 'type' and 'token'. This does not go far
enough, for a possible point in Derrida's argument is that repeated use of a type does not
leave it unchanged, i.e. it attacks it from the level of the token.

their use-in-a-situation. There is admittedly a gulf between the potentiality of general schematism and the concrete use of the schema; but it is a gulf not between two real meanings, but between a meaning-possibility and its creative realisation. There is no rule which would determine its own use as a necessary consequence of its premises.

Now Derrida too says that 'the minimal making-sense of something (its conformity to the code, grammaticality, etc.) is incommensurate with the adequate understanding of intended meaning' (*LI*, r, possibility 1,c). One could take this formulation (to which there is nothing comparable in Searle) to mean that Derrida wishes to distinguish a necessary precondition for the meaningfulness of signs (their grammaticality) from an efficient cause of their making-sense, and that he regards their use-in-a-situation as the criterion for actual meaningfulness. Then the codification would be the instance without which it is impossible to speak, but this does not in itself make it that which brings about the possible significance of the signs. A system of signs – like any apparatus of instructions and prescriptions – must remain silent so long as no-one interprets it. A rule of a game is never the same as a move in the game itself. Above all this is because (as C. S. Peirce has shown) the signs, in order to be able to relate to objects from a particular perspective, require a commentary or an interpretation which cannot be understood as the outcome of a simple deduction from their grammar. Deductions can in principle be given only in the homogeneous area of structure (of what Peirce calls *idea* or *object*) and not in that of the applied sign (the interpreted *representamen*). The structurally horizontal relationship of the sign to all other signs and their objects is crossed over by a second, as it were vertical relationship, that of the signs to their users. The system of signs functions on the level of the spoken word only when a community of interpretation and ultimately an individual has previously fixed the sense of its use, i.e. has created from scratch the relationship of representation between the codified signs and their objects, and has then in the course of history continually fixed it anew. In this way the system of signs remains tied to symbolic actions and to normative decisions which emanate from the level of social interaction.

Derrida has expressed a view on Peirce, not in 'Limited Inc.' but in *Grammatologie*.[30] I will briefly summarise this, as I can then more easily contrast it with the way in which Searle follows on from Peirce. Derrida understands the project of a semiotics as a suggestion for a game model released from its boundaries, which comes some way towards his own concept of the 'texte général'.[31] Signs – which Peirce calls 'symbols' – are never the product of original intuitions which they symbolically represent, but always of other signs (if not necessarily of the same type): 'It is only out of symbols that a new symbol can grow. Omne symbolum de symbolo.'[32] This seems to cut off every attempt to pass beyond the level of semiotics – which for its part is now no longer tamed by a truth-value functional (i.e. non-formal) logic. Derrida sees the 'indefiniteness of reference' as Peirce's real discovery. And this also implies that there can be no thing in itself to which the differential game of the 'marks' could relate as its real centre or its origin. 'The so-called "thing itself"', he writes, 'is always already a *representamen* which is removed from the simplicity of intuitive evidence', and he continues, 'The *representamen* can only function by creating an *interpretant* which in turn becomes a sign, and so on *ad infinitum*. The identity of the signified with itself is constantly concealing itself and shifting.'

That final sentence stresses most clearly the conclusion that Derrida believes to be crucial: Peirce showed, he claims, that the sign never finds its confirmation in the concrete presence of something represented, that it lacks a firm identity with itself, that it is forced by its structure 'to be itself and an Other, to come into being as a structure of reference and to separate itself from itself'. What he assiduously overlooks, however, is the function attributed by Peirce to the *interpretant*, which is by no means, as Derrida writes, 'produced by the *representamen*'. This formulation is at the very least open to misunderstanding. True, in the language process the interpretant is constantly being assigned to the sign, because it modifies and constitutes its meaning ('The interpretant becoming

---

[30] *Grammatologie* (Frankfurt am Main, 1974), pp. 83–7 (I refer to this passage in the following summary).

[31] Jacques Derrida, *Positions* (Paris, 1972), p. 82.

[32] C.S. Peirce, *Selected Writings* (London, 1940), p. 115.

in turn a sign, and so on *ad infinitum*' – these are Peirce's own words)
– but this process of the interpretant becoming a symbol is unidirectional and not reversible. It never happens that a sign 'generates' an interpretant through whose mediation it acquires meaning
here and now. Rather, the interpretant is a unique creation of the
individuality which understands and projects itself on to its world.
And if this individuality comes into play the closed circuit of an
autonomous context of reference of the signs is interrupted after
all, though not in the sense that there would consequently be a
quantity not tied to a system, wandering freely or ghost-like, which
would escape the conditions of symbolisation. The 'unspeakabil-
ity' of the individual interpretant at the moment of its creation is
not a kind of logical alternative to the 'sayable' of communication
effected by means of signs. It is precisely what causes the sayable
here and now to have this particular meaning.

Now, this condition of the possibility of significance cannot be
significant in the same sense as that which receives its specific
meaning by virtue of its withdrawal. What is individual about the
interpretant escapes the sign with a necessity inherent in the
structure, for it is the meaning of this sign in the process of its
coming into being (but there can be no intersubjectively recognised key to a meaning that is coming into being). This needs to be
understood in the same way as Saussure's famous statement that in
the *langue* there are only differences. That statement identifies
differentiality as the condition for the possibility of significance – a
condition which as such cannot of course be significant. Sartre
calls the meaning which is coming into being the 'sense' or the
'non-significant element in the language'[33] and Schleiermacher
spoke of the 'non-transferability' of the meaning at the moment of
its invention (*HuK*, pp. 361–2f.). The creation of meaning is non-
transferable and individual, in the precise sense that it is unshareable and thus immediate (both ideas are expressed by the English
'shareable'). As the interpretation, unique for the time being, of a

---

[33] Jean-Paul Sartre, *Situations VIII* (Paris, 1972), p. 449. Similarly Michael Polanyi writes:
'The relation of a word to the thing that it designates is produced by an inexplicit
integration (etc.)' ('Sinngebung und Sinndeutung', in Gadamer and Boehm, *Die Hermeneutik und die Wissenschaften*, p. 128). See also Wittgenstein: 'What is not expressed in the
sign is shown by its application' (*Tractatus*, 3.262).

chain of *representamens* relating to objects it exists as a singular thing with no others of its kind (as a 'sense') until at least one other individual actualises the virtual meaning potential contained in it from the signs uttered. Now it cannot be said that the interpretant (the meaning-potential of a sign-bearer) is instructed by a semantic rule: the validity of the rule is not cancelled, but for the duration of its application it is virtualised and it is only re-actualised if communication has taken place with at least one other subject. If this were not so, understanding could indeed be deduced from rules. The rules are, however, suspended up to the moment at which the interpretant disappears into the sign: it has then succeeded in making the breakthrough into the domain of the communal, it has made its mark on the general language type as a semantic characteristic among others; the sense – the meaning in *statu nascendi* – has become meaning (*Bedeutung*).

The reverse of such an act of imparting meaning occurs in the interpretation of meaning. The interpreter of meaning must perform a hermeneutic exercise which is analogous to the creative act of the originator. Here too rules are suspended. There is no guarantee that the interpreter will reassemble the speech act within the precise boundaries in which the speaker believed that he had synthesised it. Thus – vaguely guided by a convention which at best offers no more than a necessary but never an adequate condition for understanding, and at worst has been transformed by the speech act – he must, in an act which is motivated by grammar and context but is nonetheless creative, provide a given 'mark' with a meaning of his own invention. (The suggestion, often heard, that the interpretation of meaning implies the requirement of an authentic empathy with the intention of the author is thus shown to be arbitrary.) The interpretation of signs is in principle not a fact that could be grounded within the framework of a semiology (or universal pragmatics). At the crucial moment no rules are at hand which would permit one to generate 'the' valid interpretation of the speech act in question quite immanently, that is, 'independently of any external input' on the basis of given axioms and by the application of rules.[34] From the gulf

---

[34] Dan Sperber, *Über Symbolik* (Frankfurt am Main, 1975), pp. 120ff.

which exists between the 'system' – as the order of the 'schemata' –
and its 'use', Schleiermacher concludes that understanding is an
art: 'Not [in the sense] that its execution results in a work of art, but
that the activity merely has about it the *character* of an art, because
the rules do not also prescribe the manner of their application, i.e.
this cannot be mechanised' (*HuK*, p. 81; see also p. 360). Polanyi
too, to cite a modern source, sees the demand for 'rules which are
supposed to replace the inexplicit meaning of a chain of expression' as 'the false ideal of strictly explicit cognition at work'. It is
false because it leads to an infinite regression; for the rules explaining meaning would need in turn to be determined by rules, and so
on. 'Also, one can only understand such rules at all on the basis of
the meaning of the very expressions which the rules are supposedly
meant to replace.'[35]

The understanding of utterances cannot, to introduce another
idealistic term, be 'necessitated'. It can only be motivated, i.e.
triggered and completed by the mediation of an interpretant. But
this interpretant is not a factor that could be generated from the
code or which would remain external ('parasitical') to the interpreted signs. It affects their meaning internally; it shakes – to
return to an image I have used before – the very foundations of the
synthesis which held the signs together as that particular unit of
sound and meaning, and equally – but are these really two different things? – the foundations which constitute the speech act as
that particular and conventional interpretation of its proposition.

In short, there is no guarantee that even one participant in the
language assembles the sign or the utterance (the sign animated by
an intention) in exactly the same way as another and does not shift
its parts – the intelligible and the sensual side – very slightly in
relation to each other. And nothing prevents the two interlocutors,
for understandable reasons such as a change in their 'construction

---

[35] M. Polanyi, 'Sinngebung', p. 129. See also, however, Wittgenstein, *Philosophische Untersuchungen*, §84: 'Can we not imagine a rule which regulates the application of the rule?
And a doubt that is lifted by *that* rule – and so on?' It is indeed conceivable, Wittgenstein
answers, but this idea influences the intuitive certainty of the everyday use of rules 'in
general' as little as the fact that no *final* explanation of the expressions that I use can be
given hinders me in speaking: 'exactness' is a function of use; 'inexact' does not
(necessarily) mean 'useless' (§88). 'On the other hand it seems clear that where there is
meaning there must be perfect order' (§78).

of knowledge' (*HuK*, pp. 458ff.), from changing the linguistic units in the course of their debate, i.e. carrying out afresh the underlying intentional synthesis.[36]

The most important thing (for our purposes) is to see that the construct of a unit of language or utterance fulfils a merely structural requirement, and thus has the status of a methodological postulate, the validity of which could not be strengthened at all on the level of empirical communication. (It could only actually be contested on the basis of a fully worked out theory of intentionality and self-consciousness. I will leave that to the end of this chapter, first continuing to follow the train of Derrida's and Searle's arguments.)

THE UNDECIDABILITY OF THE 'LITERAL MEANING' OF UTTERANCES AND THE THEORY OF 'INFELICITIES'

Here, as Derrida stresses, there is a real problem of undecidability. It is made no less explosive by the fact that it can be objected that this problem does not – for practical reasons of everyday life – actually crop up in every speaking situation. The fundamental fact remains that I can never with apodictic certainty deduce the meaning intended by the Other from his utterances because firstly I cannot slip into his skin and secondly, even if I could, I possess no trans-communicative clue to suggest according to what law the synthesis of meaning and expression can be carried out with definitive 'correctness' (i.e. I do not know for certain in any particular case which semantic characteristics this particular expression covers and which it does not). 'Every instance of speaking', says Schleiermacher, 'is a constant continuation of the attempt to see whether all human beings construct identically' (*HuK*, p. 460). This is at bottom no different from juridical decisions: the laws are given, but even so the validation of the verdict is never completed, at least not by virtue of the nature of the case. In the last instance it is only with the help of the authority of the state that the judge's decision can be implemented. But with facts of history

---

[36] 'This leads us to another fact, namely the changeability of the linguistic unit itself, which is precisely related to the changeability of communal life' (Schleiermacher, *Psychologie*, ed. L. George (Berlin, 1862), p. 174).

and especially of everyday language there is no final instance. Derrida's own words are: 'Once iterability has established the possibility of parasitism . . . altering at once . . . the system of (il- or perlocutionary) intentions and the systems of rules . . . or of conventions, inasmuch as they are included within the scope of iterability . . . everything becomes possible against the language-police . . . everything is possible except for an exhaustive typology that would claim to limit the powers of graft . . . and classification in genus and species' (*LI*, x, see also z).

Derrida sees undecidability as a direct implication of iterability: it is a structural characteristic of the use of signs and cannot be disposed of either by statistics of real speech events or by rigorous idealisation.

Of course Searle is not unaware of all this. For one thing he admits that even if speech-act intentions are in principle *conscious* they do not have to be so *as* intentions. I may very well be mistaken about the intentional character of the speech act I perform (for instance I may not actually say what I meant to say: I may grossly misunderstand its real meaning, etc.): but this – Searle adds – is not a structural problem of intentionality but a matter of reflection. It is in principle possible, in the uttering of a speech act, to bring as it were intuitive awareness under control by means of reflection (provided, at any rate, that I am a competent participant in the convention in question). In this way the unconscious really does remain, as Derrida writes, 'absolutely excluded by the axiomatics . . . of current speech act theory, in particular as formulated by Searle' (*LI*, r, penultimate section). The 'unconscious' in this context does not mean some mysterious thing associated with the 'dark sides of the life of the soul' (which could only be believed in by someone who is a Romantic or an adherent of a particular school of psychoanalysis) but the 'structural unconscious' (*ibid.*) which overcomes any speaker when he is urged to state the 'sole correct criterion' for the conventional synthesis of meaning and expression. And indeed this not-knowing could not be eliminated on the level of a private effort of thought; for it is of course the Others who decide about the meaning of my utterances (and when I communicate myself, I do it as an Other, 'en autre, en position de l'Autre'); in that respect I, as an individual, am never master of the supra-individual meaning of what I say. 'Every day and every speaker', says Sartre, 'changes the meanings *for everyone,* indeed the others turn them around in my mouth.'[37]

Secondly, Searle himself emphasises that 'one of the most important insights of recent work in the philosophy of language is that most non-technical concepts in ordinary language lack absolutely strict rules. The concepts of *game,* or *chair,* or *promise* do not have absolutely knockdown necessary and sufficient conditions' (*SA,* p. 55). This is because there is no a priori or, as Wittgenstein says, 'natural' association between particular intentions and expressions on the one hand, or speech acts and contexts on the other (this follows from the concept of conventionality itself, since it implies arbitrariness, as David Lewis has shown). The synthesis of the linguistic types, that is reinforced by habit, shifts, as Schleiermacher says, according to the underlying construction of knowledge (*HuK,* p. 461) and ultimately – for in a system any alteration of one element causes an alteration of all the others – according to the underlying projection of the world. Every scientific construction manifests itself in an order of types. But the possibility of coming down from it by a process of step-by-step deduction to the domain of individual facts does not by itself do away with the merely *hypothetical* and model-like character of the structure *from* which the deductions are made. In other words, the systematic order in which a scientific view of the world – a Kuhnian *paradigm* – presents itself is not in itself evidence that 'the individual factor is wholly eliminated' (*HuK,* p. 465). That factor constantly arises anew, as the undismissable possibility of schematising the totality of what is in a different way, that is, of forming a different hypothesis about the order of the world. 'The identity of the construction of thought', says Schleiermacher, 'is not something general but is enclosed within boundaries . . . If, then, the process of schematisation is sufficient to lure forth language, then there must already be in that process itself a difference and the relativity of knowledge which expresses itself in the difference of languages' (*HuK,* p. 461).

But not only the synthesis of meaning and expression is histori-

---

[37] Sartre, *Critique de la raison dialectique* (Paris, 1960).

cal and relative. There is also – as is shown especially by the example of written texts – no 'natural' and supra-historically general association between particular speech acts and contexts (see also *LI*, s, 1).[38] This follows firstly from the changeability of ways of life and societal conventions, but it also has structural causes. For one thing, no context is, as Austin's concept of the 'complete context' suggests, 'capable of saturation'; for it points to the infinity of further contexts (pragmatically these need not necessarily become relevant, but their possible relevance cannot be excluded – by theoretical decree, as it were – from the outset). As such, in every speech act, the meaning becomes separated, however minimally, from the event: the utterance makes the meaning to a certain extent 'external'; it externalises it. Every 'mark' which – through the action of being uttered – has distanced itself from its original situation ('me speaking here now') can in other surroundings make new meaning which cannot be restricted in advance by any convention. (As we have seen, Derrida called this the 'non-present remainder of the mark'.)

What conclusions does Searle draw from this? Chiefly the conclusion that it is simply the case that 'certain forms of analysis, especially analysis into [in detail] necessary and [altogether] sufficient conditions, are likely to involve . . . idealization of the concept analysed' (*SA*, p. 55). We are speaking here, as Grice says in 'Logic and Conversation', of an 'inquir[ing] into the general conditions, that, in one way or another, apply to conversation as such, irrespective of its subject matter' (p. 43). We are already familiar with this conclusion. It entails abstracting from the communicative reality of the complications of everyday language until the demands of the pure theory no longer present any problems. What is wanted is a pure construct, the 'serious', the 'normal' and 'complete' case of a promise; but the criterion of normality is provided by the norm set up by the theory, and thus in a circular manner the norm affirms itself in its results. 'I am ignoring marginal, fringe or

---

[38] It was Wittgenstein who had spoken of the 'natural surroundings' of a word. He meant 'the totality of behaviours regulated by habit or by convention and thus in some sense institutionalised'; the correctness of these behaviours is the precondition for our understanding the meaning of the signs. (See also W. Stegmüller, *Hauptströmungen der Gegenwartsphilosophie* (Stuttgart, 1975), vol. II, p. 68.)

partially defective promises', Searle says (*SA*, p. 55). He will equally
fail to take into account the possibility that the explicitly illocutionary role[39] of a complete case of a promise could nevertheless be
misunderstood, for instance that only its descriptive content might
be comprehended: for this would go against the nine necessary
conditions and the five rules of linguistic interaction. Searle pays
no heed to Friedrich Schlegel's amusing objection that one cannot
possibly give offence to someone who will not take it: he does not
take offence just as logically as he presents the complete promise as
something that must necessarily be accepted.

But had not even Searle admitted that 'corruptibility' is a
constant, because structural, possibility of speech acts? Certainly,
but a 'strict theory' cannot take account of that possibility. 'I am
going', Searle explains, 'to deal only with a simple and idealized
case. This method, one of constructing idealized models, is analogous to the sort of theory construction that goes on in most sciences . . .
Without abstraction and idealization there is no systematization'
(*SA*, p. 56). Thus Searle does not really demonstrate that there are
universals of linguistic usage, but simply asserts – quite logically in
the context of his argument – that idealisation is a methodological
requirement of any activity aspiring to the title of a 'strictly scientific
theory': *if* there is to be a theory of speech acts *then* it can only be on
condition of a rigorous abstraction of the 'non-literal', the 'parasitical', the 'non-serious', the threatening possibilities of elliptical turns
of phrase, hints, metaphors, etc. (*SA*, pp. 55–6).

In this context I would remind readers of the warning which
Whitehead addressed to the philosophers: that it is 'a temptation
. . . that they should weave a fairy-tale of the adjustment of factors;
and then as an appendix introduce the notion of frustration, as a
secondary aspect'.[40] The theory of 'infelicities' has this appearance
of having had to be included in an appendix. It is a typical product
of an abstraction – not from the 'individual factor' of the elements
(such an abstraction is constitutive of the theory) but from the

---

[39] Searle himself shows that Austin's explicit illocutions cannot manage without certain –
inexplicit – presuppositions, for instance the presupposition that the addressee of a
promise prefers the fulfilment of the act to its non-fulfilment, that the fulfilment cannot
be taken for granted, etc.

[40] Whitehead, 'Understanding', pp. 69–70.

dependence of the 'construction of knowledge' that has just been applied on a quite definite and itself individual theory-paradigm. In other words, the perspective from which the abstraction is made is in the object-realm of the empirical sciences and still more of 'ordinary language' and is never a natural given. I can reduce the infinite multiplicity of facts and their properties to very different shared characteristics (concepts, meanings, schemata, etc.) and then of course also state the rule which I have been following. What I cannot avoid in the process of forming concepts is that 'the substantial individuality of the many things leads to conflicts between particular forms of schematisation. Therefore', White-head concludes, 'the summation of the many into the one, and the derivation of importance from the one into the many, involves the notion of disorder, of conflict, of frustration.'[41]

Austin himself categorically excludes the unsuccessful performatives only from the order of the *explicit* speech acts. In the domain of the so-called 'primary illocutionary acts' he accepts their validity. However, what raises the list of the unsuccessful speech acts to the status of a theoretical order is the fact that all these infelicities can be explained with reference to failures to comply with the norm and thus complementarily with reference to the explicit rule itself. Where the infelicity does not succeed, the theory of the infelicity does. It cures the defect by deducing it *ex negativo* from the norm. In a way analogous to the calculation of the rule of three it supplies what real communication lacks in terms of conformity to a rule, and thereby makes a rule: misunderstanding is only the shadow cast by the pinnacle of full understanding upon the incomplete framework of its structural base.

This is made far clearer by H. P. Grice than by Austin. In 'Logic and Conversation' he first sets up a general principle of conversation (a so-called 'principle of co-operation') and four flanking maxims relating to conversation which – on the model of Kant's categories – put forward suggestions for a 'maximally effective exchange of information', or for maximally economical methods

[41] *Ibid.*, pp. 70–1. 'Also, in the same sense, the selection of the particular item for emphasis is . . . arbitrary. It is the convention by means of which the Infinite governs its concentration of attention' (p. 71). 'The assignment of the type of pattern restricts the choice of details' (p. 79).

of 'influencing the interlocutor' (p. 47). This universal framework of categories is then laid over a collection of examples of conversational speech acts in which non-conventionalised but deliberately formed 'implicatures' are produced. Now, the fact that these are not coded by no means necessarily leads to ambiguities; for since the unspoken implicatures were created deliberately and serve the purpose of communication, there is no infringement of either the general principle of co-operation or the maxims of economy. The receiver of the over-determined message can thus exclude the possibility of his partner's 'opting out from the conversational contract'. And from the manner of the apparent breaking of the rule he can then conclude with precision that there is an implicature and what it is. All he has to do, to continue with the comparison used just now, is to work out the x in the calculation of the rule of three from the other elements in the apparatus of maxims. The non-determinacy of the understanding of *nonconventional* or *conversational implicatures* (*ibid.*, pp. 57–8) is thus only apparent and can be extrapolated from a knowledge of the convention.

Searle does not go as far as this. Nonetheless, for him too the possibility of failure remains calculable and can thus be assigned to a supplementary part of the actual theory – for instance of his study of 'pretended' or 'fictional speech acts'.[42] The tendency to idealisation appears more openly here than it did in Austin. The systematic ignoring of disorder *as* disorder saves the theoretician the trouble of undertaking a fundamental reflection on the price which his theory pays with its exclusion of the 'unintentional implicatures' and its premise that speech acts have such a thing as a universal and explicable 'essence'. For Derrida this premise is at the heart of the debate. And he thinks that an idealisation in the form of a speech-act theory which excludes from itself the problem of undecidability tends towards mere fiction. It explains nothing but what follows automatically from its choice of epistemology, in other words nothing but itself (see also *LI*, r, final section). This is why this theory cannot provide its own foundation so long as, acting as both judge and jury, it does not attempt to prove its legitimacy by any other method than that which its methodological premise had already chosen.

---

[42] Searle, 'The Logical Status of Fictional Discourse', *New Literary History* 5 (1975).

That Searle finds this circularity unproblematic may well arouse suspicion towards a linguistic philosophy dedicated to the analysis of utterances, that is, of *historically* situated and interpreted sentences: how is it supposed to be able to do this within the theoretical framework of a synchronic 'taxonomy of illocutionary acts'? Comparing him with Austin, Derrida finds in Searle an impoverishment of the spectrum of speech-act theory. Austin did at least recognise that he must free himself from the dictatorship of the epistemic premises of the natural sciences if he wanted to focus on what was peculiar to performatives. For instance it seemed to him useful to qualify the classical opposition of true and false (which only covers statements) and to complement it by a rhetoric of the 'strength' and 'weakness' of speech acts (*illocutionary force, soundness and weakness of arguments*, etc.).[43] Linked with this was his calling into question the opposition of *fact* and *value*, since after all every speech act communicates a performatively evaluated fact (see also *LI*, j).

Before I pass over the field of the immanent dispute between Searle and Derrida and take up a meta-critical position in relation to the debate, I would just like to indicate what are the concrete steps which Searle feels himself impelled to take as a result of his choice of methodology. How 'serious' is the 'standard speech-act promise' to which he devotes such a close analysis? In relation to the two persons between whom this speech act takes place this could never be decided with Cartesian certainty: they are involved in a linguistic event and can never control their understanding at that moment by means of ideal types. Of course in the extremity of their need to decide they can consult the third chapter of *Speech Acts*, where they will find set out a catalogue of criteria of necessary and adequate conditions for the presence or otherwise of

---

[43] It is very characteristic that in his account of speech-act theory W. Stegmüller speaks of an 'analogy' between the success or failure of speech acts and the truth or falsehood of statements (*Hauptströmungen*, vol. II, pp. 72, 74; see also 'Limited Inc.', *Firstly*). This distinction converges, incidentally, with a differentiation which is familiar in the language of the Greek enlightenment: the distinction between *nómos* and *alétheia*. *Nómos* – later synonymous with *thésis* – no longer designates the 'valid, the sacred and generally binding order', that which is necessary by nature (*tê phýsei*) or that which has been 'ordained on the basis of truth', but 'that which is valid merely generally – through convention' or the 'general but usually false opinion of the many' (*nomothetémata*). Here the *nomisthén* becomes in effect opposed to the *alétheia*. On this see Felix Heinimann, *Nomos und Physis* (Darmstadt, 1965).

'complete', 'non-defective', 'unmutilated' promises, and finally what Searle calls the 'crucial' additional condition that not only must these criteria be fulfilled *de facto* but also that 'the promisee wishes (needs, desires, etc.) that something be done, and the promisor is aware of this wish (need, desire, etc.)' (*SA*, p. 58). To this Searle adds a brief examination of 'apparent counter-examples'. These are cases in which the indicator of the illocutionary role of the promise is in fact used to express a threat or an assertion. Searle declares these cases to be 'derivative from genuine promises' and concludes that 'the point stated in [this] condition . . . is that if a purported promise is to be non-defective, the thing promised must be something the hearer wants done, or considers to be in his interest, or would prefer being done to not being done, etc.; and the speaker must be aware of or believe or know, etc., that this is the case' (*SA*, p. 59). In both quotations the *consciousness* of the speaker, who is competent in applying the rules, becomes the instance which decides whether it is really a promise or, perhaps, a threat. Can we not all recall everyday instances where two speech acts – threat and promise, say – are inextricably combined in one and the same utterance? This is not necessarily a matter of 'derivative forms' of ideal speech acts. For the synthesis of intention and expression which precisely distinguishes a particular type of speech act from another type is uncontrollably shifted in use.

If this is the case – and no speaker/hearer ever has an extra-communicative criterion for the exclusion of the opposite – then every promise, and every speech act in general, is 'structurally ambivalent' (*LI*, r, penultimate section); 'in a manner so as to prevent any *simple* logic (desire/non-desire, for example) from being able to decide . . . their meaning' (*ibid.*). In short, what Searle calls the 'crucial feature' of such contextual conditions for the complete promise, namely the *knowledge* of one's own intention or that of the person addressed – precisely this is in question, not only here and now but in principle. It is after all – to repeat – a function of the communication event as such, which cannot be methodically controlled from an Archimedean position outside itself. The ambivalence of the decision about the real meaning of an utterance has the character of a principle. It is not a function of linguistic competence, which always points to the past of circulating discourses; even the most perfect linguistic competence (but what can this concept mean here?) never guarantees a full understanding of what a speaker really 'wants to say'. 'A thousand possibilities will always remain open even if one understands something in [an utterance]' (*LI*, r, first possibility, 3rd paragraph) – which does not mean 'necessarily always and everywhere', but 'in principle'. But precisely because a theory idealises and can only take account of characteristics of linguistic usage that are present in principle, it will have to pay attention to these possibilities. The state of undecidability *theoretically* continues to exist even when neither of the interlocutors articulates the need to end it. 'It is sufficient', says Derrida, 'merely to introduce, into the manger of speech acts, a few wolves of the type "undecidability" . . . for the shepherd to lose track of this flock: one is no longer certain where to find the identity of the "speaker" or the "hearer" . . . of an intention . . . or of an effect' (*LI*, r, penultimate paragraph). Let us add that not only desire but also the involvement of historically situated subjects with traditions falls into the category of the 'unconscious'. One can perfectly well make meaning with linguistic types without in the process becoming 'conscious' of their historical freight. Of course this not-becoming-conscious does not guarantee that the implications of a tradition will not nevertheless come through in the actual speaking and over-determine the utterances. The positive insistence on the synchronic framework within which communication *de facto* takes place turns a blind eye to the pernicious spirit which may possibly be at work in it. One can only escape it by – as a matter of principle, and not only in the case of unsuccessful communication – stepping over, by reflection, the simplicity of the conventions, i.e. trying to become aware that even the most rational discourse is 'indebted' to the 'more or less anonymous tradition of a code, a heritage, a reservoir of arguments' (*LI*, f).

DIFFÉRANCE AND INDIVIDUALITY

In the final section of this chapter I would like to return to what Derrida calls his 'minimal consensus' with Searle (*LI*, r, 1st section, after c.): '[Searle] and I seemed to be in agreement, both concerning iterability itself and concerning the systematic link between iterability and code, or to put it differently, between iterability and a kind of conventionality'. How far does this consensus, which Derrida himself assures us applies only to the existence and the effects of conventionality, not also extend to its basis?

Now it is striking that both Searle and Derrida avoid having any recourse to the instance of an individuality that spontaneously creates meaning. For Searle this follows directly from his choice of the method of the exact sciences: but a transcendental subject escapes the criteria of strict cognition (no intuition and no concept could be adequate to it) and there is therefore no place for it in the realm of analytical philosophy.

But Derrida? Does he not say that the differential activity which forms a space in the tissue of the sign system, splitting 'mark' from 'mark' and so laying the basis for the identity of the elements – does he not say that *différance* is the creator of meaning? And does he not add that – as the basis of the positivity of the signs – it is itself not positive and so escapes the system itself? At first glance his description of *différance* is very similar to the description which idealism and phenomenology have given of transcendental subjectivity: it too, to the extent that it provides the systematic foundation for the ordering of the elements, escapes the categories of what it founds. The same applies to *différance*: it 'escape[s] the jurisdiction of all ontotheological discourse even if [it] render[s] the latter at times possible' (*LI*, t, third to last paragraph). 'No constituted logic, nor any rule of a logical order can . . . impose its norms upon the subject of these prelogical possibilities' (*LI*, v; translation amended). Derrida explains this sentence using Kantian terminology, and then distances himself from the ontological inclusions of the terms 'principle', 'condition of possibility', or 'basis' (*ibid.*). I find the most emphatic distinction in the following formulation: 'Iterability is . . . not a transcendental condition of possibility making citation and other phenomena (parasites, for example) into conditioned effects. This kind of (classical) logic is fractured in its code by iterability' (*LI*, x).

What can this mean? Derrida clearly thinks that the subject of transcendental philosophy – be it that of Fichte or that of transcendental hermeneutics which has become so much more modest – must be imagined as a core of presence to the self and of granite identity. Then the 'self' would escape the law of iterability and conventionality which prevents meaning and expression from ever being irrevocably joined: all the signs in a system are 'merely' conventional and thus transformable.

If, however, transcendental philosophy really regarded the 'self' as a supra-conventional identity of meaning and expression, then of course Derrida could show that the wolf of undecidability invades this sheepfold too. For either the 'I' (or the 'self') is acquainted with itself because it has a distinct meaning; then, however, it is true of it as of all other meanings that its identity is mediated via all other meanings – a consequence which would challenge the view that its nature is that of a principle; or – this would be the alternative – the self is acquainted with itself necessarily and without inner otherness; in this case its meaning would not be differentially determined and could thus, like the linguists' nil-phoneme, not be distinguished from any other meaning – an equally unacceptable conclusion, which would once again leave the fact of our familiarity with ourselves unexplained.[44]

There is here a dilemma which Fichte himself recognised in his *Wissenschaftslehre nova methodo* of 1798 and made strenuous efforts to solve in the following decade. It is that neither of the two demands can be given up but that they are incompatible with one another. Even if Derrida, from his position, is unable to give any account of the phenomenon of the immediacy of the self – he knows the self only as a case of reflection – he is still justified in pointing out that the principle of classical transcendental philosophy does not escape what he calls the 'graphics of the *iter*'. For what is true of the concepts of ideality, of meaning and of significance – that it is necessary to 'define them *differently*, through a differential system'[45]

---

[44] David Hume, in his criticism of his own denial of 'personal identity' in the Appendix to the *Treatise* (ed. L. Selby-Bigge (Oxford, 1888)), reflects similarly (pp. 633ff.): 'In short there are two principles, which I cannot render consistent; nor is it in my power to renounce either of them, viz. *that all our distinct perceptions are distinct existences*, and *that the mind never perceives any real connexion among distinct existences*. Did our perceptions either inhere in something simple and individual (e.g. a principle of connexion, which binds them together, and makes us attribute to them a real simplicity and identity), or did the mind perceive some real connexion among them, there wou'd be no difficulty on the case. For my part, I must plead the privilege of a sceptic, and confess, that this difficulty is too hard for my understanding' (pp. 635, 636).

[45] Derrida, *Positions*, p. 90.

– is in his view true 'also, one might say especially, of the concept of *representation* and of the *subject*'.[46] He concludes from this[47] that the self – like meaning – is firstly plural, that is, without inner unity, secondly not the (real) basis of itself, and thirdly non-spontaneous, i.e. the self itself comes into being as a semantic effect of differential activity or iterability. All meaning-forming effects like the synthesis of signs and the interpretation of signs are attributed to this activity which is autonomous and anonymous (not performed by a subject).

It seems to me that this conclusion brings with it epistemological problems for Derrida's position. Before indicating in more detail what these are, I will just once more briefly go back to Whitehead's lectures on *The Modes of Thought*. There we found not only serious objections to a static and taxonomic abstraction which consigns the list of infelicities to the appendix. Whitehead also makes his plea for a dynamic and innovative scientific praxis using a theoretical instrument that is akin to Derrida's *différance*. This is the concept of *incompatibility*. Henry Sheffer had developed it at the beginning of this century and had shown that, and how, all logical links between utterances could be developed from it.[48] Now, the concept of incompatibility – according to Whitehead – implies that of finiteness. 'For as Spinoza pointed out, the finite is that which excludes other things comparable to itself.'[49] Derrida's concept of *différance* does the same in relation to semiology. It explains the finiteness of sign systems and thus the revocability of the differentiations realised on any occasion. If each sign acquires its identity from its incompatibility with the identities of all others, then – we may conclude, with Whitehead – the actual incompatibility of any two signs can only be overcome in the course of a process. For 'process is the way by which the universe escapes from the exclusions of inconsistency'.[50] Precisely this seems to me to be the conception that Derrida has of linguistic change: it is the

---

[46] *Ibid.*, p. 110.
[47] Like the American empiricists/pragmatists, in whose tradition he otherwise does not feel particularly at home.
[48] The incompatibility of two sentences is the negation of their conjugability: $-(p \cdot q)$. That all utterances can be reduced to conjunction (with the help of negation) is already shown by De Morgan's laws.
[49] Whitehead, 'Understanding', p. 72.   [50] *Ibid.*, p. 75.

work of unstoppable formations and shifts of difference which at the same time grounds the mass of signs as an order and challenges it: for none of the infinitely many arrangements of signs that have historically appeared could claim to have achieved the 'true' or 'definitive' systematisation. An unlimited number of competing schematisations of the object material are possible, according to the differentiations of the material of expression that have been undertaken in any given case. 'The assignment of the type of pattern restricts the choice of details.'[51] In short, the formation of scientific concepts is a task of differentiation; and because differentiation presupposes the recognition of finiteness the structures which subdivide the mass of what exists and link it to concepts carry an index of historicity. (The adherents of scientism would be happiest if the advance of knowledge consisted merely of adding in hitherto unknown details to the established structures of the prevailing theory – so that there might perhaps be a proliferation of the number of *tokens*, but the table of categories of *types* would remain the same. 'This is the safe advance of dogmatic spirits, fearful of folly. But history discloses another type of progress, namely the introduction of novelty of pattern into conceptual experience. In this way, details hitherto undiscriminated or dismissed as casual irrelevances ["parasitical"] are lifted into coordinated experience. There is a new vision of the great Beyond.')[52]

Although Derrida's conception of linguistic change finds support in this quarter – against Searle – it still seems to me that, like Searle, he encounters insoluble difficulties as soon as he tackles the problem of the *application of signs* without having recourse to a subject. This follows directly from the 'minimal consensus'. For Searle, as for Derrida, the *use* of signs remains a matter which is decided by the code. Certainly – at any rate in Derrida's case – it is hardly possible any longer to speak of meaning being generated or deduced in Chomsky's sense. There are no fixed rules – iterability destroys their identity; but the real achievement of the creation or interpretation of signs is a matter which is not troubled in the slightest by the 'graphics of the *iter*'. Articulations

---

[51] *Ibid.*, p. 79.   [52] *Ibid.*, p. 80.

and interpretations of signs happen; they set themselves going –
that is all.[53]

However, this disregarding of the irreducibility of the (Peircian)
interpretant brings its revenge, for Derrida (whether he wants to or
not) has to make the differential activity the *author* of meaning
formation and its transformation. Very well: no originator acts,
everything takes place *by itself*. But the use of the reflexive pronoun,
here as elsewhere in neo-structuralist writings, genuinely functions
as a signal: to speak of the 'self' has no meaning without the
interpretation based on familiarity with oneself. If one transfers the
experience of this familiarity with oneself to the automatism of the
linguistic event, one cannot help thinking of this event as (analogous to) the subject. It is no use asserting (as Gadamer does) that one
thinks of this super-subject of language 'as a substance' (in the
Hegelian sense); the anonymous 'It' which now acts in place of the
eliminated subject has cunningly absorbed all its characteristics
into itself: spontaneity, unity/continuity, familiarity with itself. It is
able to preserve traditions, to create a 'continuum of meaning'; it is
structured just as 'speculatively' as the Hegelian mind, and it can
at any time make innovations in the repertoire of the language. It
is, in a word, organised like a self and cannot possibly be an
alternative to the classical transcendental subject.

What one must do, wrote Derrida, is not abolish the subject but
'explain it *differently*'. Certainly; but in my view his critique of
Searle does not provide an effective instrument for doing this. In
the discourse of criticism the structure of what is being criticised
crops up again. This does not necessarily reflect unfavourably on
the criticism, but merely shows the powers of resistance of what is
being criticised: it asserts itself, against the author's will, so to
speak, in his argumentation.

I will show this in relation to the failure of the 'subsumption
model of cognition'. Admittedly Derrida explicitly calls this model

[53] In Saussure the dialectic of differentiality and the creation of meaning is still strictly
adhered to: since the unarticulated mass of sound is in itself as meaningless as the
pre-significant meaning is amorphous, and meaning thus only appears at the intersection
(differential) of the two – and as the result of an articulatory differentiation – neither can
be regarded as the ground of the other – nor can differentiality be regarded as the
anonymous ground of both: 'It is the difference which makes significant and it is
significance which also creates the differences' (*Cahiers F. de Saussure* 15 (1957), p. 76).

into question when he expresses doubt that the individual speech act can be understood as a *case* prescribed by the community of action and determined down to the last detail. But he does not do this by using the argument that the individuality of historically situated speech acts is a matter that is not decided by the universal (the system, *différance*, etc.).

I will begin by referring back to Peirce. Peirce's *Semiotic and Significs* (ed. Charles Hardwick, Indiana, 1977) had challenged the so-called 'two-place model of signs' – which reduces signification to relationships between *objects* and *sign-bearers* – with the argument that the sign needs an *interpretation* by the user and is actually in itself non-signifying. Although Austin and Searle – and now Habermas – work on the basis of a pragmatically revised semantics, their sign model seems to me to be in the Peircian sense 'simply degenerate'. True, the trinity of the relationships seems to be preserved when communication about objects is made dependent upon 'successful agreement on the intersubjective level about the particular pragmatic meaning of the communication' having previously been achieved.[54] But this specific act of understanding – the creation of the interpretant, according to Peirce – is in its turn subjected to a 'code'.[55] Eike von Savigny expresses this in a particularly striking way: 'Illocutionary acts are the acts which they are [only] by virtue of a convention which makes them so.'[56] In that case the task of pragmatics is not to emphasise the impossibility of deriving individual uses of language and thus the creative aspect of 'semiosis' from a system, but – as Habermas says, characteristically invoking Chomsky's transformational grammar – 'to reconstruct the system of rules according to which communicatively competent speakers make sentences into utterances [i.e. situatively interpreted sentences] and re-shape them into other utterances'.[57]

---

[54] Jürgen Habermas, 'Vorbereitende Bemerkungen zu einer Theorie der kommunikativen Kompetenz', in J. Habermas and Niklas Luhmann, *Theorie der Gesellschaft oder Sozialtechnologie* (Frankfurt am Main, 1971), p. 106.

[55] *Ibid.*, p. 108.

[56] Eike von Savigny, *Die Philosophie der normalen Sprache* (Frankfurt am Main, 1974), p. 172.

[57] Habermas, 'Vorbereitende Bemerkungen', p. 107. In this schema individuals are considered only as 'systematic variation[s] of the general structures', 'of the linguistic code' – or at best as a 'variable of the personality structures', etc. (p. 108).

The elegance with which the 'code model' is transferred from the domain of the 'constatives' to that of the 'performatives' veils the real epistemological problem which is posed here. Since it could not possibly be the pragmatic convention *itself* which performs this act of interpretation – what would the 'self' of a convention consist of? and what would 'the linguistic code'[58] be, other than a lifeless abstraction, a retrospective idealisation of the discourses that have really been uttered? – since, then, the code could not possibly, except at the cost of a metaphysical hypostasisation, be its own interpreter, who then interprets the code or the convention? 'We are being asked to believe', says Sartre, 'that thought is merely *langage*, as if the *langage* itself were not *spoken*.'[59] And elsewhere he writes, '*Langage* has been made into *a langue which speaks itself all by itself.*'[60] A language which spoke itself would – as we have seen – necessarily be constituted like a subject, as in Gadamer and Wittgenstein: it is not *my* interpretation which helps the tradition to create language (Wittgenstein, *Philosophische Untersuchungen*, §198), but 'the rule, once stamped with a particular meaning, draws the lines of its observance [wholly independently (my addition, MF)] through the whole space' (*Philosophische Untersuchungen*, §219). If this is the case, then clearly the methodological recourse to a code (or in Gadamer's case to a 'traditional event') no longer has the effect of an alternative explanation. For the very thing that it was supposed to achieve – the elimination of a subjectivity which applies and changes rules – failed to happen, as can be seen from a simple analysis of the use of reflexive pronouns in the rhetoric of these theories. Given that the 'self-applying rule' still allows a subject to be involved, it becomes apparent that there is no way round the 'subjective factor' in speaking: the only certain starting-point in the search for the instance that applies the rules is the single subject, the individual. All the conclusions that result from the failure of the code model point in this direction.

Before pursuing it further, I wish to underline the terminological difference between subjectivity and individuality. I know that Peirce himself has little use for either of these expressions, and Richard J. Bernstein has analysed the reasons for this aversion

---

[58] *Ibid.*, p. 108. [59] 'Jean-Paul Sartre répond', *L'Arc* 30 (1968), p. 88.
[60] Sartre, *L'être et le néant* (Paris, 1943), p. 599.

very well.[61] But Peirce's criticism of the fetishism of the self-applying rule stands in an idealistic tradition of which – with the exception of Kant – he seems to have had no knowledge. In this tradition of modern linguistic theory, 'individuality' plays a decisive role. The epistemological reasons for the 'individualistic option' – for instance on the part of Humboldt, Steinthal, Schleiermacher and Boeckh – have been so uniformly and so thoroughly misunderstood or misrepresented in the anti-traditional self-justifications of analytical philosophy, structuralism and existential-ontological hermeneutics that to reach back into history in this way today seems positively progressive.

Now, Schleiermacher (I name him only as an example, in order to situate my reflections historically) makes the following distinction between subjectivity and individuality: subjectivity is something general; it is never fundamentally in opposition to systems, as is shown in exemplary manner by Hegel's famous formulation about the 'subjectivity of the substance'. Individuals, on the other hand, are never parts of systems (not even of systems of subjectivity such as Fichte's *Wissenschaftslehre*): they are not general. One cannot deduce them from rules as one can deduce the particular (and the particular is never the same as the individual)[62] from the general. Thus the individual cannot be subsumed under any concept and it is not amenable to definition. It is therefore of paramount importance, in Fichte's view, that in the interests of reason – of universal subjectivity – 'individuality should be forgotten in theory and denied in practice'.[63] But the ungraspable nature of the individual element does not really lead to the failure of scientific discourse about language and speaking; rather it rescues

---

[61] See also Richard J. Bernstein, *Praxis und Handeln* (Frankfurt am Main, 1975), pp. 70–1.

[62] Every human being, says Schleiermacher, 'is on the one hand an exemplar, on the other an individual' (*Die christliche Sitte*, 2nd edn, ed. L. Jonas (Berlin, 1884), p. 17, §51). As far as I can see, this difference was first clearly perceived by Gilbert de Poitiers. He distinguishes between the individuality of something that exists and its specialness (singularitas): 'Singularitas is, according to Gilbert, the more comprehensive term which designates everything that exists to the extent that it is in "conformity" to everything else via the property of singularity which is common to all, whereas the individuality of something that exists is based on the partial "dissimilarity" of its property to other things that exist' (article on *Individualität* in Ritter and Gründer, *Historisches Wörterbuch der Philosophie*, (Darmstadt, 1971–), column 303 of the appropriate volume).

[63] J.G. Fichte, *Sämtliche Werke*, ed. I.H. Fichte (Berlin, 1845–6), vol I, p. 517.

it from an aporia. For the place where the rule is suspended at the moment of its application is after all the place of speaking itself and thus precisely the object of a theory of language which is orientated towards application. When the linguistician abstracts his rules from the empirical material of speech acts, resisting as he does so the temptation to fetishise these rules into super-subjects, he knows very well that for reasons of logic it is impossible to subject the mastery of rules and the application of rules to yet more rules. Since, however, rules are constantly being used and altered, the only conclusion to be drawn is that at this point in the explanation the option of regularity can be of no further use and must – there is no other alternative – abandon the field to what is not general and not covered by rules. But not to the incomprehensible: for originality in understanding is based on the fact that it *invents* the interpretant for a given sentence. A surplus of meaning comes into play; the result of understanding exceeds the stock of the input and output of the code; the sum bursts the limits of the economic calculation which controls the strict parity of input and output. How could the interpretant conform to rules or be conventional if it is in fact a characteristic that cannot be immanent in the uttered sentence and its rules of constitution? 'Grammatically', says Schleiermacher, 'one cannot sum up any individuality in a concept . . . One cannot give a concept of a style [i.e. of any individual use of language]' (*HuK*, p. 172). For a 'concept' – as Saussure uses the term – is an intersubjectively anchored previous projection of understanding which, before it succeeded in breaking through into the repertoire of generality, existed as a singular interpretant and is one of those 'particular things' which, as Rilke says, are at first 'only intended for *one* and cannot be said'[64] – assuming that 'saying' here means 'communicating'.

Schleiermacher speaks of 'concepts' (*Begriffe*) or 'meanings' (*Bedeutungen*) whenever he wishes to refer to the communicable product of a process of communication, but of *Sinn* (literally: 'sense') when he focuses upon the process of the 'formation of meaning' as such.[65] In his opinion every concept has its roots in the *Sinn* and

---

[64] Rilke, *Sämtliche Werke*, vol. XI, p. 796.
[65] See also Wilhelm Köller, Peter Rusterholz and K. H. Spinner on 'Bedeutung und Sinn', in *Zeichen, Text, Sinn. Zur Semiotik des literarischen Verstehens* (Göttingen, 1977), pp. 49ff.

every (conventional) meaning (*Bedeutung*) is based on spontaneous understanding (which can be motivated by habits, patterns of discourse or conventions, but never explained by them). Sartre takes a very similar view: 'Meanings', he says, 'are only quasi-meanings, and their totality constitutes only a quasi-conceptual knowledge: *firstly* because they have been chosen by the sense [*sens*] as its instruments and *have their roots in the sense* [*sens*] (because, in other words, they are constituted from the individual style, expressed according to the individual style and, as such, are clouded already in their origin); *and then* also because in the domain of the universal they appear split away from themselves as if by an individuality.'[66]

As long as linguistic philosophy fixed its gaze solely on the descriptive content of utterances, it could suppress the factor of sense (*sens*) or attach little importance to it. If two names designate the same thing then they simply have the same meaning and may be substituted for one another in any sentence without the truth value of the sentence being altered. In this way the 'sense' becomes a logical stopgap: it has no part to play in verification. But, for an expression, having 'meaning' means being a usable element in what Stegmüller calls a 'fully interpreted language'.[67] Now linguistic expressions do not fall from the heaven of ideas complete with the whole dowry of their significance. As codified schemata of a communal world-view they are based on interpretations made by socialised individuals. Meanings can thus only be related to things in a positive truth-functional manner if they have previously been systematically interpreted, i.e. (as Sartre puts it) if they have come under the control of sense (*sens*). To this extent the possibility of scientific verification and of correct description is itself founded in the forms of life, world-views and projects of meaning of linguistically acting individuals.

It is important to recognise that meaning and understanding come into being as individuals even if they are subsequently appropriated by other individuals and, as we say, become communicatively acceptable. Because it cannot be penetrated by

---

[66] Sartre, *Situations VIII*, p. 450.   [67] Stegmüller, *Hauptströmungen*, vol. II, p. 96.

concepts, individual understanding sets a permanent limit to the convention of meaning (in a positive sense as its framework, in a negative sense as a challenge to it). The elements of the convention are, as Sartre says, deprived by individuality of their fullness and universality; they are 'as it were split off from themselves', never to regain the substantiality of a saturated concept. Their 'correctness' has remained hypothetical, without their usability having suffered by this lack of definition. To pursue this image, the cut (*Schnittfläche*) which separates the identity of the sign from the identity of another sign (both 'marking' and 'differentiating' it) is like an infinitely movable boundary (*marge*). It unpredictably cuts across the possibility of completely successful, total understanding, of 'meaningfulness' or the ideal 'complete speech act', in that firstly it reminds the codified meanings of their differential origin and secondly it reminds the tissue of all existing differentiations that it can be undone by new (individual) interpretations. In this way the individual is not the opponent but the (in itself not significant, quasi-transcendental) ground of the significance of the system. It could only be seen as the opponent of the system on the circular premise that the system is the ground of its own significance and needs no meaning-giving instance that transcends it.

I have made this historical excursus in order to promote the idea that talk of the meaning-creating 'gap' between the 'marks', or of 'transforming iterability' should be placed in the hermeneutic context, where talk of the individuality of meaning-creation also belongs. If Derrida (to whom I am alluding here) does not accept this offer (and indeed in some ways he participates in the inadequacies of the code model), he has of course a reason for this. For Humboldt's and Schleiermacher's concept of individuality is noticeably at odds with a far more powerful tradition of the idea of individuality which had already in the nineteenth century begun to superimpose itself on that one and gradually absorbed it into itself. Derrida seems to know only this – more powerful – tradition. It has its roots in classical antiquity and largely determines the everyday meaning of 'individuality' even today. For David Hume, for instance, the 'principium individuationis' is 'nothing but the *invariableness* and *uninterruptedness* of any object, thro' a suppos'd variation of time'.[68]

In the present context I can only invoke this tradition and not discuss it. It saw the individual as a place of abundance, as 'the completely determined being ("ens omnimodo determinatum")', as the substance wholly possessed by itself and unsplittable ('undivided in itself and shared by others'). The individual is that which exists singly ('individuum sive unum'), which consists exclusively only of itself, has internal relationships 'only' with itself and – like Plato's *átomon eîdos* – possesses the characteristics of permanence and self-preservation (in later times there might be the addition of *syneídesis*, familiarity with itself). Although there have always been attempts (for instance those of Gilbert of Poitiers and Richard of St. Victor) to distinguish between individuality and particularity, the scholastic doctrine, in particular, of the various degrees of individuality and the *principium individuationis* makes it clear that the peculiarity of the individual cannot only be reached by a categorical leap from the general but can be derived by continuous transitions from the universal. This means, of course, that the 'incommensurability' of individuals in relation to each other is limited; they are – according to the unanimous teaching of, say, St. Thomas Aquinas and Leibniz – centred towards God and can also communicate with one another through him – through shared participation in the 'esse commune'.

So it is not logical incommensurability that has the last word, but the symbolic representation of unity in the individuals: in a contracted form they represent the universe ('Individua sunt actu, in quibus sunt contracte universa', we read for instance in Nicolaus of Cusa (*De Docta ignorantia* 2,6)). Finally, Leibniz' infinitesimal calculus brings about by strictly scientific means the disappearance of the gulf between the universal concept and the *species infima*, by showing that the universal can in an infinite gradation be defined downwards to the single thing: both share the same nature. This is the thesis of the sameness in kind between the general and the individual (with the characteristic

---

[68] David Hume, *Treatise*, p. 201.

implication that the individual is a 'kind', a 'species', albeit the very smallest). God – the highest species – determines 'a priori' the concept of all individuals.[69] Can one say that this premise, which remains equally binding for the systems of Fichte or of Hegel as – *mutatis mutandis* – for the natural sciences, constitutes the concept of science in general?

With this tradition of the idea of individuality I will now contrast the other one which I invoked earlier by means of a few quotations from Schleiermacher and Sartre. According to it, the individual is not a place of abundance, not a core of selfhood which can never be worn away,[70] and – above all – not a concept which could be developed by processes of deduction from an ideal of reason. On the contrary, 'The "individual feeling" (i.e. the familiarity with itself of something that exists individually) is the "complement" of a constitutive "lack" in the interior of every self-consciousness, even the highest.'[71] It 'adds to' and 'completes' the 'missing unity'[72] of that movement in which the single self-consciousness strives to represent in itself the *general* condition of truth. The gap which separates it from the abundance of the (Hegelian) concept and denies it the identity of an original and complete self-presence causes the individual 'I' to be 'open to the totality of the Outside-us'.[73] In other words the lack of a natural meaning which would define its nature once and for all forces the individual on to the path of interpretation: he must project his meaning anew at every moment, and will never be able to 'resolve into an identical way of thinking' the changing

---

[69] Kant admittedly adheres to this view, by demonstrating the transcendence of the concept of God and thus the impossibility of achieving the task of reconciling individual and universal, but nonetheless emphasising that the concept of the 'ens omnimodo determinatum' logically presupposes that of the 'epitome of all predicates' – a concept which precisely expresses nothing individual but the highest universality (see *Kritik der reinen Vernunft* (*Critique of Pure Reason*), pp. 599–605).

[70] Thus for instance Johannes Volkelt in *Das Problem der Individualität* (Munich, 1928), p. 38: One cannot say 'that the I dissolves in multiplicity and combination and lacks anything firm, core-like, gathered together in itself. But this firmness consists precisely in the consciousness of thisness, uniqueness, individuality . . . Here that which is like a core, which stands firm, appears in every stream of consciousness . . .' Volkelt, incidentally, regards individuality as a 'determination of the *essence (Wesen)*' of a human being.

[71] Schleiermacher, *Dialektik*, ed. Rudolf Odebrecht (Leipzig, 1942), pp. 290 and 295–6.

[72] *Ibid.*, pp. 298 and 290.

[73] Schleiermacher, *Psychologie*, p. 77.

aspects under which his own being and that of the world present themselves to him 'and remove all differences' (*HuK*, p. 411).

In this way the individual does become the transcendental condition of meaning and understanding: it creates the meanings through the exchange of which communication and thus intersubjectivity become possible. But among these meanings there is none that could guarantee a 'complete' understanding, i.e. one which shakes off the 'individual addition',[74] and could re-present the totality of the Outside-us objectively and thus definitively (no representation without previous presence). Everything that has once had contact with individuality escapes the requirement of generality and verifiability, if truth is understood as 'readequation or reappropriation as a desire to stop up the gap'.[75] Truth is hollow. In the heart of the Hegelian idea a hole gapes, as it were, devouring its identity and finality. For precisely this reason the 'true' meaning of the world is an open question: it remains relative to all the judgments which have been made about it and which can in principle not be completed. Equally the linguistic world-view prevailing at a given time (the code, the convention, etc.) in which these judgments are combined to form a consensus for that epoch must be regarded as an unstable, historically open context, the meaning of which changes according to interpretative judgments by individuals and never attains the state of being of a 'truth' which shakes off interpretation and commands from outside. But not only is a final judgment on the truth of what exists unattainable: one must also – as August Boekh says – 'remain aware (of the fact) that one can never reach a complete understanding of any element of language'.[76] For every understanding is productive: it shifts the boundaries of meaning of the signs in the act of creating interpretants, and the extent of this shift can never – because of its individuality – be controlled by a system, i.e. with the help of a convention. All idealisations miss their target, all understanding is understanding-differently. 'And

---

[74] August Boeckh, *Enzyklopädie und Methodologie der philologischen Wissenschaften*, ed. E. Bratuschek (reprinted Darmstadt, 1966), p. 83.

[75] Derrida, 'Le facteur de la vérité', in *Poétique. Revue de théorie et d'analyse littéraires* 21 (1975), p. 115.

[76] Boeckh, *Enzyklopädie*, p. 106 (see also Schleiermacher, *HuK*, pp. 80-1 [§ 9] and 94 [§18.4]).

therefore one can never produce the same thing again',[77] says Boeckh, quite in the spirit of Derrida.[78] Not that there is no self-consciousness of any given interpretant. But what Derrida writes about intention applies to it too: 'What is limited by iterability is not intentionality in general, but its character of being conscious or present to itself (actualized, fulfilled and adequate), the simplicity of its features, its *undividedness*' (*LI*, z). Of course Humboldt already knew this: 'Understanding is not a meeting of ways of thinking in one indivisible point, but a meeting of spheres of thought *where the more general part [of each] is congruent while the more individual part protrudes.* The intellectual progress of the human race thereby becomes possible, because every expansion of thinking that is achieved can pass into the possession of others without fettering the freedom in them which is necessary for that appropriation and for further expansion.'[79]

Thus not only does individuality not imply the concept of 'complete determinacy' but logically it also does not imply that of full presence to oneself. One could characterise individuality in a striking manner as that being whose nature it is to exist without an essence (*Wesen*). By *Wesen* I mean *what* a thing is – its *way* of being, that is permanent and preserves itself identically in changing conditions. Now obviously one cannot ascribe essentiality (*Wesenhaftigkeit*) to that which helps determinations of the *Wesen* – its own and that of others – to appear, in the same sense as one can ascribe it to that which has an identifiable *Wesen* (essence) *by virtue of it*. To this extent individuality is a pure deed-*action* (*actus purus*), without the fact (deed-*thing*) founded by it being wholly equated with the act. I quote Derrida: 'The iteration structuring [the intention] a priori introduces into it a dehiscence and a cleft [*brisure*] which are essential' (*Sec*, p. 192). Here, as often, Derrida uses an artificial expression; *Littré* defines *brisure* as ' "faille" et "articulation", par charnière, d'un ouvrage de serrurie' (as a hinge-like gap and as a linking bridge within a piece of iron-

---

[77] Boeckh, *Enzyklopädie*, p. 126.
[78] An attempt to see the individual as a being 'not subject to the principle of identity' is also made in Richard Müller-Freienfels's *Philosophie der Individualität* (Leipzig, 1921), pp. 3, 54ff.
[79] Humboldt, *Werke*, 5 vols., ed. Andreas Flitner and Klaus Giel (Stuttgart, 1979–86), vol v, p. 418.

work). The metaphor is also an appropriate one to characterise the dissonant unity of consciousness: two elements which relate to one another in the framework of a reflection constitute – as Sartre says – a synthetic *unity* ('unification synthétique'), but they do not turn into a seamless *identity* (*identité*).[80] The synthesis of self-consciousness is 'a quality which *is* unity, a reflex which *is* its own reflection',[81] but in such a way that the two parts do not simply coincide. If that were the case the phenomenon of self-hood, which always presupposes a minimal distance – the gap of re-presentation – would inevitably destroy itself.[82] The very grammar of reflexive pronouns tells us that. The expressions 'self', 'oneself', etc., point to a unity which *as such* neither appears (there is an irreducible duality of reflection and that which reflects), nor is simply suspended (the non-identity of the self with itself does not remove the possibility of the self's familiarity with itself, does not remove the unity of subjectivity).

Sartre thus distinguishes – like Schelling before him – the identity which is unrepresentable because it is self-less from its manifestation as a synthetic organisation of elements which relate to each other. This manifestation is incomplete: it exists (just like 'immediate self-consciousness' in Schleiermacher) on the basis of a principle which escapes it. What escapes there – identity or being – is still a precondition of the structure of self-consciousness. The self exists as a call for being, as a demand for this its transcendent precondition. (This is what Sartre calls the 'ontological proof of consciousness'.)

Once again Derrida's words can readily be brought into these reflections: 'Iterability supposes a minimal remainder . . . in order that the identity of the *selfsame* be repeatable and identifiable *in*, *through*, and even *in view of* its alteration. For the structure of iteration . . . implies *both* identity *and* difference. Iteration in its "purest" form – and it is always impure – contains *in itself* the discrepancy of a difference that constitutes its iteration' (*LI*, o). To prove the compatibility of the two positions I will continue with Sartre: 'The *self* [*soi*] thus represents an ideal distance in the

---

[80] Sartre, *L'être et le néant*, p. 116, 2nd section.
[81] *Ibid.*, p. 118. Since Sartre did not know Fichte's philosophy, the expression 'reflet reflétant' is probably his translation of Hegel's 'Reflexion-in-sich'. [82] *Ibid.*, pp. 118–19.

immanence of the subject in relation to itself, a way of *not being its own coincidence*, of escaping from identity while positing it as a unity, in short of being in a permanently unstable equilibrium between identity as absolute cohesion without a trace of diversity and unity as the synthesis of a multiplicity.'[83]

That *as which* the singular act determines itself to be can be iterated, established and written in a system of signs – but not the act itself, which escapes the category of the something, of iterability and of reflexivity. Was it not this that caused Schelling late in life (and following him Kierkegaard, Heidegger and Sartre) to think of pure existence as individuality (*Sämtliche Werke*, pp. 583ff.)[84] and to attribute to its pure actuality the fact that it precedes the essence (*Wesen*) or – which is the same thing – that it is that being whose nature it is to project its way of being freely, without it being possible to characterise it on the basis of that way of being? Existence is always 'my particular' existence, but its essential project never coincides with the act of the one who projects it. 'Existence', says Sartre, (and in reading this one must recall Derrida's formulation), 'is distance from oneself, separation. What exists is what it is not and is not what it is. It "nothings" itself [Il se "néantise"].'[85]

'Minimal distance' (*distance, décalage*), 'gaping apart', 'bursting open' (*déhiscence*), 'breaking', 'identity and difference': Sartre's characterisations of (individual) existence and Derrida's catalogue of characteristics of the iteration–transformation can be interchanged easily and without loss of meaning. Derrida appears not to notice this convergence. This is especially clear in his engagement with Lacan ('Le facteur de la vérité'). In Lacan – as I have shown elsewhere – the differential activity of investing with meaning[86] appears under the heading of a *singulier*: its individuality, and that means its non-generalness, makes it impossible for

---

[83] *Ibid.*, p. 119, 1st section.

[84] Schelling, *Sämtliche Werke*, ed. K.F.A. Schelling, I Abtheilung vols. I–x, II Abtheilung Bde. I–4, (Stuttgart, 1856–61), II/1, pp. 583ff.)

[85] Sartre, 'Conscience de soi et connaissance de soi', *Bulletin de la Société Française de Philosophie* 42 (Paris, 1948), p. 50.

[86] Of course this is not a term used by Lacan: for the sake of simplicity I am translating Lacan's theorem of the missing signifier, the loss of which enables all other signifiers in the 'symbolic order' to attain meaningfulness, by Derrida's artificial term, *différance*.

the signs created by it to be repeated identically. There is always something 'which cannot be articulated' involved, which makes what Searle calls the 'repetition of the same' problematic because in the act of its application it gnaws at the prevailing boundaries of the taxonomic system. Derrida on the other hand believes that the use of the concept of *singularité* appeals to a system of presuppositions, including in particular that of the unity and permanence of the person amid the changing conditions and events in which he/she is involved. He says that in Lacan individuality appears, as in the European tradition, as 'the locus of an agreement of the truth with itself',[87] as the adequate and terminal reflection of the truth within itself. This may be true of a certain tradition of the philosophy of the subject and of reason – but the Romantic idea of individuality (and Lacan's) does not fall within the classical reflection model, and moreover the Romantic tradition was the first to attack this model and lay the foundations of a linguistic philosophy in the tradition of which Derrida himself stands.

It would be sufficient simply to point this out if it were just a matter of achieving some clarification in the analysis of concepts, as a contribution to the history of philosophy. But I had a further ambition: I wanted to show that Derrida encumbers his criticism of the convention model of analytical philosophy (and this applies also to Foucault's 'archaeology' and to Gadamer's and Ricœur's hermeneutics)[88] with a theoretical handicap. This consists in the fact that he locates the scientistic or normative option which shows itself in the rule-fetishism of the *human sciences* back in the tradition of Western reflection philosophy. This, he claims, found its appropriate expression, its *télos* as a scholarly discipline, in the idea of a complete presence of subjectivity to itself (Descartes, Fichte, Hegel). This is a diagnosis from the philosophy of history which prevents Derrida from deploying the idea of subjectivity critically against the objectivism of speech act theory. This is admittedly logical if one accepts Derrida's premises. These, how-

---

[87] Derrida, 'Le facteur de la vérité', p. 112.
[88] Derrida explained this more fully in an interview with Lucette Finas, 'Avoir l'oreille de la philosophie', in *Ecarts. Quatre essais à propos de Jacques Derrida* (Paris, 1973). See also the end of *LI*, g.

ever, have the drawback that they take over Hegel's (and Husserl's) idea of subjectivity as self-presence – though certainly with critical intent. But what escapes from Derrida's 'deconstructive' work through this critical fixation on the reflection model is that (heretical) version of the idea of the subject which one finds for instance in Schleiermacher or Sartre. These theoreticians also rejected the reflection model, using an argument of which Derrida nowhere takes any account: they assert that while the characteristic of the self only ever comes into being *in* the reciprocal play of two reflections (and is thus differentially determined), it cannot be explained merely *by* the play of reflection (or difference). One must distinguish here between a *conditio sine qua non* and a positively efficient cause and see that the reflexive differentiation of the idea 'I' does not *on its own* explain our familiarity with ourselves. The play of differential marks, left to itself, offers the as it were 'amorphous' self-consciousness a place where it can acquire a profile and a distinct existence (it is its ground in the sense of its ideal ground); but it cannot produce it, in the sense of positively bringing it about. The circles in which every attempt to explain the self-consciousness of intentionality on the basis of an experience of something other (for instance of a reflection) inevitably becomes entangled are well known – and Derrida ought to know them too. Sartre avoids them by saying that the self does not owe its familiarity with itself to the act of a positing or a thematisation (it is 'non-thetic'); its nature is also not dyadic but unitary (this is why he places brackets round the preposition 'de' in the expression 'conscience (de) soi'). Schleiermacher had equally strictly distinguished 'individual feeling' from 'I-ness', 'where one has become an object to oneself'[89] and had added that this explanation did not seek to deny that it was only in the event of differentiation that the self became an object of explicit knowledge: *différance* is the ideal ground of the self and of meaning (terms which in this context play largely the same role: there is no meaning without a self whose meaning it would be); but – once again – differentiality does not produce meaning, and it does not bind it to the *status quo* of the prevailing convention.

---

[89] Schleiermacher, *Dialektik*, pp. 288, 290–1.

It could be said that the meaning grasps itself on the basis of an already constituted cultural system: it is the internalising of this system. The error of conventionalism lies in the belief that this internalisation does not modify the system by the fact that it *interprets it individually* and then re-externalises it differently. The reflection – or *différance* – is split: it has access to itself, but not simply through the game of self-mediation as such but via the detour of a free interpretation which is made by the individual and in which the instances of convention, of tradition, of differentiality have their absolute boundary. Only individual self-consciousness explains what Derrida claims constantly (and rightly against Searle): that every repetition of a sign affects, transforms or simply conserves its meaning, but that this iteration radically cannot be understood as an anonymous fulfilling of the requirements of a code or as the permanence of a 'type'. Schleiermacher already vehemently opposed this hermeneutic conservatism, and Sartre now follows (evidently without knowing it) in his footsteps.

If a theoretical explanation enables one to explain all that another, divergent theory explains by other means, and if, moreover, this first theory avoids the aporias which its rival fails to resolve, then it is reasonable to accept it. In its attack on the scientism of the convention model Derrida's theory reaches conclusions which are the same as, or very similar to, those of a hermeneutics of individuality. Where it needs to name the driving force behind the transformation of meaning it finds itself in difficulties and has recourse to the notion of a 'language which speaks itself all by itself' (Sartre), that is, a language which is itself the subject of the speaking. No 'erasure' and no 'placing in inverted commas' can remove this metaphysical legacy. It is not merely a blemish on the surface of Derrida's arguments,[90] but binds what they can explain positively on the basis of their premises to a faulty model of relation to the self. If one agrees with his diagnosis that the paradigm of reflection still shows through where it has been wiped from the consciousness of its adepts, namely in scientific objectivism, then of course one must also critically 'deconstruct' the 'minimal consensus' between Searle

---

[90] Rather as in Aristophanes' *The Frogs* the verses of Euripides are marred by the jar of pomade.

and Derrida. The denial of the subject in positivism has – like any simple negation – merely resulted in the subject being retained the other way round. One might say that it has merely changed its position, fleeing from the heart of human consciousness into the idea of a self-organising and self-applying system. Does not this explain why Derrida's *différance* and his other neologisms are hedged about with so many prohibition signs and signalling systems? Developed on the basis of the rejected and negatively determined reflection model, these concepts (which no longer want to be 'concepts') have to combat on all fronts the consequences which follow from that fact.

And indeed Derrida does this with the greatest care and admirable precision. This is why a critical theory of understanding and of interpretation can learn so much more from 'Limited Inc.' than from speech act theory. Austin, Searle and Grice seek to reduce the meaning-effects to as few principles of communication as possible: their work is in the service of reduction. Derrida, by contrast, is a master of differentiation; he champions multiplicity and the release of meaning from limits. Faced with the challenge of his writings, transcendental hermeneutics (for instance) must seriously ask itself whether it is not breaking off its work too soon. Satisfied with the fact *that* meaning is produced, transcendental hermeneutics far too rarely questions the value of an understanding that deciphers in the utterances of a text only the prevailing language game or the dominant context of tradition (traditions too, where they can be grasped as such, are structured and thus organised according to rules). After all, understanding in the emphatic sense takes place only when the leap is made from the universal system (the code, the convention, the linguistic type) to the individual style of a historically situated subject. Only through this leap does the general schema attain its individual meaning. The gap which separates the schema from the unique meaning pulls away the counterpart of reflection: the linguistic type is reflected in its application, without being able to 'represent' itself 'authentically' in it; for the mirror-image bears the index of a transformation which no conceptual and scientific effort can reduce to its original. Precisely this is the effect of the individual productive power of giving meaning and understanding meaning. And it is this power which drives the fetishism of the code and convention models to its limits.

'Limited Inc.' is an important contribution to a better understanding of that 'minimal consensus' between classical reflection theory and the nomologism of the exact sciences. It is a pity that Derrida's 'deconstruction' shares in this consensus. It recognises that the living meaning of individual subjects who are open to the world is infiltrated, both in modern societies and in the theories which formulate the self-consciousness of those societies, by the cage of omnipresent constraints imposed by rules: to argue is to state the rules by which this or that must be constructed in order to be recognised as 'true'. That the productive power of human individuality is fading away under the constraint of being allowed to be valid only as a 'case' which is subsumed under a rule, is of course not Derrida's view. Having recognised that the exact sciences' forgetfulness of the subject in the last analysis merely remains faithful to idealistic subjectivism, he uses this insight to argue for theoretical anti-humanism. It seems to me that by so doing he reaches the outermost curve of the spiral of alienation: instead of perceiving a subject tormented and reduced to silence beneath the strait-jacket of a rationality that has become totalitarian, he finally abandons it. To do so is to suppress for a second time that tradition of the idea of individuality which was itself not able to withstand the triumphal progress of the spirit of positivism. Derrida's example shows how easily history can come to be in the wrong towards itself, as soon as the lessons which it learns from its course become radical and lack redemptive criticism. Of course the idea of the irreducibility of the individual is not very important from the scientific point of view: the world will continue to exist without it. But – as everyone knows – it can continue to exist even more easily without human beings.[91]

[91] See also Sartre, 'Qu'est-ce que la littérature', in *Situations II* (Paris, 1948), p. 316.

Manfred Frank: bibliography of main works in German and English, and English translations

BOOKS

1. *Das Problem 'Zeit' in der deutschen Romantik. Zeitbewußtsein von Zeitlichkeit in der frühromantischen Philosophie und in Tiecks Dichtung* ('The problem "time" in German Romanticism. Time-consciousness and consciousness of temporality in early Romantic philosophy and in Tieck's literary work'), Munich: Winkler, 1972. Reprinted with Afterword, Paderborn, Munich, Vienna, Zurich: Schöningh, 1990.

2. *Der unendliche Mangel an Sein. Schellings Hegelkritik und die Anfänge der Marxschen Dialektik* ('The endless lack of being. Schelling's critique of Hegel and the beginnings of Marxist dialectic'), Frankfurt am Main: Suhrkamp, 1975. Second substantially extended and revised edition, Munich: Fink, 1992.

3. *Das Individuelle-Allgemeine. Textstrukturierung und -interpretation nach Schleiermacher* ('The individual-universal, text-structuration and -interpretation according to/after Schleiermacher'), Frankfurt am Main: Suhrkamp, 1977. Reprinted 1985.

4. *Die unendliche Fahrt. Ein Motiv und sein Text* ('The endless journey. A motif and its text'), Frankfurt am Main: Suhrkamp, 1979. Second substantially extended and revised edition, Leipzig: Reclam, 1995.

5. *Das Sagbare und das Unsagbare. Studien zur deutsch-französischen Hermeneutik und Texttheorie* ('The sayable and the unsayable. Studies in contemporary French hermeneutics and textual theory'), Frankfurt am Main: Suhrkamp, 1980. Second very substantially extended edition, subtitled *Studien zur französischen Hermeneutik und Texttheorie*, 1989, 1993[3]. The essays in the present volume come from this latter edition.

6. *Der kommende Gott. Vorlesungen über die Neue Mythologie* I ('The coming God. Lectures on the new mythology'), Frankfurt am Main: Suhrkamp, 1982. Sixth, revised edition 1995.

7. *Was Ist Neostrukturalismus?*, Frankfurt am Main: Suhrkamp, 1984. English translation by Sabine Wilke, Richard Gray, *What is Neostructuralism?*, Minneapolis: University of Minnesota Press, 1989.

8. *Eine Einführung in Schellings Philosophie* ('An introduction to Schelling's philosophy'), Frankfurt am Main: Suhrkamp, 1985. Second, revised edition 1995.

9. With Rolf Kauffeld and Gerhard Plumpe. *Gott im Exil. Vorlesungen über die neue Mythologie* II ('God in exile. Lectures on the new mythology part II'), Frankfurt am Main: Suhrkamp, 1988.

10. *Die Unhintergehbarkeit von Individualität. Reflexionen über Subjekt, Person und Individuum aus Anlaß ihrer 'postmodernen' Toterklärung* ('The incontrovertibility of individuality. Reflections on subject, person and individual on the occasion of the "post-modern" announcement of their death'), Frankfurt am Main: Suhrkamp, 1986.

11. *Die Grenzen der Verständigung. Ein Geistergespräch zwischen Lyotard und Habermas* ('The limits of agreement. A fictional conversation between Lyotard and Habermas'), Frankfurt am Main: Suhrkamp, 1988. English translation in preparation.

12. *Kaltes Herz. Unendliche Fahrt. Neue Mythologie. Motivuntersuchungen zur Pathogenese der Moderne* ('Cold heart. Endless journey. New mythology. Investigations of motifs in the pathogenesis of modernity'), Frankfurt am Main: Suhrkamp, 1989.

13. With Gianfranco Soldati. *Wittgenstein. Literat und Philosoph* ('Wittgenstein. Writer and philosopher'), Pfullingen: Neske, 1989.

14. *Einführung in die frühromantische Ästhetik* ('An introduction to early Romantic aesthetics'), Frankfurt am Main: Suhrkamp, 1989. English translation in preparation.

15. *Zeitbewußtsein* ('Time-consciousness'), Pfullingen: Neske, 1990.

16. *Selbstbewußtsein und Selbsterkenntnis. Essays zur analytischen Philosophie der Subjektivität* ('Self-consciousness and self-knowledge. Essays on the analytical philosophy of subjectivity'), Stuttgart: Reclam, 1991.

17. *Stil in der Philosophie* ('Style in philosophy'), Stuttgart: Reclam, 1992.

18. *'Conditio Moderna'* – *Essays, Reden, Programme*, Leipzig: Reclam, 1993.

19. *'Unendliche Annäherung.' Die Anfänge der philosophischen Frühromantik* ('Endless approximation. The beginnings of philosophical early Romanticism'), Frankfurt am Main: Suhrkamp, 1997. English translation to appear with SUNY Press.

EDITIONS

1. With Gerhard Kurz. *Materialien zu Schellings philosophischen Anfängen* ('Material relating to Schelling's philosophical beginnings'), Frankfurt am Main: Suhrkamp, 1975.

2. *F.W.J. Schelling, Philosophie der Offenbarung 1841–2* ('F.W.J. Schelling, philosophy of revelation 1841–2'), Frankfurt am Main: Suhrkamp, 1977. Revised edition 1993.

3. *F.D.E. Schleiermacher, Hermeneutik und Kritik. Mit einem Anhang sprachphilosophischer Texte Schleiermachers* ('F.D.E. Schleiermacher, hermeneutics and criticism. With an appendix of texts by Schleiermacher on the philosophy of language'), Frankfurt am Main: Suhrkamp, 1977. An English translation and edition by Andrew Bowie of *Hermeneutik und Kritik*, with other texts by Schleiermacher, will be appearing in the Cambridge University Press 'Texts in the History of Philosophy' series in 1998.

4. *Das kalte Herz und andere Texte der Romantik* ('The cold heart and other Romantic texts'), Frankfurt: Insel, 1978. Revised edition 1981. Fifth revised and extended edition 1996.

5. *Schellings Ausgewählte Schriften* ('Schelling's selected writings'), six volumes, Frankfurt am Main: Suhrkamp, 1985.

6. *Ludwig Tieck, Phantasus*, Frankfurt am Main: Deutscher Klassiker Verlag, 1985.

7. *Selbstbewußtseinstheorien von Fichte bis Sartre* ('Theories of self-consciousness from Fichte to Sartre'), Frankfurt am Main: Suhrkamp, 1991.

8. *Analytische Theorien des Selbstbewußtseins* ('Analytical theories of self-consciousness'), Frankfurt am Main: Suhrkamp, 1994.

9. With Véronique Zanetti. *Kritische Edition und Kommentar von Immanuel Kant, Kritik der Urteilskraft. Kants Schriften zur Ästhetik und Naturphilosophie* ('Critical edition and commentary on Immanuel Kant, *Critique of Judgement*. Kant's writings on aesthetics and philosophy of nature'), Frankfurt am Main: Deutscher Klassiker Verlag, 1996.

10. *Aenesidemus oder über die Fundamente der von dem Herrn Professor Reinhold in Jena gelieferten Elementar-Philosophie. Nebst einer Verteidigung des Scepticismus gegen die Anmaßungen der Vernunftkritik*, 1792 ('Aenesidemus or on the foundations of the elementary philosophy provided by Herr Professor Reinhold in Jena. With a defence of scepticism against the presumptions of the Critique of Reason'), Hamburg: Meiner, 1996.

ESSAYS, REVIEW ESSAYS[1]

1. 'Die Philosophie des sogenannten "magischen Idealismus"', *Euphorion* 63 1969, pp. 88–116.

2. 'Heine und Schelling', *Heine-Studien* 1973, pp. 281–306.

3. With Gerhard Kurz. 'Ordo inversus. Zu einer Reflexionsfigur bei

---

[1] This list does not include the original publications in journals of essays reprinted in the books already listed, and only lists the *book* publication of essays which have appeared in both journals and books. It also lists only the revised and extended later (including English) versions of essays which have appeared in more than one form. This list also does not include the many book reviews by Frank in the area of German studies, or newspaper articles and interviews.

Novalis, Hölderlin, Kleist und Kafka', in *Geist und Zeichen*, Festschrift für Arthur Henkel, Heidelberg, 1977, pp. 76–97.

4. 'Die Dichtung als "Neue Mythologie". Motive und Konsequenzen einer frühromantischen Idee', in K.H. Bohrer (ed.), *Mythos und Moderne*, Frankfurt am Main: Suhrkamp, 1983, pp. 15–40.

5. 'Das Individuum in der Rolle des Idioten. Die hermeneutische Konzeption des *Flaubert*', in Traugott König (ed.), *Sartres Flaubert lesen*, Reinbek: Rowohlt, 1980, pp. 83–108.

6. 'The Infinite Text', *Glyph* 7 1980, pp. 70–101.

7. ' "Kaum das Urthema wechselnd". Die alte und die neue Mythologie in "Doktor Faustus" ', *Fugen. Deutsch-Französisches Jahrbuch für Textanalytik*, 1980, pp. 9–42. English translation by Jason Gaiger in Michael Minden (ed.), *Thomas Mann*, London and New York: Longman, 1995, pp. 194–209.

8. 'The World as Will and Representation: Deleuze's and Guattari's Critique of Capitalism as Schizo-Analysis and Schizo-Discourse', *Telos* 57 1983, pp. 166–76 (revised and extended version of essay from *Das Sagbare und das Unsagbare*).

9. 'Auf der Suche nach einem Grund. Über den Umschlag von Erkenntniskritik in Mythologie bei Robert Musil', in K.H. Bohrer (ed.), *Mythos und Moderne*, Frankfurt am Main: Suhrkamp, 1983, pp. 317–61.

10. 'Das "fragmentarische Universum" der Romantik', in Lucien Dällenbach and Christiaan L. Hart Nibbrig (eds.), *Fragment und Totalität*, Frankfurt am Main: Suhrkamp, 1984, pp. 212–24.

11. 'Schelling's Critique of Hegel and the Beginnings of Marxian Dialectics', trans. Joseph P. Lawrence, *Idealistic Studies* XIX, 3 1989, pp. 251–301 (translation of the new Introduction to the 1992 edition of *Der unendliche Mangel an Sein*).

12. 'Zwei Jahrhunderte Rationalitätskritik und ihre "postmoderne" Überbietung', in Willem van Reijen and Dietmar Kamper (eds.), *Die unvollendete Vernunft: Moderne versus Postmoderne*, Frankfurt am Main: Suhrkamp, 1987, pp. 99–121. English translation by Dieter Freundlieb and Wayne Hudson, 'Two Centuries of Philosophical Critique of Reason and Its "Postmodern" Radicalisation', in Dieter Freundlieb and Wayne Hudson (eds.), *Reason and Its Other. Rationality in Modern German Philosophy and Culture*, Oxford: Berg, 1993, pp. 67–85.

13. 'Die Grenzen der Beherrschbarkeit der Sprache. Das Gespräch als Ort der Differenz von Neostrukturalismus und Hermeneutik', in Philippe Forget (ed.), *Verstehen und Interpretieren. Die Hermeneutik-Grammatologie Debatte in elf Originalbeiträgen*, Munich, Paderborn, Vienna: Schöningh, 1984, pp. 181–213. Partial English translation in Diane Michelfelder and Richard E. Palmer (eds.), *Dialogue and Deconstruction. The Gadamer–Derrida Encounter*, Albany: SUNY Press, 1983, pp. 150–61.

14. 'Zwei Jahrhunderte Rationalitätskritik und die Sehnsucht nach einer "Neuen Mythologie"', *manuskripte. Zeitschrift für Literatur* 23 Jahrgang 82, Graz 1983, pp. 34–40.

15. 'Subjekt – Person – Individuum', in Manfred Frank, Gérard Raulet and Willem van Reijen (eds.), *Die Frage nach dem Subjekt*, Frankfurt am Main: Suhrkamp, 1988, pp. 7–28.

16. 'Wahrheit der Kunst? Überlegungen zur Stellung der Ästhetik im Blick auf Heidegger', *Zeitschrift für die Didaktik der Philosophie*, Heft 2 1986, pp. 74–83.

17. 'Religionsstiftung im Dienste der Idee? Die "Neue Mythologie" der Romantik', in Gerhard vom Hofe, Peter Pfaff and Hermann Timm (eds.), *Was aber (bleibet) stiften die Dichter? Zur Dichter-Theorie der Goethezeit*, Munich: Fink, 1986, pp. 121–37.

18. ' "Intellektuale Anschauung". Drei Stellungnahmen zu einem Deutungsversuch von Selbstbewußtsein: Kant, Fichte, Hölderlin/ Novalis', in Ernst Behler and Jochen Hörisch (eds.), *Die Aktualität der Frühromantik*, Munich, Paderborn, Vienna: Schöningh, 1988, pp. 96–126.

19. 'Gespräch mit Florian Rötzer', in Florian Rötzer (ed.), *Denken, das an der Zeit ist*, Frankfurt am Main: Suhrkamp, 1987, pp. 110–28.

20. 'Is Self-Consciousness a Case of *présence à soi*? Towards a Meta-Critique of the Recent French Critique of Metaphysics', English translation by Andrew Bowie of essay from *Das Sagbare und das Unsagbare*, in David Wood (ed.), *Derrida: A Critical Reader*, Oxford: Blackwell, 1992, pp. 218–34.

21. 'Selbstsein und Dankbarkeit. Dem Philosophen Dieter Henrich', *Merkur*, Heft 4, 42 Jahrgang 1988, pp. 333–42.

22. 'Vom Bühnenweihefestspiel zum Thingspiel. Zur Wirkungsgeschichte der Neuen Mythologie bei Nietzsche, Wagner und Johst', in W. Haug and R. Warning (eds.), *Das Fest (Poetik und Hermeneutik* XIV) Munich, 1989, pp. 573–601.

23. 'Anti-bourgeoise Anarchie und Revolutionskritik. Von der zwiespältigen Haltung der Frühromantik zur Französischen Revolution', in Henning Krauss (ed.), *Folgen der Französischen Revolution*, Frankfurt am Main: Suhrkamp, 1989, pp. 221–44.

24. 'Ist Selbstbewußtsein ein propositionales Wissen?', *Acta analytica. Philosophy and Psychology*, 7 1991, pp. 97–124.

25. 'Identität und Subjektivität', in Hans Michael Baumgartner and Wilhelm G. Jacobs (eds.), *Philosophie der Subjektivität? Zur Bestimmung des neuzeitlichen Philosophierens*, Schellingiana 3, Stuttgart, Bad Cannstatt, 1993, pp. 321–41. English translation by Peter Dews, 'Identity and Subjectivity', in Simon Critchley and Peter Dews (eds.), *Deconstructive Subjectivities*, Albany: SUNY Press, 1996, pp. 127–48.

26. 'Subjektivität und Intersubjektivität', *Revue internationale de philosophie*

194, vol. 49, 4, 1995, pp. 521–50.

27. 'Die eigentliche Zeit in der Zeit', in Peter Sloterdijk (ed.), *Vor der Jahrtausendwende. Berichte zur Lage der Zukunft*, vol. 1, Frankfurt am Main: Suhrkamp, 1990, pp. 151–69.

28. 'Towards a Philosophy of Style', trans. Richard E. Palmer, *Common Knowledge* vol. 1, no. 1, 1992, pp. 54–77.

29. 'Kants "Reflexionen zur Ästhetik". Zur Werkgeschichte der "Kritik der ästhetischen Urteilskraft"', *Revue internationale de philosophie* 175, vol. 44, 4, 1990, pp. 552–80.

30. 'Hölderlin über den Mythos', *Hölderlin-Jahrbuch* 1990–1, Stuttgart, 1991, pp. 1–31.

31. 'Selbstbewußtsein und Rationalität', in Petra Kolmer and Harald Korten (eds.), *Grenzbestimmungen der Vernunft*, Bonn, 1994, pp. 389–438.

32. 'Welchen Nutzen bringt uns die analytische Philosophie?', *Merkur*, Heft 518, 46 Jahrgang 1992, pp. 415–25.

33. 'Die Wiederkehr des Subjekts. Drei neuere Arbeiten zum Thema Selbstbewußtsein', *Internationale Zeitschrift für Philosophie*, Heft 1 1992, pp. 120–45.

34. 'Vom Lachen. Über Komik, Witz und Ironie. Überlegungen im Ausgang von der Frühromantik', in Thomas Vogel (ed.), *Vom Lachen*, Tübingen: Attempto, 1992, pp. 211–31.

35. 'Wider den apriorischen Intersubjektivismus', in Micha Brumlik and Hauke Brunkhorst (eds.), *Gemeinschaft und Gerechtigkeit*, Frankfurt am Main: Fischer, 1993, pp. 273–89.

36. 'Die *Kritik der Urteilskraft* als Schlußstein des kantischen Systems', *FilozoFski Vestnik* 2 1992, pp. 59–77.

37. 'Allegorie, Witz, Fragment, Ironie. Friedrich Schlegel und die Idee des zerrissenen Selbst', in Willem van Reijen (ed.), *Allegorie und Melancholie*, Frankfurt am Main: Suhrkamp, 1992, pp. 124–46.

38. 'Nachdenken über Deutschland. Aus Anlaß der Kommemoration der Reichspogromnacht vom 9. November 1938', in Siegfried Unseld (ed.), *Politik ohne Projekt? Nachdenken über Deutschland*, Frankfurt am Main: Suhrkamp, 1993, pp. 250–82. English translation, 'Nationality and Democracy: Defining Terms in Germany', *Common Knowledge* vol. 2, no. 3, 1993, pp. 65–78.

39. 'Philosophische Grundfragen der Frühromantik', *Athenäum* Jahrgang 4, Paderborn, Munich, Vienna, Zurich: Schöningh, 1994, pp. 37–130. Radically shortened English translation by Günter Zöller and Karl Ameriks, 'Philosophical Foundations of Early Romanticism', in Karl Ameriks and Dieter Sturma (eds.), *The Modern Subject. Conceptions of the Self in Modern German Philosophy*, Albany: SUNY Press, 1995, pp. 65–85.

40. 'Ist Subjektivität ein Unding? Über einige Schwierigkeiten der naturalistischen Reduktion von Selbstbewußtsein', in Sybille Krämer (ed.),

'*Bewußtsein*'. *Philosophische Positionen*, Frankfurt am Main, 1996, pp. 66–90. English translation by Karl Ameriks, 'Is Subjectivity a Non-Thing, an Absurdity (*Unding*)', in Ameriks and Sturma (eds.), *The Modern Subject*.

41. '"Weltgeschichte aus der Saga". Wagners Widerruf der "Neuen Mythologie"', in Wolfgang Wagner (ed.), *Programmbuch der Bayreuther Festspiele*, Bayreuth, 1994, pp. 16–37. English translation by Stephen Reader, '"The History of the World in Legend". Wagner's disavowal of the "New Mythology"', in *ibid*.

42. 'The Subject v. Language. Mental Familiarity and Epistemic Self-Ascription', translation by Lawrence K. Schmidt and Barry Allen, *Common Knowledge*, vol. 4, no. 2, 1995, pp. 30–50.

43. '"Alle Wahrheit ist relativ, alles Wissen symbolisch". Motive der Grundsatz-Skepsis in der frühen Jenaer Romantik (1796)', *Revue internationale de philosophie* 197, vol. 50, 3, 1996, pp. 403–36.

44. 'Über Subjektivität. Rede an die Gebildeten unter ihren Reduktionisten', in Jörg Huber and Alois Martin Müller (eds.), *Interventionen 5: 'Die Wiederkehr des Anderen'*, Stroemfeld, Basle: Roter Stern, 1996, pp. 83–101.

45. '"Wechselgrundsatz". Friedrich Schlegels philosophischer Ausgangspunkt', *Zeitschrift für philosophische Forschung*, vol. 50, 1/2, 1996, pp. 26–50.

46. 'So kam ich unter die Philosophen', in Christine and Michael Hauskeller (eds.), *. . . was die Welt im innersten zusammenhält*, Hamburg: Junius, 1996, pp. 152–7.

Index

This index does not give references for such central topics as 'subject', 'self-consciousness', 'hermeneutics', 'individual', 'interpretation', 'language', 'literature', 'meaning' etc., which occur too frequently to be usefully listed. Bold numerals indicate an extended discussion of the author or topic.